Jaguar S Type, 420 1963-68 Autobook

By Kenneth Ball

Graduate, Institution of Mechanical Engineers
Associate Member, Guild of Motoring Writers
and the Autopress Team of Technical Writers.

Jaguar 3.4S 1963-68
Jaguar 3.8S 1963-68
Jaguar 420 1966-68

Autopress Ltd. Golden Lane Brighton BN1 2QJ England

The AUTOBOOK series of Workshop Manuals is the largest in the world and covers the majority of British and Continental motor cars, as well as all major Japanese and Australian models. For a full list see the back of this manual.

CONTENTS

ISBN 0 85147 113 7

First Edition   1970
Reprinted   1971
Reprinted   1972
Reprinted   1973

703

Printed and bound in Brighton England for Autopress Ltd by G Beard & Son Ltd   A

ACKNOWLEDGEMENT

My thanks are due to Jaguar Cars Ltd. for their unstinted co-operation and also for supplying data and illustrations

I am also grateful to a considerable number of owners who have discussed their cars at length and many of whose suggestions have been included in this manual.

Kenneth Ball
Graduate, Institution of Mechanical Engineers
Associate Member, Guild of Motoring Writers
Ditchling Sussex England.

INTRODUCTION

This do-it-yourself Workshop Manual has been specially written for the owner who wishes to maintain his car in first class condition and to carry out his own servicing and repairs. Considerable savings on garage charges can be made, and one can drive in safety and confidence knowing the work has been done properly.

Comprehensive step-by-step instructions and illustrations are given on all dismantling, overhauling and assembling operations. Certain assemblies require the use of expensive special tools, the purchase of which would be unjustified. In these cases information is included but the reader is recommended to hand the unit to the agent for attention.

Throughout the Manual hints and tips are included which will be found invaluable, and there is an easy to follow fault diagnosis at the end of each chapter.

Whilst every care has been taken to ensure correctness of information it is obviously not possible to guarantee complete freedom from errors or to accept liability arising from such errors or omissions.

Instructions may refer to the righthand or lefthand sides of the vehicle or the components. These are the same as the righthand or lefthand of an observer standing behind the car and looking forward.

CHAPTER 1

THE ENGINE

1:1 Description

The six-cylinder in-line engines are of watercooled unit construction with a stroke of 106 mm and bores of 83 mm, 87 mm and 92 mm for the 3.4, 3.8 and 4.2 litre capacities respectively. Two overhead camshafts are provided. One operates the inlet valves and the other the exhaust valves. There is no provision for routine adjustment of valve clearances. Valve timing is the same for all models. The camshafts are roller-chain driven.

FIGS 1:1 and **1:2** show end and side elevation cross-sections of the 3.4 litre engine and are representative of the 3.8 and 4.2 litre versions.

The chromium iron cylinder block is integral with the crankcase. The 3.8 and 4.2 litre cylinders have dry liners. The cylinder head is of aluminium alloy with machined hemispherical combustion chambers. Valve seat inserts, valve and tappet guides are of cast iron and are shrunk into the head.

The counterbalanced crankshaft has seven pressure lubricated shell bearings. Axial thrust is accommodated at the centre bearing position. A torsional vibration damper is fitted externally to the front end of the crankshaft. The generator or alternator, water pump and cooling fan, power assisted steering pump and air conditioning system compressor (if these are fitted) are belt driven from the forward end of the crankshaft.

The oil pump, which is located inside the sump, draws oil through a strainer from the rear of the sump. Pressure oil is fully filtered by an external filter of the fullflow type which incorporates a balance valve and also a relief valve through which excess oil is returned to the sump.

Forged steel connecting rods have shell type bearings at the big-ends while the gudgeon pin bushes are of phosphor/bronze. The rods are drilled to provide pressure oil to the fully floating gudgeon pins. The pistons are of low expansion aluminium alloy and different pistons give compression ratios of 7:1, 8:1 and 9:1.

The twin SU carburetters are side-draught type. The air cleaner also provides air intake silencing. The breather, which is located at the front of the cylinder head, is piped to the air intake. Ignition is by coil and the distributor is a vacuum and centrifugal automatic advance/retard type.

The engine is supported on two rubber mountings at the front and a spring type at the rear. All engines have a stabilizer which is located immediately behind the cylinder block. 3.4 and 3.8 litre models are, in addition, fitted with two stabilizers at the front of the engine.

Twin exhaust manifolds, each serving three cylinders, connect with a multi-silencer exhaust system and twin tailpipes.

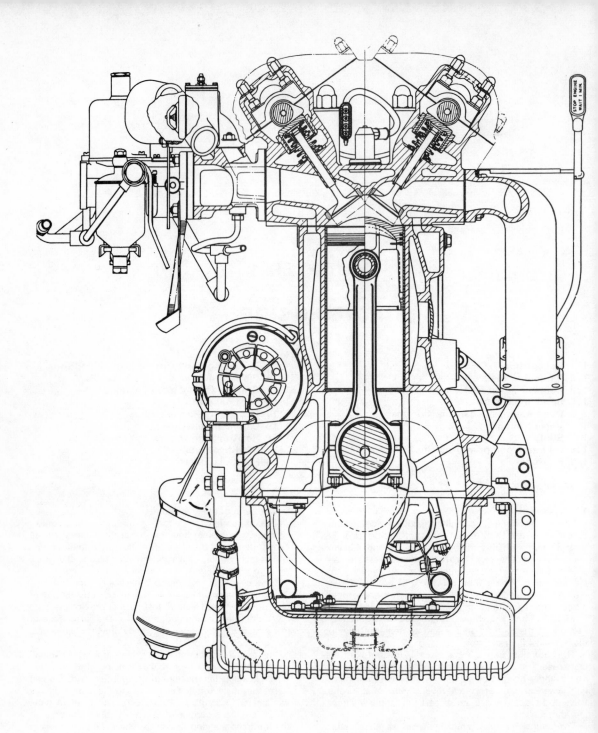

FIG 1:1   Cross section of engine (3.4 litre)

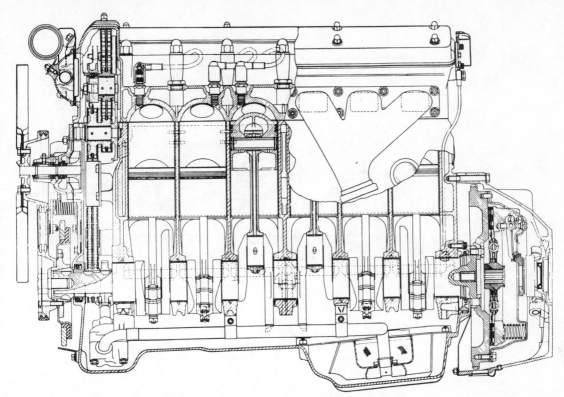

FIG 1:2 Longitudinal section of engine (3.4 litre)

1:2 Removing the engine

Big-ends can be worked on, pistons can be removed, decarbonizing and servicing the cylinder head can be carried out with the engine in the car. A major overhaul however can only be carried out if the engine and gearbox have been removed from the car.

If the operator is not a skilled automobile engineer, it is suggested that he will find much useful information in Hints on Maintenance and Overhaul which will be found in the Appendix Section at the end of this manual and that he should read it before starting work.

If the car is fitted with air conditioning, the system's condenser must be removed before the radiator can be withdrawn. As the removal of the condenser requires the use of special tools and as **it is dangerous for any unqualified person to attempt to disconnect or remove any part of the air conditioning system, the operation must be carried out only by Authorized Jaguar Distributors, Dealers or qualified Refrigeration Engineers.**

The engine and gearbox, together with the overdrive if fitted, is removed by lifting the unit out of the car and the procedure is as follows

1 Remove the bonnet. To facilitate refitment, mark the position of the hinge plates before unscrewing the two setbolts which attach each plate to the bonnet. Disconnect the leads and remove the battery.

2 Drain the cooling system as described in **Chapter 4**.

If antifreeze is in use, conserve the coolant. Remove the dipstick. Drain the engine sump.

3 On automatic transmission 420 models, refer to **Chapter 7** and drain and remove the oil cooler.

4 Refer to **Chapter 2**. Remove the air cleaner, disconnect the carburetter linkage, the filter to carburetter fuel feed pipe and the cable to the starting carburetter thermostat. Remove the carburetters from the manifold.

5 Remove the brake and heater vacuum pipes from the inlet manifold. Disconnect the cables and pipe and remove the windscreen washer bottle.

6 Slacken off the clips on the radiator and heater hoses. Remove and examine the hoses. If there are any signs of deterioration, obtain replacement hoses.

7 If the car is fitted with power assisted steering, refer to **Chapter 10** and remove the hoses from the pump. Blank off the unions. In the case of 420 cars, slacken off the adjuster nuts and press the pump towards the engine to its minimum adjustment point.

8 Disconnect the leads and remove the generator or alternator as described in **Chapter 12**. Remove and examine the drive belt which should be renewed if it shows any signs of wear or deterioration.

9 On S type cars, unscrew the four nuts securing the cooling fan cowl and allow it to rest temporarily on the water pump behind the cooling fan. On 420 type cars, separate the two halves of the cowl at the bottom joint and remove after unscrewing the four securing bolts. Refer to **Chapter 4** and remove the radiator.

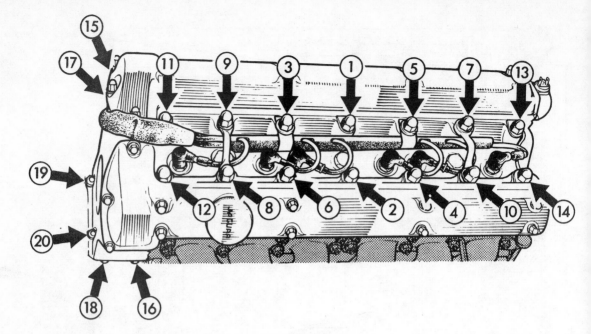

FIG 1:3   Slacken and tighten the cylinder head nuts in this order

The need for care when lifting out the matrix is stressed to preclude accidental damage against the fan blades.

10 Disconnect the earth strap and the starter motor cable(s). Disconnect the water temperature and oil pressure transmitter cables. On 420 models, disconnect the high-tension lead from the coil and, on S type cars, disconnect the lead from the SW terminal on the ignition coil.

11 On S type cars only, detach the tachometer leads from the AC generator which is located at the rear of the righthand camshaft cover. Refer to **Chapter 8, Section 11:8** and uncouple the clutch fluid pipe at the bracket which bridges the two rear cylinder head holding down studs.

12 Disconnect the two snap connectors from the gearbox harness at the rear of the exhaust manifolds on S type cars. Refer to **FIG 1:3** and fit an engine lifting plate (Churchill tool No. J8) under nuts numbered 3, 6, 8 and 9. This illustration shows the two lifting brackets which, on 420 models only, are standard fitments. On 420 type cars, refer to (**Section 11:8** and uncouple the flexible hose from the clutch slave cylinder.

13 Disconnect the exhaust pipes from the manifolds as described in **Chapter 13, Section 13:12.**

14 On manual gearbox models, remove the gearlever knob, refer to **Chapter 13, Section 13:10** and remove the console. Remove the gearlever rubber grommet. Disconnect the reverse light switch and, if fitted, the overdrive switch cables.

15 On automatic transmission models, refer to **Chapter 7** and remove the selector cable from the lever on the transmission unit after uncoupling the selector cable

clamp. On S type cars, remove the governor control rod from the governor lever, disconnect the leads from the anti-creep pressure switch and the intermediate hold lead at the snap connector. On 420 type cars, disconnect the kick-down linkage.

16 On all models, remove the speedometer drive cables from the gearbox or transmission unit.

17 Support the engine on lifting tackle. Refer to **Section 1:15** and **Chapter 8**, remove the rear mounting and the propeller shaft. Uncouple the stabilizer at the rear of the cylinder block, remove the two front mountings and, on S type cars, remove the two front stabilizers as also described in **Section 1:15**.

18 Check that everything linking the engine unit to the frame has been disconnected or removed. Lower the rear of the unit and guide it forwards and upwards out of the car. Clean off the exterior of the unit before proceeding with any dismantling operations.

1:3 Removing and refitting the head

Warning:

Before carrying out the removal or dismantling of the cylinder head it is most important to accept three warnings which are given to avoid the possibility of valves fouling the pistons and of the inlet and exhaust valves fouling each other.

1 **Do not rotate the engine or the camshaft after the camshafts have been disconnected from the drive sprockets until the cylinder head has been removed.**

2 **Once the cylinder head has been removed, do not rotate either camshaft unless the other has been removed.**

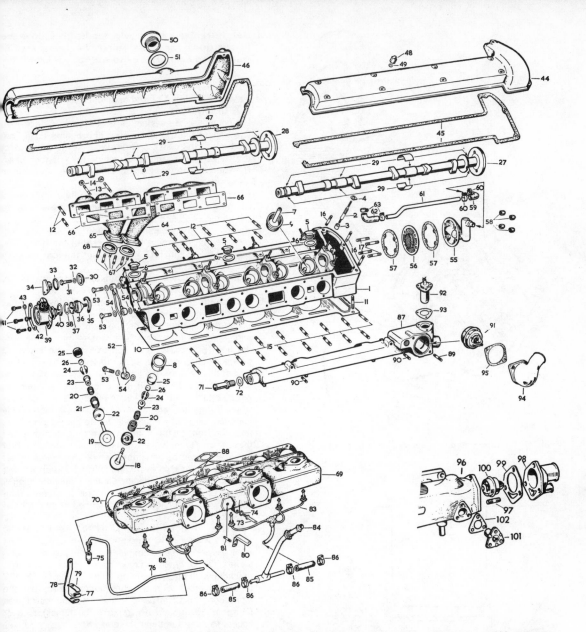

FIG 1:4 Components of the cylinder head. The S type is illustrated except for items 96 to 102 which are 420 type parts

Key to Fig 1:4   1 Cylinder head   2 Stud   3 Ring dowel   4 D-washer   5 Core plug   6 Copper washer
7 Guide   8 Insert   9 Guide   10 Gasket   11 Stud   12 Stud   13 Stud   14 Distance piece   15 Stud
16 Stud   17 Stud   18 Inlet valve   19 Exhaust valve   20 Valve spring (inner)   21 Valve spring (outer)   22 Seat
23 Collar   24 Cotter   25 Tappet   26 Adjusting pad   27 Inlet camshaft   28 Exhaust camshaft   29 Bearing
30 Oil thrower   31 Screw   32 Copper washer   33 Sealing ring   34 Sealing plug   35 Seal   36 Adaptor
37 Driving dog   38 Circlip   39 Revolution counter generator   40 O-ring   41 Screw   42 Plate washer   43 Lockwasher
44 Righthand camshaft cover   45 Gasket   46 Lefthand camshaft cover   47 Gasket   48 Dome nut   49 Copper washer
50 Oil filler cap   51 Fibre washer   52 Oil pipe   53 Banjo bolt   54 Copper washer   55 Front cover and breather
housing   56 Gauze filter   57 Gasket   58 Dome nut   59 Hose elbow   60 Clip   61 Breather pipe   62 Hose elbow
63 Clip   64 Front exhaust manifold   65 Rear exhaust manifold   66 Exhaust gasket   67 Stud   68 Sealing ring
69 Inlet manifold   70 Gasket   71 Adaptor   72 Copper washer   73 Pivot pin   74 Spring washer
75 Vacuum servo adaptor   76 Vacuum servo pipe   77 Rubber sleeve   78 Hanger bracket   79 Clamp
80 Anti-creep throttle switch bracket   81 Stud   82 Starting pipe (lefthand manifold)   83 Starting pipe (righthand manifold)
84 Carburetter starting pipe   85 Neoprene tube   86 Clip   87 Water outlet pipe   88 Gasket   89 Stud   90 Stud
91 Thermostat   92 Thermostat (automatic choke)   93 Gasket   94 Water outlet elbow   95 Gasket   96 Inlet manifold
97 Stud   98 Water outlet pipe   99 Gasket   100 Thermostat   101 Thermostat (automatic choke)   102 Gasket

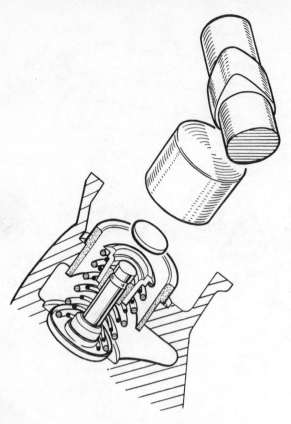

FIG 1:5 Tappet and valve clearance adjusting pad

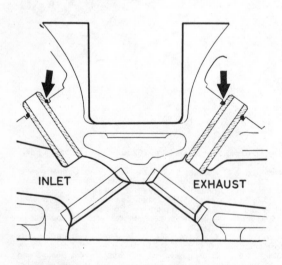

FIG 1:6 Valve guides. Arrows show the circlips

3 Before replacing the cylinder head, follow the instructions for positioning the camshafts in relation to each other and to the crankshaft.

Removal:

1 Refer to **Section 1:2** and carry out operations number 1, 4, 5, 11 and 13.

2 Drain the cooling system as described in **Chapter 4**. Disconnect the top water hose and bypass hose from the front of the inlet manifold water jacket. Disconnect the heater pipes from the rear of the cylinder head. Disconnect the cable from the water temperature transmitter.

3 Remove the leads from the sparking plugs and remove the plugs. On S type models, disconnect the wires to the ignition coil and remove the coil.

4 Remove the two banjo connections of the branched camshaft oil feed pipe from the rear of the head. This pipe is item 52 in **FIG 1:4**. Collect the four washers and two banjo bolts 53 and 54.

5 Remove the eleven domed nuts and copper washers from each camshaft cover and lift off the covers.

6 Release the tension in the top camshaft drive chain as described in **Section 1:5**.

7 Break the locking wire on the setbolts which secure each sprocket to its camshaft. Rotate the engine until the front piston No. 6, is approximately on top dead centre on the firing stroke (both valves closed). Note that in this position the keyway in each camshaft is as shown in **FIG 1:13** and that one of the two setbolts which attach each sprocket to a camshaft is inaccessible. Rotate the engine until these setbolts can be removed. After their removal rotate the engine back until the front piston is again on top dead centre and the camshaft keyways are again as shown in **FIG 1:13**. Remove the remaining setbolt in each camshaft sprocket. **From this point Warning 1, given earlier applies.** Tap the sprockets off the camshaft flanges and slide them up the slots in the front mounting bracket where they can remain 'parked' until the head is refitted.

8 Following the order shown in **FIG 1:3**, slacken off the twenty cylinder head nuts by part of a turn at a time until they are free. Remove the sparking plug lead carrier. On S type engines, collect the clutch pipe bracket which bridges stud numbers 13 and 14. On 420 type cars fitted with air conditioning, dismount the alternator (see **Chapter 12**) and the compressor (see **Chapter 13** and do not remove the hoses) to gain access to nuts numbered 16 and 18.

9 Lift off the head. Remove and discard the joint gasket. **Observe Warning 2.**

When the valves are fully open they protrude below the level of the cylinder head joint face and the cylinder head should therefore be supported on the bench by a block of wood at each end.

Refitting:

Observe Warning 3. Rotate the engine until the front, No. 6, piston is on top dead centre of the firing stroke. Check that the head is prepared for refitment as instructed at the end of **Section 1:4**. Fit the new head gasket ensuring that the side marked 'Top' is uppermost. Refit the head, noting that the stud in position 8, **FIG 1:3**, is a

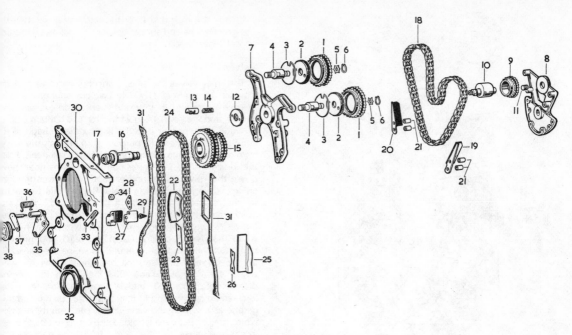

FIG 1:7 Components of the camshaft drive

dowel stud. Refit the washers and brackets in their original positions, refit the nuts and tighten them part of a turn at a time in the order shown in **FIG 1:3**, and finally to a torque of 54 lb ft on S type engines and to 58 lb ft on 420 type engines.

Refitment is now the removal procedure in reverse except that instruction 7 in reverse is not appropriate and the whole of the procedure given in **Section 1:6** will apply instead. Fit new camshaft cover gaskets.

1:4 Servicing the head

Since the cylinder head is of aluminium alloy, it is relatively easily damaged, and attention is drawn to the need for appropriate care. The joint face in particular should be well guarded from the possibility of it being scratched or scored. When removing sealing compound, old gasket material or carbon deposits avoid the use of pointed tools and use worn emerycloth and paraffin only for cleaning off operations.

Dismantling:

As soon as the cylinder head has been removed as described in **Section 1:3**, the camshafts 27 and 28 in **FIG 1:4**, should be removed so that the possibility of them being accidentally turned and the consequential possibility of inlet and exhaust valves fouling may be avoided.

1 Remove the tachometer generator in the case of S type models from the righthand rear of the head. Remove the Allen setscrews and collect the copper washers from under their heads.

2 Check that the identification marks on the camshaft bearing caps are clear so that they can be refitted to the same positions. Each camshaft has four whitemetal steel-backed shell bearings 29. End float is taken on the flanges at each side of the front bearing. Release, a turn at a time, the eight nuts which secure the four bearing caps on each camshaft. Remove the caps, note that they are located to the lower bearing housings with hollow dowels, and collect the nuts, spring washers and D-washers. Identify the bearing shells so that, if they do not require to be renewed, they may be refitted to their original positions. The camshafts can now be lifted out.

3 The twelve tappets 25 and valve clearance adjusting pads 26 should now be removed with the assistance of a valve grinding suction tool. Identify them to their positions and record the thickness letter etched on each of them. The tappets and pads are also shown in **FIG 1:5**

4 If the exhaust manifolds 64 and 65, in **FIG 1:4**, are to be removed, this is effected by removing the eight brass nuts and spring washers which secure each manifold to the head. Check the condition of the gaskets 66.

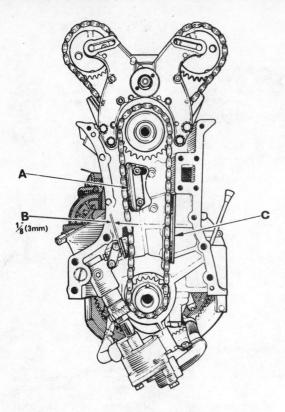

FIG 1:8   Arrangement of camshaft drive

Key to Fig 1:8   **A** Intermediate damper
B Gap between rubber slipper and hydraulic tensioner body
C Lower damper

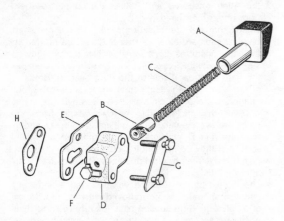

FIG 1:9   Components of the hydraulic chain tensioner

Key to Fig 1:9   A Plunger   **B** Restraint cylinder
C Spring   **D** Body   **E** Backing plate
F End plug and tabwasher   **G** Body securing bolts and tab-
washer   **H** Shim

5 If the inlet manifold is to be withdrawn, remove th
eighteen nuts and spring washers. Check the conditio
of the gasket 70.

Valves:

The inlet valves are of silicon chrome steel and th
exhaust valves are of 21-4-N5. Two coil springs are fitte
to each valve and they are retained by collars and spl
cotters, and are items 18 to 24 in **FIG 1:4**. Obtain a bloc
of wood and contour it to the approximate shape of th
combustion chamber. Its purpose is to prevent the valve
from opening while the springs are being removed. Plac
this block in No. 1 cylinder combustion chamber, pres
down the valve collars and extract the split cotters, th
collars, springs and spring seats. Repeat this procedur
for the remaining cylinders. In later engines, inlet valv
guides are fitted with oil seals which must be remove
before the valve spring seats. The valves are numbere
(note that No. 1 cylinder is at the rear) and must b
refitted in their original positions. Examine the valves fo
pitting, burning or distortion and their stems for wea
which should not exceed .003 inch from the origina
diameter of .310 —.001 inch. Valves which are too pitte
to clean up on grinding to their seats may be refaced by
garage as also may the valve seats. The amount of meta
which may be removed is limited and it may not be possibl
to salvage valves or valve seats. It may be necessary t
obtain new valves and to fit new seat inserts as describe
later. The valve seat angle is 45 deg. in all cases.

Valve springs:

The valve springs should be tested for their ability t
apply their functional load to the valves. This may be don
either by comparison with the figures given in Technica
Data in the Appendix Section of this Manual or b
comparison with a new valve spring. To compare with
new spring, insert both the old and the new end to en
with a metal plate between them into the jaws of a vic
or under a press. Apply load to compress them by a tota
of about .75 inch and compare their individual lengths
If the loaded length of the old spring is less than that c
the new by more that 5 or 6 per cent it should be rejecte

Valve seats, guides and tappet guides:

These are shrunk into the head and should be examine
to ensure that they do not require to be replaced. The valv
seats have already been mentioned and, if they will n
clean up without removal of excess metal they must b
replaced. Examine the valve guides for excessive wea
The clearance between the valve stems and guides whe
new was .001 to .004 inch and the normal acceptabl
maximum would be .009 inch. It may be possible, b
fitting new valves to restore this clearance to an acceptabl
figure. If not, new guides should be fitted. The clearanc
between the tappet guides 9 (see **FIG 1:4**), and th
tappets was .0008 to .0019 inch when new. It is suggeste
that .005 or .006 inch is acceptable. New tappets have
diameter of 1.3742—.0004 inch. Measurement of th
tappet guide bore diameter will indicate whether ne
tappets will restore the clearance to within that suggeste
or whether new tappet guides are also required.

Should replacement valve seat inserts, valve guides c
tappet guides be necessary, only genuine factory replace

ment parts should be used. The facilities required however, to machine out the old parts, shrink in the new and carry out the further machining and honing operations will necessitate the work being carried out by or through a competent garage. Seat inserts and tappet guides should have an interference fit of .003 inch and the cylinder head will have to be oven heated for one hour at 300°F (150°C) before fitting them. The new valve seats must be cut so that the dimension between the top of the valve stem and the back of the cam is .325 inch to ensure that the correct valve clearance will be obtainable at about the middle of the range of adjusting pad thicknesses. The tappet guide internal diameter must finally be reamed to 1.375 + .0007 inch and concentric with the valve guide bore. After pressing out the old valve guide, its location must be reamed to a diameter which will give an interference fit of .0005 to .0022 inch with the new oversize guide. Heat the head in boiling water for half an hour, fit the circlip to the guide, coat the stem with graphite grease and, with a piloted drift, drive it in until the circlip registers in the groove as shown in **FIG 1 : 6**. Inlet guides which are fitted with oil seals have a second groove above the circlip groove. Ensure that the correct type replacements are obtained.

Decarbonizing and valve grinding:

Avoid the use of sharp pointed tools and scrapers which could damage the aluminium surfaces. Remove all traces of carbon deposits from the combustion chambers, inlet and exhaust ports and joint faces with worn emerycloth and paraffin. Remove the carbon depoits from the crowns of the pistons. Grind the valves to their seats, using a suction type valve grinding tool and, on completion, ensure that all traces of grinding paste are removed from the valves and the head.

Valve clearance adjustment:

Assemble the valves, spring seats, springs, collars and cotters. The use of Churchill tool No. J.6118 to compress the springs will, if access to one is possible, greatly simplify this assembly. Fit the adjusting pads and tappets and, temporarily, one camshaft only. Measure and record the valve clearance using feeler gauges between the back of each cam and its tappet. Remove the first camshaft and fit the other. Measure and record the clearances as before. The correct clearances are: Inlet .004 inch; Exhaust .006 inch.

Adjusting pads are available increasing in .001 inch steps from .085 to .110 inch thick and are identified with the letter 'A' to 'Z' etched on the surface. From the record of valve clearances just taken and from the record of pad thicknesses, taken earlier, which gave these clearances the adjusting pads which are now required to give the correct clearances can be determined. Provided that the original pads are not indented they may be switched to any position which may require that thickness of pad. Obtain the other pads which are required.

Reassembly:

With the appropriate adjusting pads in position, finally fit one camshaft complete with D-washers, spring washers and nuts which should be torque tightened to 15 lb ft. Position this camshaft, as shown in **FIG 1 : 13** with the keyway at right angles to the cover face. The

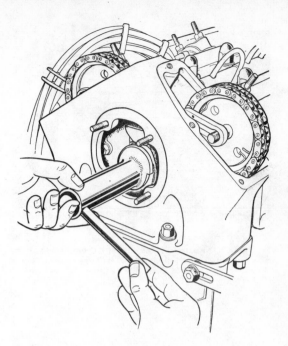

FIG 1:10   Tensioning the top chain

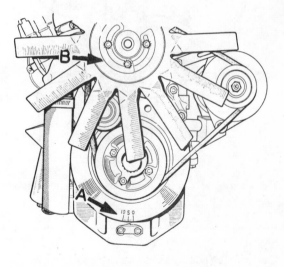

FIG 1:11   The arrow A indicates the timing scale on the S type crankshaft damper. O is TDC. The arrow B indicates the cooling fan balance pieces

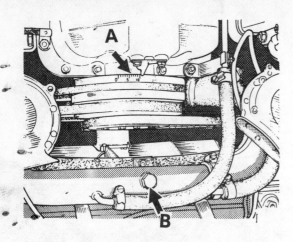

FIG 1:12 The arrow A indicates the timing scale on the 420 type crankshaft damper. O is TDC. The arrow B indicates the drain plug for the automatic transmission oil cooler

FIG 1:13 Camshaft timing gauge in position. The gauge must seat at the points indicated by the arrows

second must now be similarly positioned with the keyway at right angles to its cover face, fitted finally and the nuts torque tightened up. **From this point observe the warning given in Section 1:3**, that the camshafts must not be rotated until the timing procedure has been completed. Reassembly of the inlet and exhaust manifolds is their removal procedure in reverse.

1:5 Overhauling the camshaft drives

The components which comprise the camshaft drives are shown in **FIG 1:7** and the assembled drives in **FIG 1:8**. A bottom duplex endless roller chain 24 in **FIG 1:7**, driven from a sprocket on the crankshaft, engages round the larger of the double intermediate sprocket assembly 15. A second, top duplex chain is driven by the smaller intermediate sprocket and loops round the two camshaft sprockets 1 and under the idler sprocket 9 which runs on an eccentric shaft 10. The eccentricity of this shaft provides a means of adjusting the tension in the top chain while the bottom chain is automatically tensioned by the hydraulic tensioner 27 and which is also shown in **FIG 1:8** in its functional position immediately to right of and slightly above the oil pump and distributor drive. Two chain vibration dampers 19 and 20 in **FIG 1:7**, are associated with the top chain and two, 22 and 25, serve the bottom chain. The adjusting plates 2, which are bolted to the camshafts, have serrated peripheries which engage into the serrated bores of the camshaft sprockets 1 and create the vernier between the sprocket teeth and the holes in the adjusting plates so providing the means of timing the camshafts in relation to the crankshaft.

The hydraulic chain tensioner components are illustrated in **FIG 1:9**. Pressure oil from the crankcase oil gallery is fed through a gauze filter to the body 'D'. Under the combined influence of the hydraulic pressure and the light spring C which is cased in the restraint cylinder B, the plunger A causes the oil resistant rubber slipper which is mounted on it to bear upon the duplex chain and maintain it in correct tension. The slipper head is prevented from retracting by the limit peg at the bottom of the body plunger bore which engages in the nearest tooth in the helical slot in the restraint cylinder. A hole on the slipper head allows pressure oil to lubricate the chain. The plate E provides a face along which the slipper head works.

Removal:

1 Remove the cylinder head as instructed in **Section 1:3**. Remove the sump as instructed in **Section 1:7**. Remove the crankshaft torsional damper as described in **Section 1:12**. Remove the radiator, cooling fan and water pump as described in **Chapter 4**.

2 Remove the front cover 30 (see **FIG 1:8**), by unscrewing the setbolts which attach it to the front face of the cylinder block and collect the washers from beneath their heads.

3 Remove the hydraulic chain tensioner. Untab and remove the plug F (see **FIG 1:9**). Insert an Allen key (.125 inch across the flats) and turn it clockwise until the slipper remains in the fully retracted position. Untab and remove the securing bolts G and detach the unit. Collect the backing plate E the shim I and the gauze filter H.

4 Remove the four setbolts which attach the front mounting bracket 7 (see **FIG 1:7**), to the cylinder block. Remove the setscrews which secure the intermediate and bottom dampers, 22 and 25, to the block. Remove the two slotted setscrews securing the rear mounting bracket and withdraw the timing gear assembly.

Dismantling :

Remove the nut, shakeproof washer and adjustment plate 12 from the idler shaft 10, and withdraw the locking plunger and spring 13 and 14. Separate the front mounting bracket from the rear mounting bracket by removing the four nuts which hold them together and remove the bottom chain. The intermediate sprocket shaft 16 is retained in the rear mounting bracket by a circlip. Remove this, press the shaft out of the bracket and remove the intermediate sprockets.

Overhaul :

If the chains show signs of wear or stretch, fit new ones. Fit new dampers and a new hydraulic tensioner plunger if any of these are worn. Fit new sprockets if the original ones are worn.

Reassembly :

1 Fit the eccentric shaft to the front mounting bracket, insert the spring and locking plunger, fit the serrated adjustment plate and secure with the shakeproof washer and nut. Fit the idler sprocket (21 teeth) to the eccentric shaft.

2 Fit the intermediate sprockets onto the shaft with the large sprocket forwards. Press the shaft into the lower hole in the rear mounting bracket and secure it with the circlip at the rear of the bracket.

3 Fit the longer top chain to the smaller intermediate sprocket and the shorter bottom chain to the larger intermediate sprocket.

4 Loop the top chain under the idler sprocket and offer up the front mounting bracket to the rear mounting bracket with the chain dampers 19 and 20, together with their distance pieces 21 interposed between the brackets. Thread shakeproof washers onto the four setbolts, pass them through the front bracket, the chain dampers and distance pieces and secure the two brackets together with four nuts and shakeproof washers.

5 Refitting the remainder of the assembly is the removal procedure in reverse. After fitting the bottom chain but before fitting the front cover, the hydraulic tensioner must be reinstalled as follows. Fit the oil-feed conical filter. Fit the tabwasher and the two body bolts and secure the body including the shim and backing plate. Tighten the bolts and tab them. Do not release the tensioner locking mechanism until it has been finally fitted into place with the bottom chain in position. Insert the Allen key and turn it clockwise until the plunger moves forward under spring pressure against the chain. Do not turn the key anticlockwise or force the plunger onto the chain by external force. Refit the plug and secure it with the tabwasher. Refer to **FIG 1 : 8** and adjust the intermediate damper A on its slotted securing holes so that, with a new chain, the slipper projects from the body by $\frac{1}{8}$ inch as shown at B. With a stretched chain this dimension will have to be increased. Set the bottom damper C in light contact with the chain.

Tensioning the camshaft drive top chain :

Refer to **FIG 1 : 10** and, through the breather aperture, slacken the locknut which secures the serrated adjustment plate 12 in **FIG 1 : 7**. Depress the locking plunger 13 and

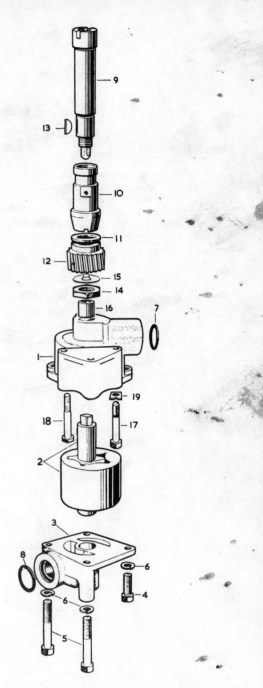

FIG 1 :14   Components of the oil pump and distributor pump drive

Key to Fig 1 :14   1 Pump body   2 Rotor assembly   3 Cover   4 Setscrew   5 Setscrew   6 Spring washer   7 O-ring   8 O-ring   9 Drive shaft   10 Bush   11 Washer   12 Helical gear   13 Key   14 Nut   15 Special washer   16 Coupling sleeve   17 Dowel bolt   18 Bolt   19 Tabwasher

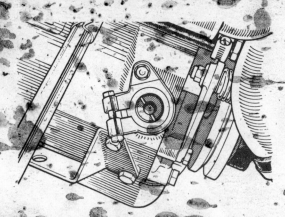

FIG 1:15 The distributor drive shaft offset slot when No. 6 piston is on TDC of the compression stroke

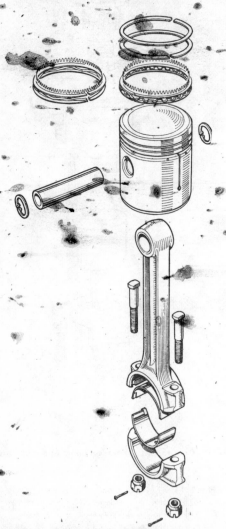

FIG 1:16 Components of the piston and connecting rod

rotate the adjustment plate by means of the two holes in an anticlockwise direction. When correctly tensioned there should be slight flexibility on both outer sides below the camshaft sprockets, that is, the chain should not be dead tight. Rotate the crankshaft slightly each way and recheck the chain tension. Release the locking plunger and tighten the adjustment locknut. The use of Churchill tool No. J2 for this procedure is shown in FIG 1:10. The tension of the chain may be released by following this procedure but turning the adjustment plate in a clockwise direction.

1:6 Valve timing

1 Set the front piston No. 6 accurately on TDC on the firing stroke, that is with the distributor rotor arm opposite No. 6 cylinder segment. The location of TDC marks are shown in FIGS 1:11 and 1:12.

2 Tension the top camshaft drive chain as described at the end of Section 1:5.

3 Accurately position the camshafts with the timing gauge which is included in the tool-kit and the use of which is illustrated in FIG 1:13. Ensure that the gauge is seated on the camshaft cover face at the points indicated by the arrows.

4 Refer to FIG 1:7 and withdraw the circlips 3 which retain the serrated adjuster plates 2 to the sprockets 1. Press the adjuster plates towards the front of the engine until their serrations disengage from the sprocket. Fit the sprockets to the flanges on the camshafts. Carefully line up the two holes in the adjuster plates with the two tapped holes in the camshaft flanges. It is most important that this lining up operation is done exactly to preclude the camshafts from being moved off their gauge-set position when the setbolts are fitted. If difficulty is experienced in aligning the holes precisely, the adjuster plate should be turned through 180 deg. and this, due to the relative indexing of the two holes and the serrations, will facilitate the operation. Engage the serrations of the adjuster plates with those of the sprockets, fit the circlips and the one setbolt which is accessible in each adjuster plate. Turn the engine until the other holes are accessible, fit the second setbolt and secure them in pairs with new locking wire.

1:7 Sump

Removal:

Drain and discard the sump oil. Disconnect the relief oil return pipe from the filter. Remove the front suspension unit as described in **Chapter 9**. On S type models, remove the twenty-six setscrews and four nuts and, on 420 type cars, remove the twenty-four setscrews and two bolts and detach the sump. Note, on all models, that a short setscrew is fitted at the righthand front corner of the sump. On 420 type models fitted with automatic transmission, the two pipes from the transmission to the oil cooler must be removed before the sump can be detached.

Refer to FIG 1:17. Remove oil pipe 66 and check the condition of O-ring 67 and hose 69. Clean all sludge from the sump, wash the gauze strainer in petrol and ensure that all traces of gasket and jointing compound are removed from the sump, crankcase and bearing cap faces.

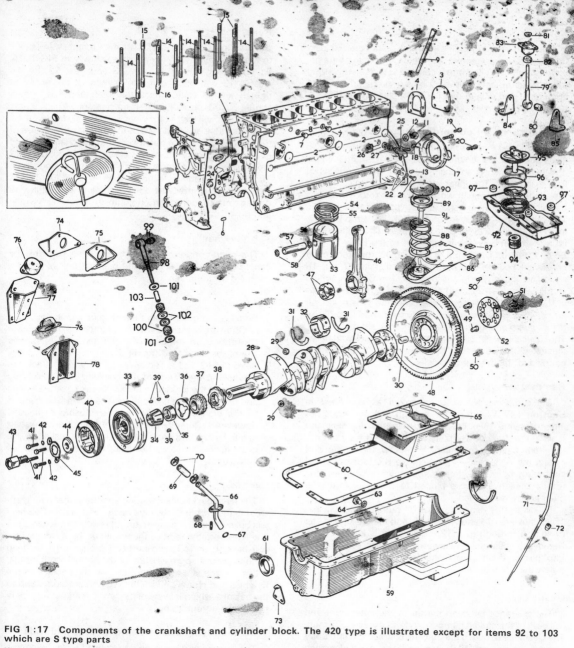

FIG 1:17 Components of the crankshaft and cylinder block. The 420 type is illustrated except for items 92 to 103 which are S type parts

Key to Fig 1:17   1 Cylinder block assembly   2 Core plug   3 Blanking plate   4 Gasket   5 Front timing cover   6 Dowel
7 Setscrew   8 Copper washer   9 Dipstick adaptor tube   10 Plug   11 Headed plug   12 Copper washer   13 Dowel
14 Stud (plain)   15 Stud (plain)   16 Stud (dowel)   17 Cover assembly   18 Ring dowel   19 Cap screw (centre)
20 Cap screw (outer)   21 Banjo bolt   22 Copper washer   23 Sealing ring   24 Filter gauze   25 Drain tap   26 Copper
washer   27 Fibre washer   28 Crankshaft   29 Screwed plug   30 Bush   31 Thrust washer   32 Main bearings
33 Crankshaft damper   34 Cone   35 Distance piece   36 Oil thrower   37 Timing chain sprocket   38 Gear
39 Key   40 Pulley   41 Bolt   42 Lockwasher   43 Bolt   44 Washer   45 Tabwasher   46 Connecting rod
47 Big-end bearing   48 Flywheel   49 Dowel   50 Dowel   51 Setscrew   52 Lockplate   53 Piston
54 Pressure ring (upper)   55 Pressure ring (lower)   56 Scraper ring (Maxiflex)   57 Gudgeon pin   58 Circlip   59 Oil sump
60 Gasket   61 Seal   62 Seal   63 Drain plug   64 Copper washer   65 Baffle assembly   66 Pipe assembly
67 O-ring   68 Stud   69 Hose   70 Hose clip   71 Dipstick assembly   72 Washer   73 Ignition timing pointer
74 Bracket assembly (righthand)   75 Bracket assembly (lefthand)   76 Front engine mounting   77 Support bracket assembly
(righthand)   78 Support bracket assembly (lefthand)   79 Stabilizing link   80 Bush   81 Stepped washer   82 Stepped bush
83 Rubber mounting   84 Bearing bracket (righthand)   85 Bearing bracket (lefthand)   86 Bracket assembly (rear mounting)
87 Packing piece   88 Coil spring   89 Spring seat (rubber)   90 Coil spring retainer   91 Pin assembly   92 Channel
support   93 Spring seat   94 Centre bush   95 Spring retainer assembly   96 Coil spring   97 Packing piece
98 Stabilizing link (front)   99 Bush   100 Rubber bush   101 Washer   102 Dished washer   103 Distance tube

Refitting :

This is the reverse of the removal procedure. Fit new gaskets 60 and a new seal 62 which, to facilitate its fitment, should be rolled into a coil and retained with string for some hours before fitting. Use a good quality jointing compound and ensure that the short setscrew is fitted in its correct position.

1 : 8 Oil pump, oil pump/distributor drive

An exploded view of the oil pump and its drive (which is common to the distributor) is shown in **FIG 1 : 14**. The pump which is an eccentric rotor type, consists of four main parts. The inner rotor and shaft unit has four male lobes and is driven within the outer rotor which has five female lobes. Item 2 shows these parts in engagement. The outer rotor locates in the bore of the pump body 1, in which the oil delivery port is situated. The suction port is in the cover 3 which is attached to the body by four bolts 4 and 5. The pump is secured to the front main crankshaft bearing cap by three dowel bolts 17 and 18 which are locked by tabwashers 19. The O-rings, which should always be replaced at overhaul, locate in grooves in the suction and delivery bores and into which suction and delivery pipes are a push fit. Items 9 and 14 comprise the oil pump and ignition distributor drive shaft assembly. The helical gear 12 is driven from the crankshaft as illustrated in **FIG 1 : 8**. The inner pump rotor shaft is coupled to the drive shaft by sleeve 16.

Removal :

The sump must first be removed as described in **Section 1 : 7**. Withdraw the suction and delivery pipes after removing their brackets. Untab the washers and remove the three dowel bolts which attach the pump to the front main bearing cap. Withdraw the pump and collect the coupling sleeve. Remove the four bolts and spring washers and detach the cover. Withdraw the rotors. The drive shaft is pinned to the inner rotor and must not be dismantled.

Following the removal of the oil pump, untab washer 15. Remove nut 14 and washer 15, and tap the square end of shaft 9 through gear 12, to which it is keyed by 13. Remove the gear and thrust washer 11. Bush 10 is pressed into the cylinder block and should not be removed unless a new bush is required.

Overhaul :

The clearance between the tip of the inner rotor and the peak of the curved hump should not exceed .006 inch. The clearance between the outer rotor and the pump body should not exceed .010 inch and the axial clearance between the rotors and the face of the pump body should not exceed .0025 inch. If necessary this axial clearance may be reduced to this figure by judicious lapping of the body and/or the unchamfered face of the outer rotor on a suitable surface plate. Inspect the cover and body; if they are scored or if the bores show signs of wear, new parts should be obtained. Check that the inner rotor is tightly pinned to its shaft and note that, should replacements be required, the inner rotor and shaft unit and the outer rotor are only supplied as an assembly.

If a new bush is fitted it must be reamed in position to a diameter of .7497 + .0008 inch.

Reassembly :

With No. 6 piston on TDC of the compression stroke, fit the drive shaft with the offset, as shown in **FIG 1 : 15**. Fit the thrust washer 11, key 13 and gear 12. Fit the washer 15 with its peg in the keyway of the gear and tighten nut 14 fully. Check the shaft end float which should be .004 to .006 inch. If no clearance exists, a new driving gear will restore the clearance. Finally retab nut 14.

Reassembly and refitment of the pump is the reverse of the removal procedure but ensure that the chamfered end of the outer rotor is entered into the pump body. On refitment care must be taken to check that the coupling sleeve 16 has appreciable end float when in position. This is important as it indicates correct fitment and otherwise damage may occur to the oil pump/distributor drive gear and bush assembly.

1 : 9 Flywheel

The operations covered by this section can only be carried out after the engine and gearbox unit have been removed from the car.

Removal :

1 Remove the gearbox and clutch housing as described in **Chapter 6** and the clutch assembly as described in **Chapter 5**. In the case of cars fitted with automatic gearboxes, refer to **Chapter 7**.
2 Refer to **FIG 1 : 17**. The ten bolts 51 which attach the flywheel to the flange of the crankshaft are locked by the tabs of the locking plate 52. Knock back these tabs and remove the bolts and plate. The flywheel is centred to the crankshaft flange by two mushroom-headed dowels 49. Remove the flywheel from the crankshaft flange by tapping gently with a rawhide mallet or, if a plain hammer has to be used, interpose a block of hardwood.

Overhaul :

The flywheel is a steel forging and the starter gear teeth are integral with it. If they are badly worn a new flywheel will be required. If, however, only a few teeth are damaged it will be possible to have them built up by welding. This will have to be followed by hand-profiling the built up teeth to a close approximation of the normal tooth profile. If this salvage is adopted, ensure that the balance of the flywheel and clutch unit is checked and any correction to the balance which may be necessary is made as for a new flywheel before refitting.

1 : 10 Removing and refitting pistons and rods

The pistons and rods can be removed with the engine in the car. The pistons, however, will not pass the crankshaft and it is therefore necessary to remove the cylinder head and withdraw the pistons and rods up through the top of the cylinder bores.

Removal :

Remove the cylinder head and sump as described in **Sections 1 : 3** and **1 : 7**. If all the pistons and rods are to be removed, it will be found convenient to deal with them in pairs and, by turning the engine, to work on the pair which are at BDC. The components are shown in **FIG 1 : 17** and, in greater details, in **FIG 1:16**. Remove and discard the splitpins from the connecting rod bolt nuts and remove the nuts. Remove the connecting rod caps noting that each cap is matched to its rod and must not be interchanged with that from another rod. Remove the connecting rod bolts and, after removing any carbon from round the top of the cylinder bore, push the rod and piston up and out of the bore. Wire each cap and rod together and note that they are each marked with the cylinder number and that these marks are on the same side of the rod and its cap.

Big-end bearings can be examined and changed without removing the pisons and rods and, consequently, without the need to remove the cylinder head. With that exception, proceed as described but, when the connecting rod cap has been removed, lift the connecting rod off the crankpin and detach the bearing shells. If there has been a big-end bearing failure, the crankpin must be examined for damage and for the transfer of metal to its surface. The oilway in the crankshaft must be checked to ensure that there is no obstruction.

Refitting:

If connecting rods have been in use for a very high mileage or if a severe bearing failure has occured it is advisable to fit a new set to avoid the possibility of failure due to fatigue. If the original rods are being refitted, ensure that all oil holes are clear. Under no circumstances should the rod or cap be filed to take up wear nor should bearing shells be hand-scraped.

The connecting rods and pistons are refitted through the cylinder bores to the same cylinders from which they were removed. Ensure that the pistons are refitted with the split skirt on the lefthand or exhaust side of the engine. To facilitate correct fitting, 'Front' is marked on the piston crown. Lubricate all parts with engine oil, position the piston ring gaps out of line with each other and use a piston ring clamp such as Churchill tool No. 3843 when entering the rings into the bores.

Fit the bearing shells and caps, check that the caps are matched to their own rods and refit the bolts and nuts. Torque tighten the connecting rod nuts to a figure of 37 lb ft and lock with new splitpins.

Refit the sump as described in **Section 1:7** and refit the cylinder head as described in **Section 1:3**.

1:11 Pistons and rings

The aluminium alloy pistons have three rings of which two are tapered periphery compression rings and the third is an oil control. The top compression ring is hard chrome plated. Tapered periphery rings must be fitted the correct way up and they are marked 'Top' or 'T' accordingly. The Maxiflex oil control ring consists of two thin steel rails with an expander between them. On new rings these parts are held together as an assembly with an adhesive. The two lugs of the expander must be positioned into the hole in the piston which is directly above the gudgeon pin bore.

Compression ratios:

The engine compression ratio is determined by the type of piston which has been fitted and, by changing the type of piston, the compression ratio may be altered. Reference should be made to **Section 1:17** for information on this.

The original, as manufactured, compression ratio is given by a stroke number after the engine number in the log book and on the car data plate.

Gudgeon pins:

Gudgeon pins, which are fully floating and retained by a circlip at each end, are selectively assembled to their pistons and consequently are not interchangeable. New pistons are supplied complete with gudgeon pins. Gudgeon pins are a tight push fit in the piston bores at normal temperature and removal and refitting is best effected by heating in oil to a temperature of 230°F (110°C). Remove the circlips, heat the piston, gudgeon pin and connecting rod small-end, and with due care for the temperature, push out the gudgeon pin. To refit, heat the piston and small-end, press in the gudgeon pin, centre it and fit the circlips.

Overhaul:

Standard size pistons are graded for selective assembly purposes in steps of .0003 inch and are identified 'F', 'G', 'H', 'J' and 'K'. The sizes which correspond with these letters are given in Technical Data in the Appendix. Pistons and cylinder blocks, adjacent to the bores, are stamped with the relevant letter. If new standard size pistons are required, the identification letter must be quoted. There is no grading of oversize pistons which are available at +.010, +.020 and +.030 inch oversize. Reboring of the cylinder bores is normally recommended when bore wear exceeds .006 inch. If the bores will not clean up within .030 inch oversize, new liners should be fitted and bored and honed to standard size. For reasons of engine balance, pistons fitted to an engine should not vary in weight, one with another, by more than 2 drams.

Before fitting new piston rings, remove the cylinder bore glaze and check the ring fitted gap. This is measured by placing a piston well down the bore, pressing the new ring down onto it and using feeler gauges. Compression ring gaps should be .015 to .020 inch, Maxiflex oil control ring gaps should be .015 to .033 inch and side clearances should be .001 to .003 inch. Always fit and remove piston rings over the top of a piston and, when cleaning carbon deposits from the ring grooves, care must be taken not to remove metal. Ensure that all oil holes are clear.

1:12 Crankshaft and main bearings

The counterbalanced crankshaft is a manganese/molybdenum steel forging and is supported on seven shell type main bearings with axial thrust taken on two semi-circular whitemetal faced thrust washers which are fitted into recesses in the centre main bearing cap. A torsional vibration damper is fitted to the front of the crankshaft. During manufacture the crankshaft was statically and dynamically balanced as a component and, with the flywheel and clutch unit fitted, as an assembly. Keyed to the front of the crankshaft are the drives for the oil pump and distributor and the camshafts. **FIG 1:17** illustrates these components.

Removal:

Following the removal of the engine, the cylinder head, camshaft drives, sump, oil pump and drive, flywheel and the pistons and rods as described in **Sections 1:2, 1:3,**

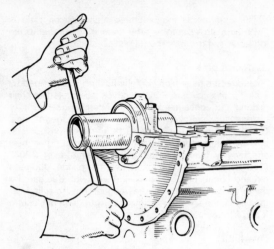

FIG 1:18 Sizing the rear oil seal using Churchill tool No. J.17

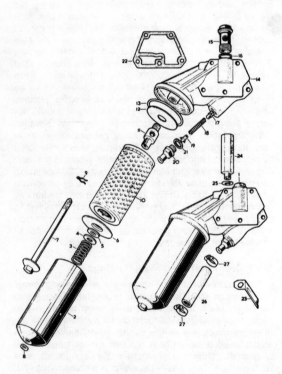

FIG 1:19 Components of the oil filter

Key to Fig 1:19   1 Oil filter assembly
2 Canister   3 Spring   4 Plain washer   5 Felt washer   6 Pressure plate   7 Bolt   8 Rubber washer
9 Spring clip   10 Element   11 Anchor insert
12 Clamping plate   13 Sealing ring   14 Filter head
15 Balance valve   16 Washer   17 Relief valve   18 Spring
19 Spider   20 Adaptor   21 Washer   22 Gasket
23 Bracket   24 Adaptor   25 Washer   26 Hose
27 Clips

1:5, 1:7, 1:8, 1:9 and **1:10** respectively, and the other preliminaries dismantling operations indicated in these sections, refer to **FIG 1:17** and proceed to:

1 Knock back the tabs and remove the two bolts which secure the locking washer 45. Remove the locking washer, unscrew the large bolt 43 and remove the washer 44. Insert two levers behind the damper 33 and ease it off the cone 34. A sharp tap on the edge of the cone will assist removal.

2 Remove the cone, distance piece, oil thrower, sprocket and gear which are 34 to 38. Collect the keys 39. Should it be necessary to separate the pulley 40 from the damper, mark them so that they may be reassembled in their original position then remove the bolts and shakeproof washers 41 and 42.

3 Untab the fourteen washers (later engines are fitted with plain washers) and remove the bolts from the bearing caps. Note that the caps are identified to their positions as also are the semicircular thrust washers to their recesses in the centre main bearing cap. The thrust washers are items 31.

4 Detach the oil return thread bottom half cover from the top half by removing the two Allen screws. The two halves 17 are located by hollow dowels. The crankshaft can now be lifted away and the remaining bearing shells removed. The top half cover of 17 is located to the crankcase by two hollow dowels 18 and attached by three Allen screws 19 and 20.

Overhaul:

The screw plugs, 29 in **FIG 1:17**, which are locked by peening should be removed and the accumulated sludge removed and the oil passages cleaned. Refit the plugs and re-peen to lock them.

Measure the main journals and the crankpins both for wear and ovality and, if this exceeds .003 inch, a factory reconditioned exchange crankshaft should be obtained or the journals and crankpins should be reground —.010, —.020, —.030 or —.040 inch undersize. Grinding by more than .040 undersize is not acceptable and this circumstance would dictate the fitment of a new crankshaft. The identificaion figures for undersize journals will be found stamped on the webs of reconditioned crankshafts.

New main bearing shells should be fitted and these will either be standard or oversize to suit the diameters of the reground journals. New thrust washers should be fitted to give an end float of .004 to .006 inch. Standard and .004 inch oversize washers are obtainable. It is permissible to mix them to obtain an end float within these limits.

Reference should be made to **Section 1:8** for the overhaul of the oil pump and distributor drive.

Refitting:

Fit new asbestos seals, noting that all of each half seal must be pressed into the groove in each half cover. Do not cut off the ends but continue pressing until the ends are flush. Fit the rear main bearing cap but omit the shell bearings. Fit and tighten its bolts to a torque of 83 lb ft. Fit the two oil return thread covers, smear the seal with colloidal graphite and, using Churchill tool No. J17, as shown in **FIG 1:18**, as if it were a reamer, size the asbestos inserts by entering the pilot end of the tool into the rear main bearing bore. Press and rotate until the sizing bar is

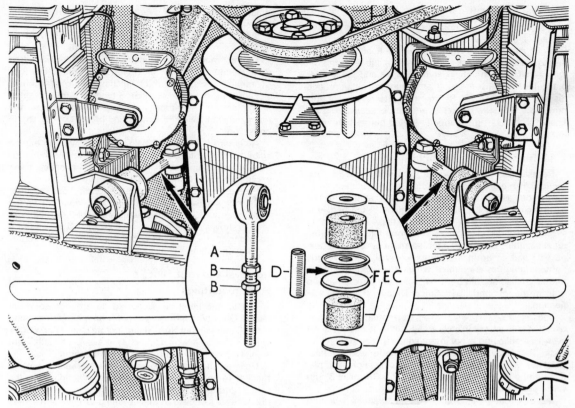

FIG 1:20   Front stabilizers fitted to S type engines

Key to Fig 1:20   **A** Stabilizing link   **B** Nut   **C** Washer   **D** Distance tube   **E** Rubber bush   **F** Dished washer

fully home. Remove by reversing the process. Remove the rear bearing cap and the bottom half cover.

With the cylinder block upside down, fit the new main bearing shells. Lay the crankshaft in position and fit the oil return thread covers. Ensure that the hollow dowels are not omitted. Fit the centre main bearing cap and thrust washers and check that the end float is within the limits of .004 to .006 inch. Fit the remaining caps to their identified positions, torque tighten their bolts to 83 lb ft, check the crankshaft for free rotation and tab up the washers.

1:13 External oil filter

Description:

The external oil filter is of the fullflow type and pressure oil is fed to it from a passage in the crankcase. The pressure relief valve is incorporated in the head of the filter and excess oil is returned to the sump through external piping. Under normal circumstances the oil which is fed to the main oil gallery has passed through the filter element but the element collects foreign matter and sludge on its surface and, as it becomes clogged, the drop in pressure across it increases. Normally a replacement element is fitted about every 3000 miles and before this pressure drop

becomes excessive but, in the event of neglect, to preclude the engine from being starved of oil, a balance valve is incorporated in the filter. This valve is spring-loaded and opens when the differential pressure across the element rises to 10 to 15 lb/sq in and allows pressure oil to bypass the element. There will usually be a drop of about 10 lb/sq in in the oil gauge pressure when this occurs, and a new filter element should be fitted as soon as possible. The oil pressure relief valve is not adjustable. It limits the pressure of oil fed to the main gallery to approximately 40 lb/sq in with a warm engine.

The components of the oil filter are illustraed in **FIG 1:19**. The electrically operated oil pressure transmitter is mounted in the head of the unit and its circuit is given in **FIG 12:20** in **Chapter 12**.

Element replacement:

Replace the element every 3000 miles. Refer to **FIG 1:19** and remove bolt 7. Collect washer 8. Oil will drain from the canister 2 as it is removed. Thoroughly wash the canister with petrol and allow it to dry before inserting a new element. Check the condition of sealing ring 13 and washer 8 before reassembly and, if their condition is at all doubtful, replace them with new parts.

Removal of the filter unit:

Disconnect the lead from the oil pressure transmitter. Slacken clip 27 and disconnect hose 26 from the unit. Remove the five bolts which secure the head of the filter unit to the cylinder block and remove the clip retaining the carburetter float chamber overflow pipes and the anchor bracket for the throttle spring. Dismount the filter unit and discard the gasket 22. Refitment is the reverse of this procedure. Fit a new gasket 22 and rubber sealing ring 13. Ensure that this ring is correctly seated before tightening the centre bolt.

1:14 Reassembling the engine

Reassembly instructions are given in the text of each section. These are largely the dismantling procedures in reverse but, as they are not always so, the point should be confirmed against the information given in the text. It is then simply a matter of tackling the tasks in the correct sequence, of applying normal automobile engineering practice, fitting only Jaguar replacement parts, using new gaskets and ensuring that joints are well made. Torque tightening figures are quoted where it is important that a torque wrench should be used. Torque figures are given both in the text and in Technical Data in the Appendix Section.

The following sequence covers the rebuild of an engine which has been completely overhauled. It does not list every operation and is not intended to replace the Section texts. Reference will have to be made also to later Chapters which cover separate subjects. For example, the ignition timing procedure is given in **Chapter 3**, and carburetter refitment and tuning in **Chapter 2**.

Start by fitting the crankshaft and torsional vibration damper. Follow with the pistons and connecting rods, the distributor and oil pump drive, the oil pump and its pipes. The flywheel, clutch unit and gearbox should now be refitted followed by the camshaft drives, front cover, sump, water pump and cooling fan. The cylinder head is fitted next and, on S type engines the engine lifting plate can be attached at this point. The top camshaft drive chain may now be tensioned and the valve timing procedure carried out. Fit the distributor and carry out the ignition timing procedure. Refitment of the carburetters should not be carried out until after the engine unit has been reinstalled.

At each stage check free rotation, clearances and end floats as may be applicable and that locking of nuts and bolts by tabwasher, splitpin or shakeproof washer has not been omitted.

1:15 Engine mountings
Description:

The front of the engine is supported on two rubber mountings. Those fitted to 420 type cars are shown in **FIG 1:17** and are items 74 to 78. The front mountings fitted to S type models are similar though not dimensionally identical.

Two types of rear mounting are shown in **FIG 1:17**. That illustrated by items 86 to 91 is fitted to all 420 type cars irrespective of the type of transmission. This type, though not dimensionally identical, is also fitted to later S type cars fitted with automatic transmissions and a similar type is fitted to overdrive models with and after chassis Nos.

3.4S	1B.2192RH	1B.25301LH
3.8S	1B.52078RH	1B.76310LH

The rear mounting illustrated by items 92 to 97 is fitted to all standard transmission S type models and to S type overdrive models earlier than the chassis numbers quoted.

Early automatic transmission S type cars are supported at the rear on two rubber mountings fitted between the rear extension case and a mounting bracket bolted to the body floor.

All engines, S and 420 type, are fitted with an engine stabilizer unit at the rear of the cylinder block. The components of this unit are items 79 to 83. It is attached to the engine by a bolt through brackets 84 and 85.

S type engines only are provided with front stabilizer units, one on each side of the engine, adjacent to the front mountings. The components of one of these stabilizer units is shown by items 98 to 103. **FIG 1:20** shows these stabilizer units in position and the inset shows the components in detail.

Removal and refitment:

Front mountings:

The engine must be supported on appropriate lifting tackle. On S type models, either lift on a sling or a lifting plate (Churchill tool No. J8) and, before taking the weight, remove the bolt which attaches the eye of each front stabilizing link (99 in **FIG 1:17**) to the engine.

Unscrew the large setbolt which secures each mounting bracket 74 and 75 to mounting rubber 76 and collect the spring and plain washers. Raise the engine until the brackets are just clear of the mounting rubbers which may then be detached from brackets 77 and 78 by removing two nuts and bolts from each.

Refitment is this procedure in reverse. On S type cars, reassemble the front stabilizer units as described later in this Section.

Rear mountings:

In all cases, **release the rear engine stabilizer** as described later in this Section **before commencing to remove the rear mounting.**

Early S type automatic transmission models:

Remove the six bolts which attach the ventilated coverplate to the bottom of the torque converter housing and remove it. Place a piece of wood under the torque converter housing and, making sure that it does not foul the converter, take the weight of the engine on a jack placed under the piece of wood. Release the engine stabilizer as described later in this Section. Mark the postion of the engine mounting bracket relative to the body floor to facilitate refitting it in its original position. Remove the six bolts and the packing washers from between the bracket and the body floor. Remove the two nuts and washers which attach the support bracket to the two mounting rubbers and the nuts and washers which secure the mounting rubbers to the bracket on the gearbox extension case. This will be facilitated if the jack is lowered slightly. Reassembly is the reverse of this procedure. Reset the rear stabilizer unit as described later.

420 models:

Support the rear mounting with a jack and remove the four setscrews which secure the bracket assembly 86 in **FIG 1 : 17**. Collect the spring and oval washers. Lower the jack slowly to release the compressed mounting spring 88. Collect the four packing pieces 87. Refitment is the reverse of this procedure. Reset the rear stabilizer unit as described later in this Section.

Later S type overdrive models:

The procedure is as described for 420 models.

Later S type automatic transmission models:

The procedure is as described for 420 models.

S type standard transmission and earlier overdrive models:

Place a jack under the gearbox and take the weight of the engine. Refer to the inset in **FIG 1 : 17**, place a large washer over the stem of the spring retainer and secure it by a piece of .125 inch diameter rod as shown. Remove the eight bolts and washers which attach the channel support 92 to the body. Collect the stiffening plates and packing pieces. Remove the two bolts and washers which secure the mounting lugs to the gearbox. The unit is dismantled by placing it upside down under a press, compressing the spring until the rod can be removed from the hole through the stem and then slowly releasing the spring pressure. The large washer, spring retainer 95, spring 96, rubber spring seat 93 and centre bush 94 may now be removed from the channel support bracket. The free length of the spring on cars fitted with an overdrive is .375 inch longer than on a car with no overdrive. The spring lengths are given in Technical Data in the Appendix Section.

Reassembly is the reverse of this procedure. Ensure that if a new spring is required, it is of the correct length. Ensure also that the spring retainer is fitted the correct way round with the washers which are welded to the lugs facing that side of the support channel which has the extra cutaway in the flange.

Rear stabilizer unit:

To release the stabilizing link, refer to **FIG 1 : 17** and remove the locknut and stepped washer 81. Screw the flanged washer 82 downwards and out of engagement with the rubber mounting 83. Following its release it may be removed by unscrewing the nut and bolt 90 and 91 in **FIG 1 : 17**, which attaches the stabilizer link 83 to the brackets on the engine. On reassembly it is important that the stabilizer is adjusted correctly and failure to observe the following procedure may result in engine vibration or in the engine being pulled up on its mountings. Refer to **FIG 1 : 17** and:

1 Screw the flanged washer 86 up the stabilizer link until its flange contacts the bottom of the rubber mounting 87. The slot in its upper face enables it to be screwed up the link by means of a narrow-bladed screwdriver.
2 Fit the upper flanged washer 85 and tighten the self-locking nut.

Front stabilizer units (S type models only):

To preclude pulling the engine down onto the front mountings it is important to assemble the front stabilizer units as follows:

Refer to the inset in **FIG 1 : 20** and run the nuts B up to the top of the thread on the link A. Fit one washer C, the distance tube D, one rubber bush E and one dished washer F. Pass the link, with these parts fitted, through the hole in the underframe bracket and bolt eye of the link to the bracket on the engine. Fit the second dished washer, rubber bush and plain washer below the bracket and retain them with the self-locking nut which should not be tightened at this stage. Screw the lower nut B into firm contact with the top washer C and lock them with the second nut B. Tighten the self-locking nut. Removal is the reverse of this procedure.

1 : 16 Refitting the engine

Refitting the engine and gearbox unit into the car is the reverse of the removal procedure given in **Section 1 : 2** and reference should be made to that Section and to the various Chapter and Section numbers quoted in it. New hoses will have been obtained to replace any which showed signs of deterioration and the required quantities of engine oil, gearbox oil or transmission fluid will have been obtained. These quantities are given in Technical Data in the Appendix Section.

Refitment of the air cleaner should be delayed until the cylinder head holding down nuts have been checked tightened. On S type engines, the lifting plate may be removed as soon as the engine unit has been reinstalled and the engine mountings have been refitted. Torque tighten the four cylinder head nuts which were used to the figure of 54 lb ft.

Refill the cooling system and, if antifreeze was in use and was retained, this coolant may be re-used. Fill the engine with the correct grade of oil. Fill the gearbox noting that the overdrive, if fitted, will automatically be filled from the gearbox. Fill the automatic gearbox and converter with the correct grade of fluid by following the procedure described in **Chapter 7**.

Top up the clutch hydraulic reservoir to the correct level. Refer to **Chapter 5** and bleed the system. If the front suspension assembly was removed, the brake hydraulic system must be topped up and the brakes bled as described in **Chapter 11**.

When installation is complete and all systems made serviceable, the engine should be run up to full working temperature and, after allowing it to cool, the cylinder head holding down nuts should be check tightened to the figure of 54 lb ft for S type and 58 lb ft for 420 types and the air cleaner refitted. When the car has been run for about a hundred miles the cylinder head holding down nuts should again be check torque tightened.

1 : 17 Modifications
Compression ratios:

The engine compression ratio is determined by the type of piston fitted and the ratio may be altered by fitting appropriate pistons. There is the choice of 8:1 or 9:1 for 4.2 litre engines and of 7:1, 8:1 or 9:1 for 3.4 and 3.8 litre engines. Reference should be made to Technical Data in the Appendix where compression height dimensions are given and these allow pistons to be identified to the compression ratio which they will provide. Reference to **Chapter 2** will indicate whether carburetter modifications are required to match them to a change in compression ratio.

Inlet valve oil seals:

Inlet valve oil seals may be introduced into earlier engines provided that **complete sets** of inlet guides, collars, cotters, spring seats and circlips are obtained. If, on overhaul, new inlet valve guides are required, it will be found a suitable opportunity to fit the later type.

1:18 Fault diagnosis

(a) Engine will not start

1 Defective coil
2 Faulty distributor capacitor (condenser)
3 Dirty, pitted or incorrectly set contact breaker points
4 Ignition wires loose or insulation faulty
5 Water on spark plug leads
6 Battery discharged, corrosion of terminals
7 Faulty or jammed starter
8 Sparking plug leads wrongly connected
9 Vapour lock in fuel pipes
10 Defective fuel pump
11 Overchoking or underchoking
12 Blocked petrol filter or carburetter jet(s)
13 Leaking valves
14 Sticking valves
15 Valve timing incorrect
16 Ignition timing incorrect

(b) Engine stalls

1 Check 1, 2, 3, 4, 5, 10, 11, 12, 13 and 14 in (a)
2 Sparking plugs defective or gaps incorrect
3 Retarded ignition
4 Mixture too weak
5 Water in fuel system
6 Petrol tank vent blocked
7 Incorrect valve clearances

(c) Engine idles badly

1 Check 2 and 7 in (b)
2 Air leak at manifold joints
3 Carburetter adjustment wrong
4 Air leak in carburetter
5 Over-rich mixture
6 Worn piston rings
7 Worn valve stems or guides
8 Weak exhaust valve springs

(d) Engine misfires

1 Check 1, 2, 3, 4, 5, 8, 10, 12, 13, 14, 15 and 16 in (a); 2, 3, 4 and 7 in (b)
2 Weak or broken valve springs

(e) Engine overheats (see **Chapter 4**)

(f) Compression low

1 Check 13 and 14 in (a); 6 and 7 in (c) and 2 in (d)

2 Worn piston ring grooves
3 Scored or worn cylinder bores

(g) Engine lacks power

1 Check 3, 10, 11, 12, 13, 14, 15 and 16 in (a); 2, 3, 4 and 7 in (b); 6 and 7 in (c) and 2 in (d). Also check (e) and (f)
2 Leaking joint washers
3 Fouled sparking plugs
4 Automatic advance not working

(h) Burnt valves or seats

1 Check 13 and 14 in (a); 7 in (b) and 2 in (d). Also check (e)
2 Excessive carbon round valve seats and head

(j) Sticking valves

1 Check 2 in (d)
2 Bent valve stem
3 Scored valve stem or guide
4 Incorrect valve clearance

(k) Excessive cylinder wear

1 Check 11 in (a)
2 Lack of oil
3 Dirty oil
4 Piston rings gummed up or broken
5 Badly fitting piston rings
6 Connecting rod bent

(l) Excessive oil consumption

1 Check 6 and 7 in (c) and check (k)
2 Ring gaps too wide
3 Oil return holes in pistons choked with carbon
4 Scored cylinders
5 Oil level too high
6 External oil leaks

(m) Crankshaft and connecting rod bearing failure

1 Check 2 in (k)
2 Restricted oilways
3 Worn journals or crankpins
4 Loose bearing caps
5 Extremely low oil pressure
6 Bent connecting rod

(n) Internal water leakage (see **Chapter 4**)

(o) Poor water circulation (see **Chapter 4**)

(p) Corrosion (see **Chapter 4**)

(q) High fuel consumption (see **Chapter 2**)

(r) Engine vibration

1 Loose generator, alternator, steering pump or compressor (if fitted)
2 Engine mountings loose or ineffective
3 Engine stabilizer wrongly adjusted
4 Cooling fan out of balance
5 Misfiring due to mixture, ignition or mechanical faults

CHAPTER 2

THE FUEL SYSTEM

2:1 Description

The layout of the fuel supply system is shown in **FIG 2:1**. An AUF 301 type SU electric fuel pump above each of the two petrol tanks is located behind the lefthand and righthand trim panels of the luggage compartment. Petrol is sucked through a gauze filter which is integral with each pump and is delivered to twin carburetters via a glass bowl type filter mounted in the engine bay. Each carburetter inlet is provided with a gauze filter.

The SU carburetters are fixed jet type and starting mixture is provided by an SU starting carburetter associated with the front carburetter. It is electrically actuated and automatically controlled from a thermostatic switch fitted in the inlet manifold water jacket. HD.6 size carburetters are fitted to 3.4 and 3.8 litre engines and HD.8 size to 4.2 litre models.

The air supply to the carburetters is from beneath the lefthand valance through a paper element type cleaner/silencer mounted on top of the cylinder head.

2:2 Routine maintenance

Every 3000 miles, remove the dampers 23 in **FIG 2:6** (7 in **FIG 2:8**) and fill the hollow piston spindle with 20W engine oil. Maintain the correct slow-running setting at all times. With a fully warmed up engine this should be 500

rev/min for early S type manual transmission models (synchromesh on 3 speeds) and all automatic transmission models and 700 rev/min for cars fitted with all-synchromesh gearboxes. Check the tuning and synchronization of the carburetters about every 6000 miles. Carburetter adjustment is described in **Section 2:10**. Check that the overflow pipes 59 in **FIG 2:8** are unobstructed and also those fitted in the base of the air intake (12 in **FIG 2:13**).

The carburetter gauze filters 27 in **FIG 2:8** should be cleaned every 6000 miles. Access is by removal of banjo bolt 28. At the same time, or more frequently if the glass bowl shows the presence of water or sediment, slacken off the nut below the bowl and swing the retaining clip to one side. Clean the gauze filter and bowl in petrol. Ensure that the sealing washer is in good condition and, on reassembly, that it is correctly seated. **Do not use cloth to clean filters as particles of lint will contaminate the gauze.**

The air cleaner requires no maintenance other than renewal of the paper element every 12,000 miles or more frequently in dusty conditions. The procedure is described in **Section 2:12**.

2:3 Pumps, removal and dismantling

To gain access to a pump, remove the trim panel from

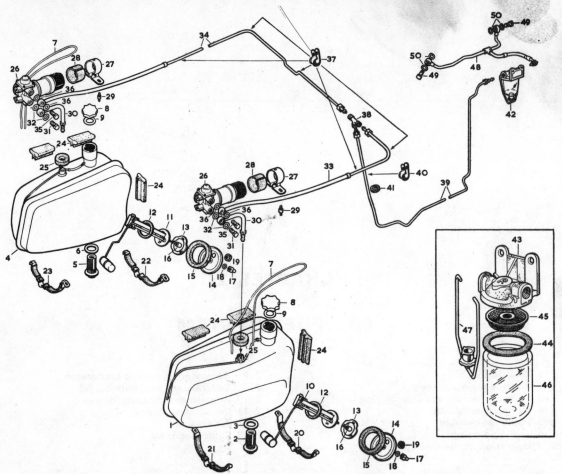

FIG 2:1   Components of the fuel supply system

Key to Fig 2:1   1 Petrol tank assembly (righthand)   2 Petrol filter assembly   3 Washer   4 Petrol tank assembly (lefthand)
5 Petrol filter   6 Washer   7 Connecting tube   8 Filler cap   9 Sealing ring   10 Petrol gauge element (righthand)
11 Petrol gauge element (lefthand)   12 Rubber seal   13 Locking ring   14 Cover ring   15 Sealing ring   16 Spacer
17 Nyloc cap nut   18 Fibre washer   19 Grommet   20 to 23 Cradle assembly   24 Locating pad   25 Sealing ring
26 Petrol pump assembly   27 Clip   28 Mounting rubber (packing)   29 Mounting rubber   30 Petrol pipe assembly
31 Banjo bolt   32 Fibre washer   33 Petrol pipe assembly (righthand)   34 Petrol pipe assembly (lefthand)   35 Banjo bolt
36 Fibre washer   37 Clip   38 T-piece   39 Petrol pipe   40 Clip   41 Grommet   42 Petrol filter assembly
43 Filter casting   44 Sealing washer   45 Filter gauze   46 Glass bowl   47 Retaining clip   48 Feed pipe
49 Banjo bolt   50 Fibre washer

the side of the luggage compartment. Disconnect the
supply and earth leads, unscrew banjo bolts 31 and 35
(see **FIG 2:1**), remove the inlet and delivery pipes and
collect the fibre washers. Remove the two nuts and
washers and dismount the pump. Inspect the condition of
the rubber mountings and replace if necessary. Refitting
is the reverse of this procedure. Ensure that fibre washers
32 and 36 are servicable and correctly seated.

Dismantling:

Refer to **FIG 2:2** and proceed as follows:

1 Take off end cover 29 after removing items 30 to 33.
Unscrew 24 and remove the capacitor terminal tag,
contact blade 22 and washer 23. Remove the capacitor
25 from its clip 26.

2 Mark the relative position of the of the body and coil
housing. Remove screws 7 and separate the body 1
from the coil housing 6. Unscrew the diaphragm and
spindle unit 2 and collect the eleven brass rollers 3. Do
not attempt to separate the diaphragm from the spindle.

3 Remove washer 20 and nut 21, cut away the lead
washer 19 and remove the two screws 28 which retain
the pedestal 16 to the coil housing. Tip the pedestal,
remove stud 17 and dismount the pedestal complete
with the rocker mechanism.

4 Push out the hardened pin 14 to dismount the rocker
mechanism which should not be further dismantled.

5 The valve assemblies may be removed after detaching
clamp plate 34 which is retained by two screws 35. The
Melinex valve discs are permanently assembled within

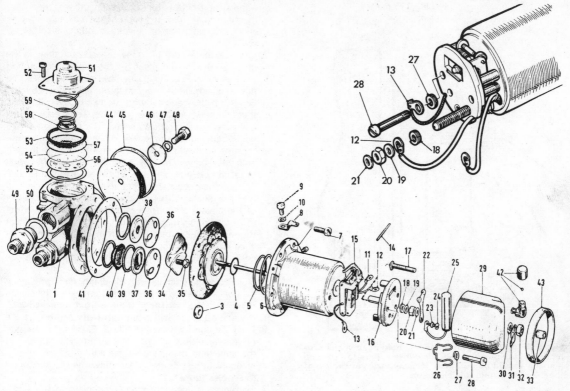

FIG 2:2 Components of the fuel pump

Key to Fig 2:2   1 Pump body   2 Diaphragm and spindle assembly   3 Armature centralizing roller   4 Impact washer
5 Armature spring   6 Coil housing   7 Screw   8 Earth connector   9 Screw   10 Spring washer   11 Terminal tag
12 Terminal tag   13 Earth tag   14 Rocker pivot pin   15 Rocker mechanism   16 Pedestal   17 Terminal stud   18 Spring
washer   19 Lead washer   20 Terminal nut   21 Washer   22 Contact blade   23 Washer   24 Screw   25 Capacitor
26 Clip   27 Spring washer   28 Screw   29 End cover   30 Shakeproof washer   31 Lucar connector   32 Nut
33 Insulating sleeve   34 Clamp plate   35 Screw   36 Valve cap   37 Inlet valve   38 Outlet valve   39 Sealing washer
40 Filter   41 Diaphragm gasket   42 Vent valve   43 Sealing band   44 Inlet air bottle cover joint   45 Inlet air bottle cover
46 Dished washer   47 Spring washer   48 Screw   49 Outlet connection   50 Fibre washer   51 Cover (delivery flow
smoothing device)   52 Screw   53 O-ring   54 Diaphragm barrier   55 Sealing washer   56 Diaphragm plate   58 Spring
end cap   59 Diaphragm spring

their cages. A gauze filter is fitted on the suction side of the inlet valve. It is not necessary for parts 51 to 59 to be dismantled.

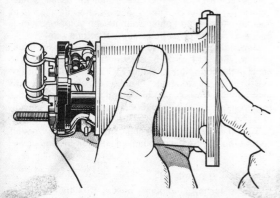

FIG 2:3   Adjusting the throw-over mechanism

2:4 Pump examination

1 If the contact points are burned or pitted renew the rocker assembly and spring blade and suspect that the capacitor may be ineffective. Check that the electrical leads are in good condition and that the tags are secure.

2 Examine the diaphragm for deterioration. Note that the diaphragm and spindle are only renewable as a unit. Note that a new lead washer will be required to replace that cut away in instruction 3, **Section 2:3**. Check the condition of all washers and seals.

3 Wash all parts except the coil in clean paraffin and rinse off in petrol. Clean the filter with a brush and, should it be cracked, fit a new one.

4 Examine the Melinex valves and check that they seat properly. Note that the retaining tongue on the cage should allow the valve to lift approximately $\frac{1}{16}$ inch. Check that the vent valve ball 42 is free to move.

5 Examine the pedestal for cracks or damage. In particular check that the projection (B in **FIG 2:4**) on which the contact blade rests is intact.

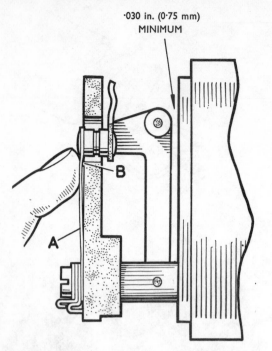

·030 in. (0·75 mm)
MINIMUM

FIG 2:4 If the contact blade A is held against the projection B, the gap between the white rollers and the coil housing should be .030 inch. If necessary, set the tip of the blade to obtain this clearance

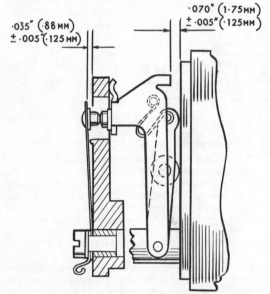

·035" (·88 mm)
± ·005" (·125 mm)

·070" (1·75 mm)
± ·005" (·125 mm)

FIG 2:5 Rocker and contact blade clearances for modified type of outer rocker

2:5 Pump reassembly

Refer to **FIG 2:2** and proceed as follows:
1 Fit the rocker mechanism 15 to pedestal 16 with the pivot pin 14. **If this pin is being renewed, use only**

a genuine SU hardened part. Ensure that the rocker mechanism is free in action. This may require very slight lubrication of the pivots or judicious setting of the arms.
2 Fit the terminal stud 17 to the pedestal and then, in the order shown in the inset, fit the double coil spring washer 18, the cable tag, the new lead washer 19, the nut 20 which should now be tightened and washer 21.
3 Re-attach the pedestal with the two screws 28. Note that (as shown in the inset to **FIG 2:2**) the earth tag 13 is secured by the lefthand screw. The capacitor clip 26 is also retained by this screw. When tightening, ensure that the earth tag does not strain the lead by turning with the screw. **Do not overtighten or the pedestal may crack. Do not fit the spring blade yet.**
4 Fit the impact washer 4 over the diaphragm spindle and into the recess in the armature. Fit the large diameter of the armature spring 5 into the coil housing. Enter the thread of the diaphragm spindle into the trunnion of the rocker mechanism and turn the diaphragm clockwise until the rocker will just not throw-over. Do not confuse this with jamming of the armature in the coil housing.
5 Hold the unit vertically with the diaphragm uppermost, turn back the edge of the diaphragm and fit the eleven rollers. **Fit the contact blade, adjust its setting as described later and then carefully remove it.**
6 Hold the unit as shown in **FIG 2:3**. Unscrew the diaphragm one-sixth of a turn at a time (one hole) and, at the same time, press and release it until the throw-over mechanism just operates. Unscrew the diaphragm by four holes further.
7 Fit the valves and their retaining plate to the body. Ensure that each is the right way round for inlet and delivery and that the filter is fitted below the inlet valve and with a sealing washer 39 on each side of it. Note that the inlet valve recess in the body is deeper than that for the delivery valve. Attach the body and coil housing in their original (as marked in instruction 2, **Section 2:3**) relative position and tighten the setscrews 7 fully. **Do not use jointing compound on the diaphragm.**

Contact blade and gap setting:

Pumps may be fitted with either the type of rocker mechanism illustrated in **FIG 2:4** or **FIG 2:5**.

Onto screw 24 fit washer 23 and then the capacitor lead tag. Fit the coil lead tag and secure the contact blade in position. Adjust and tighten so that each point wipes over the centre of the other point and not to one side.

Depending upon the type of rocker mechanism fitted, refer to **FIG 2:4** or **2:5**. Set the blade by bending to achieve the condition shown in **FIG 2:4** or, in the case of **FIG 2:5**, set the stop finger to obtain the clearance of .035 inch between the contact blade and the pedestal and the rocker finger to achieve .070 inch clearance with the coil housing.

Tuck the spare length of cable into a position where it cannot foul the rocker mechanism and refit the end cover.

2:6 Testing pump

Before testing the pump ensure that the fuel tank venting is not blocked. If it is suspected that fuel is not reaching the carburetters, disconnect the feed pipes from the carburetters and switch on. If fuel squirts from the disconnected pipe, check that the carburetter float needle valves are not stuck.

Reduced flow can be caused by blocked fuel pipes or by a clogged filter. Check the filters in the carburetter float chamber inlets and the glass bowl unit in the engine bay. If an obstructed pipeline is suspected, it may be cleared with compressed air. Disconnect the pipelines at the pumps and the carburetters. **Do not pass compressed air through a pump or the valves will be damaged.** If there is an obstruction in the pipe between a pump and its tank, remove the tank filler cap before blowing the pipe through from the pump end.

If a pump operates rapidly but delivers insufficient fuel, suspect an air leak between the pump and the fuel tank, dirt under the valves or faulty valve seatings.

If there is no flow, confirm that there is voltage at the pump terminal and, if so, remove the pump end cover. If the contact points are touching, reconnect the lead to the terminal and short across the contacts with a piece of bared wire. If the pump then makes a stroke the fault is dirty, burnt or maladjusted points. If this operation fails, suspect stiffening of the diaphragm or excessive friction in the rocker mechanism. Remove the coil housing and

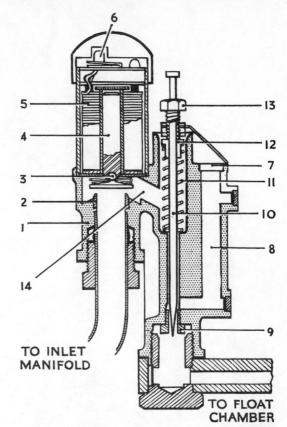

TO INLET MANIFOLD

TO FLOAT CHAMBER

FIG 2:7   Section through an SU starting carburetter

Key to Fig 2:7   1 Carburetter body   2 Valve seat
3 Valve 4 Armature 5 Solenoid 6 Electrical connections
7 Air intake   8 Air inlet passage   9 Jet   10 Jet needle
11 Spring   12 Disc   13 Adjustment screw
14 Air/fuel mixture passage

flex the diaphragm a few times, ensuring that the rollers do not fall out. When reassembling, apply a little thin oil to the pivots of the rocker mechanism. Refer to **Section 2:5** for instructions covering reassembly.

If a pump is noisy, suspect an air leak on the suction side. Check all pipe connections and unions and check also that the coil housing screws are evenly tightened. Examine the condition of the two rubber grommets in the pump mounting bracket.

2:7 Operation of the carburetters

The twin SU carburetters, one of which is shown in section in **FIG 2:6**, have no integral enrichment for starting and this is provided by an auxiliary carburetter attached to the front carburetter and shown in section in **FIG 2:7**

The choke is variable and formed by the piston 22 in **FIG 2:6**, rising and falling automatically depending upon the depression in the intake system as controlled by the throttle opening and the engine load. To maintain the correct mixture in the varying volume of intake air, a tapered jet needle attached to the piston rises and falls in the aperture of jet 18. The smallest diameter of the

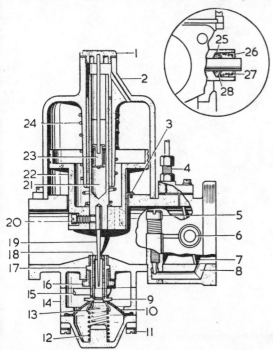

FIG 2:6   Section through an SU HD type carburetter

Key to Fig 2:6   1 Damper cap   2 Suction chamber
3 Piston guide   4 Union for vacuum advance/retard
5 Slow-running volume screw   6 Throttle spindle
7 Throttle butterfly   8 Slow run passage   9 Jet cup
10 Diaphragm   11 Float chamber securing screw
12 Jet return spring   13 Return spring cup   14 Jet unit
housing   15 Actuating lever   16 Nut (jet bearing)
17 Jet bearing 18 Jet 19 Jet needle 20 Needle retaining
screw   21 Oil reservoir   22 Piston   23 Damper
24 Piston return spring   25 Throttle spindle gland
26 Shroud for spring   27 Spring   28 Washer

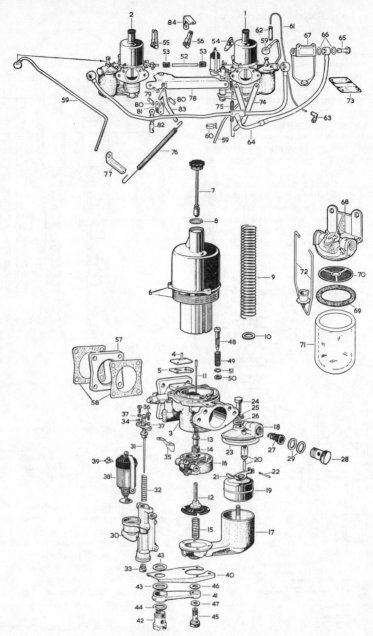

FIG 2:8 Components of the front SU HD6 carburetter. The rear carburetter excludes items 30 to 47

Key to Fig 2:8   1 Front carburetter   2 Rear carburetter   3 Carburetter body   4 Ignition union adaptor   5 Gasket
6 Suction chamber and piston   7 Damper   8 Washer   9 Spring   10 Skid washer   11 Jet needle   12 Jet   13 Jet bearing
14 Nut, jet bearing   15 Spring   16 Jet unit housing   17 Float chamber   18 Float chamber lid   19 Float   20 Needle and
seat   21 Float needle lever   22 Knurled pin   23 Gasket   24 Cap nut   25 Fibre serrated washer   26 Aluminium washer
27 Filter   28 Banjo bolt   29 Fibre washer   30 Thermostat body   31 Acceleration needle   32 Spring   33 Jet   34 Spring finger
35 Dust shield   36 Screw   37 Washer   38 Solenoid   39 Spring clip   40 Bracket   41 Connecting arm   42 Banjo bolt
43 Fibre washer   44 Fibre washer   45 Banjo bolt   46 Fibre washer   47 Aluminium washer   48 Slow-running control valve
49 Spring   50 Neoprene washer   51 Brass washer   52 Connecting rod   53 Connecting rod coupling   54 Throttle return
spring lever   55 Throttle operating lever   56 Anti-creep throttle switch lever   57 Insulator   58 Gasket   59 Overflow pipe
60 Clip   61 Suction pipe   62 Neoprene tube   63 Elbow   64 Petrol feed pipe   65 Banjo bolt   66 Fibre washer
67 Petrol filter   68 Filter casting   69 Sealing washer   70 Filter gauze   71 Glass bowl   72 Retaining strap   73 Bracket
74 Bracket   75 Throttle return spring   76 Throttle return spring   77 Bracket   78 Throttle stop bracket   79 Dowel bolt
80 Intermediate throttle link   81 Trunnion   82 Throttle link rod   83 Intermediate throttle lever   84 Bracket

needle is in the jet when the piston is at the top of its travel and the flow of fuel is then at a maximum. Rapid fluctuations of the piston are prevented by the hydraulic damper 23, oil being contained in the well 21. A spring 24 assists gravity to return the piston to its lowest point.

The recommended jet needle type (designated by two letters stamped on the side or top face of the parallel portion of the needle) for each engine capacity and compression ratio is given in Technical Data in the Appendix.

The starting carburetter takes fuel from the float chamber of the front carburetter. The solenoid, 5 in **FIG 2:7**, is energized through a thermostatically operated switch housed in the inlet water manifold at temperatures below 30°C to 35°C. The solenoid opens valve 3 and engine intake depression operates on disc 12 differentially against spring 11 to raise the jet needle 10, the tapered end of which, operating in the jet 9, adjusts the amount of fuel required by the air entering from passage. The unit cuts out when the cooling water temperature rises and the thermostatic switch de-energizes the solenoid allowing the valve 3 to close under spring pressure.

2:8 Removing, servicing carburetters

Remove the air intake and drain tubes as described in **Section 2:12**. Remove the fuel feed pipe by withdrawing the banjo bolts 28 in **FIG 2:8** and collect the filters 27 and washers 29. Disconnect the distributor vacuum pipe 61 and the overflow pipes 59. Remove the throttle return spring 76, disconnect the cables from the starting carburetter and uncouple the throttle rod. Unscrew the union connecting the starter pipe to the auxiliary starting carburetter. On 420 type cars fitted with automatic transmission, remove the spring clip securing the kick-down link at the rear of the rear carburetter. Remove the four nuts and washers which secure each carburetter to the inlet manifold and dismount the carburetters together with insulators 57.

Refitting is the reverse of the removal procedure. Fit new gaskets 58 on both sides of each insulator. Disconnect the front carburetter coupling and the rear throttle lever by releasing their clamp bolts. Check that both butterflies are fully closed then retighten the front coupling clamp bolt. Refer to **FIG 2:9** and set the intermediate throttle stop to give centre A a downwards toggle of $\frac{1}{16}$ inch in relation to centre B. Tighten the throttle lever clamp bolt.

Dismantling carburetters:

Refer to **FIG 2:8**. Items 30 to 47 cover the starting carburetter and are relevant to the front carburetter only. The starting carburetter is detached from the front carburetter by removing banjo bolts 42 and 45 and bracket 40. The four setscrews which attach this bracket to the front carburetter also secure the float chamber, jet/diaphragm unit 12 and jet unit housing 16 to the carburetter body 3. These items are shown sectioned in **FIG 2:6**. Refer to **FIG 2:7** for the sectioned details of the starting carburetter.

The thermostatic switch for the starting carburetter is shown in **FIG 1:4**. It is retained in the water inlet manifold by three setbolts. The single lead is connected under the domed nut. A quantity of coolant will escape when the switch is removed. A new cork gasket must be used when the switch is refitted.

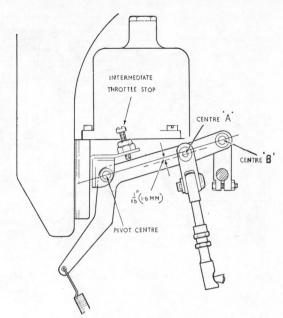

FIG 2:9 Intermediate throttle stop setting

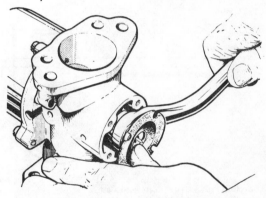

FIG 2:10 Centralizing a jet

Refer to **FIG 2:8**. Remove the suction chamber and piston assembly 6 (2 and 22 in **FIG 2:6**) complete with jet needle 11 (19 in **FIG 2:6**) after marking the position of the chamber in relation to the carburetter body 3. This will ensure that the chambers are reassembled to their original positions. The jet needles are retained in the pistons by screws (20 in **FIG 2:6**).

Servicing the carburetters:

Remove the damper and empty out the oil. Remove the piston from the suction chamber. Clean the piston diameters and the chamber bores with petrol. If the jet needle is changed or renewed, fit it so that the bottom of the shoulder is flush with the lower face of the piston. Clean the sediment from the float chambers. Examine the float needle and seat unit. If there is a noticeable shoulder on the seat, renew the unit. The setting of the float needle lever is covered in **Section 2:10**. Check that the diaphragm of the jet/diaphragm unit is in good condition.

FIG 2:11   Carburetter adjustment points

Key to Fig 2:11   **A** Slow-running volume screw   **B** Mixture adjusting screw

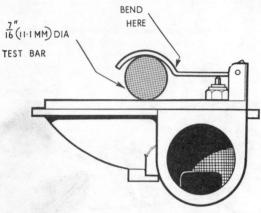

FIG 2:12   Correct setting of the float lever. Adjust by bending only at the point arrowed

Reassembly:

Reassembly is the dismantling procedure in reverse but the jet must be centralized as described in **Section 2:9**. When reassembling the piston to the suction chamber, apply a little thin oil to the hollow piston rod only. When the carburetters have been refitted to their manifold, fill the damper oil wells with 20W engine oil as described in **Section 2:2**.

2:9 Centralizing carburetter jet

This operation is always necessary if the jet bearing nut 14 in **FIG 2:8** has been loosened or removed or if a new jet needle 11 has been fitted. The jet is correctly centred when the piston falls freely and hits the jet bridge smartly and with a metallic click. With the carburetter removed from the engine and the float chamber 17, spring 15, and jet/diaphragm unit 12, the jet unit housing 16 and the damper 7 removed from the carburetter, proceed as follows:

1 Using a ring spanner, slacken off the jet bearing screw 14 until the jet bearing 13 is loosened enough to be turned with the fingers.
2 With the ring spanner still in position, fit the jet/diaphragm unit as shown in **FIG 2:10**. Align the setscrew holes in the diaphragm with those in the carburetter body and, with a soft pencil, mark the diaphragm and carburetter body. Push the jet in as far as possible and with a pencil or rod pressing the piston gently onto the bridge, tighten the jet bearing nut.
3 Lift the piston and check that is falls freely Lower the jet and repeat the test. If the sound of impact is then sharper, repeat the centring operation until successful.
4 When satisfied, remove the jet/diaphragm unit and spanner. On reassembly ensure that the jet/diaphragm unit is fitted in the relative position as marked.

2:10 Adjustments to carburetters

Tuning and slow-running:

The following procedure assumes that the cylinder compressions, valves, sparking plugs, contact breaker points, ignition timing etc, are in order. For information on the ignition system, refer to **Chapter 3**.

Before proceeding, ensure that the basic setting of each jet is correct. Remove the suction chamber and piston assemblies and the air intake manifold. Refer to **FIG 2:11**. Screw out each mixture adjusting screw B until the top of the jet is seen to be flush with the jet bridge. Turn the mixture screws clockwise by $3\frac{1}{2}$ turns beyond the point at which the jets just start to move downwards.

Check and, if necessary, adjust the throttle valves so that they are fully closed. Screw in the slow-running volume screws A until they are fully onto their seatings then unscrew each by $2\frac{1}{2}$ turns.

The engine should now be run up to normal operating temperature. Adjust the screws A until both carburetters are sucking equally and the slow-running speed is 500 rev/min for cars with early gearboxes (synchromesh on 3 speeds) and automatic transmission models and 700

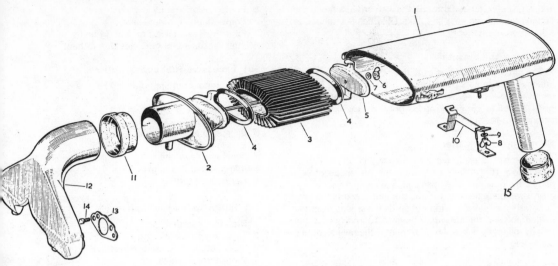

FIG 2:13 Components of the air cleaner

rev/min on cars fitted with gearboxes having synchromesh on 4 speeds. The judgement of this equal sucking synchroization is achieved by placing one end of a length of rubber tube to the ear and the other end inside each carburetter intake in turn. Recheck that both throttle valves are closed by rotating thier spindles clockwise (looking from the front) when no change in engine speed will occur if they are fully closed.

Proceed now to check the mixture strength. Raise the front carburetter piston approximately $\frac{1}{32}$ inch. If:

1 The engine speed increases, the mixture is too rich.
2 The engine speed decreases, the mixture is too weak.
3 There is no change in engine speed, the mixture of this carburetter is correct.

Repeat this check on the rear carburetter and make the appropriate adjustments to both carburetters. To enrich the mixture, the screw B must be turned clockwise and, to weaken the mixture, anticlockwise. Some slight readjustment of the slow-running speed may be required and, if so, the screws A must be turned each by exactly equal amounts.

Starting carburetter adjustment:

With the engine at normal operating temperature and running at idling speed, energize the starting carburetter solenoid by making a temporary connection between the domed nut of the thermostatic switch and one of its retaining setscrews. Adjust the screw 13 in **FIG 2:7** so that the mixture is distinctly but not excessively rich. Judge this by the exhaust gasses being discernibly black but short of the point where the engine begins to run irregularly. Anticlockwise rotation of screw 13 enriches the mixture.

2:11 Carburetter faults

A sticking piston:

This can cause difficult starting and lack of response of the throttle. Remove the air intake and lift the piston with a pencil. It should lift freely and drop back smartly. If it does not, remove the suction chamber and piston assembly and clean thoroughly as described in **Section 2:8**. If this does not effect a cure the jet should be recentred as described in **Section 2:9**. Check that the needle is not bent.

Float chamber flooding:

The usual cause is that dirt or grit has jammed open the float needle in its guide. Remove the float chamber cover and clean the needle and guide.

If the needle should be jammed shut, the engine will be starved of fuel. Check by removing the fuel feed pipe, switching on the ignition and proving that the pump is operating. Have a container ready to collect the fuel. If the needle is stuck, proceed to clear it as described earlier.

Level of fuel in float chamber:

For the correct fuel level, the float needle lever must be correctly set. Refer to **FIG 2:12** and check that when the needle valve is closed a $\frac{7}{16}$ inch diameter test bar will just slide between the cover face and the inside curve of the lever fork. Correct as necessary to achieve this by carefully bending **at the point arrowed** in the illustration in the appropriate direction. Keep both prongs of the fork level and maintain the straight portion dead flat.

Starting mixture:

If difficulty is experienced after adjusting the starting carburetter as described in **Section 2:10** when next starting from bold, the adjusting screw 13 in **FIG 2:7** should be turned anticlockwise by a half turn.

2:12 Air cleaner

The components of the air intake and air cleaner are shown in **FIG 2:13**. The cleaner/silencer is of the paper element type and is fitted across the top of the engine. Air is ducted from beneath the lefthand valance to the shell 1 and, after being filtered through the element 3, is fed to the carburetters through the air intake 12 which is attached to the carburetter flanges.

Removing the air intake :

The bifurcated intake is provided with two drain tubes attached to adaptors in its base. To dismount the intake, remove these tubes before unscrewing the attachment bolts. A gasket 13 is interposed between the intake and each carburetter flange.

Removing the cleaner :

To remove the air cleaner, disconnect the breather pipe elbow (62 in **FIG 1 : 4**) from the underside of end plate 2 by loosening the hose clip, slacken the two wing-nuts 8, roll back the seal 11, pull the unit towards the left-hand valance until the wing nut studs disengage from the slotted holes in the mounting bracket 10 and release the unit by rolling back seal 15. Refitment is the reverse of this procedure.

Changing the element :

To fit a new element, proceed as for removing the unit but do not disengage the inlet pipe from seal 15. Release the two toggle clips which retain the end plate 2. Withdraw this component together with the element. Remove the wing nut 6 and washer 7, plate 5 and rubber sealing ring 4. Withdraw and discard the element. Fit the new element and ensure that both sealing rings 4 are correctly positioned. Reassembly is the reverse of the dismantling procedure.

2:13 Fault diagnosis

(a) Leakage or insufficient fuel delivered

1 Air vent to tank restricted
2 Fuel pipes blocked
3 Air leaks at pipe connections
4 Pump filter blocked
5 Pump gaskets faulty
6 Pump diaphragm defective
7 Pump valves sticking or seating badly
8 Fuel vaporizing in pipelines due to heat

(b) Excessive fuel consumption

1 Carburetters require adjusting
2 Fuel leakage
3 Defective thermostatic switch
4 Dirty air cleaner
5 Excessive engine temperature
6 Brakes binding
7 Tyres under-inflated
8 Idling speed too high
9 Car overloaded

(c) Idling speed too high

1 Rich fuel mixture
2 Throttle control sticking
3 Incorrect slow-running adjustment
4 Worn throttle valve

(d) Noisy fuel pump

1 Worn mounting grommets
2 Air leaks on suction side or at diaphragm
3 Obstruction in fuel pipeline
4 Clogged pump filter

(e) No fuel delivery

1 Float needle stuck
2 Tank vent blocked
3 Electrical connection to pump faulty
4 Pump contact points dirty
5 Pipeline obstructed
6 Pump diaphragm stiff or damaged
7 Pump inlet valve stuck open
8 Bad air leak on suction side of the pump

CHAPTER 3

THE IGNITION SYSTEM

1 Description

Lucas 22.D6 distributors are fitted to all models covered by this manual. The distributor incorporates variable timing which is controlled by a centrifugal mechanism and by a vacuum actuated unit. To compensate for changes in engine condition or for the use of different octane fuels, a manual trimmer is provided which allows fine adjustment of the timing. As engine speed increases, the centrifugal action of rotating weights rotating against the tension of small springs, advances the contact breaker cam relative to the distributor driving shaft and progressively advances the ignition. The vacuum control unit is connected by small-bore pipe to the front carburetter intake. At high degrees of vacuum it advances the ignition but, under load, at reduced vacuum the unit progressively retards the ignition.

2 Routine maintenance

FIG 3:1 shows the distributor with the moulded cap and the rotor removed. Every 3000 miles, apply a few drops of engine oil around screw 4, one drop of oil to pivot post 1, a touch of grease to cam 3 and a few drops of oil through the aperture 2 in the contact breaker base plate below the cam. Ensure that no oil or grease contaminates the contact breaker points.

Refer to FIG 3:2 and, with the points fully open, check that the gap is correct at .014 to .016 inch. If necessary adjust by slackening screw 2 and turning a screwdriver between notches 3. Clockwise rotation decreases the gap. Tighten screw 2 and recheck the gap.

Cleaning the contact breaker points:

Use a fine carborundum stone to polish the contact points if they are dirty or pitted. Dismantle them by reference to Section 3:4. Keep their faces square and flat and wipe away all dust with a cloth moistened in petrol.

3:3 Ignition faults

If the engine runs unevenly, set it to idle at about 1000 rev/min and, taking care not to touch any metal part of the sparking plug leads, remove and replace each lead from its plug in turn. Doing this to a plug which is firing properly will accentuate the uneven running but will make no difference if the plug is not firing. Locate the faulty cylinder, remove the lead from the plug and pull back the insulator. Hold the lead so that the metal end is about $\frac{1}{8}$ inch from the cylinder head. A strong, regular spark confirms that the fault lies with the sparking plug which should be cleaned as described in Section 3:6 or a new plug fitted.

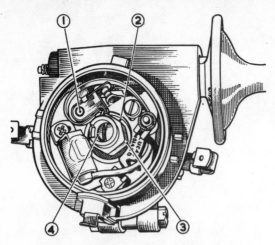

FIG 3:1   Distributor lubrication points

Key to Fig 3:1
2 Lubrication point for cam bearing
4 Rotor arm spindle

1 Pivot post
3 Cam

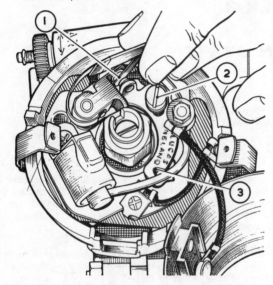

FIG 3:2   Checking the contact breaker points

Key to Fig 3:2
2 Screw securing fixed contact plate

1 Feeler gauge
3 Adjusting notches

If the spark is weak and irregular, check the condition of the lead and, if it is perished or cracked, renew it and repeat the test. If no improvement results, check that the inside of the moulded cap is clean and dry, that the carbon brush at its centre can be moved freely against its internal spring and that there is no 'tracking', which will show as a thin black line between the electrodes or to a metal part in contact with the cap. 'Tracking' cannot be rectified except by fitting a new moulded cap.

Testing the low-tension circuit:

Check that the contact breaker points are clean and correctly set. Refer to wiring diagram **FIG 14:1** in the case of S type cars and to **FIG 14:2** in the case of 420 mod and proceed as follows:

1 Disconnect the thin cable from the 'CB' terminal on coil and from the side of the distributor. Connec test lamp between these terminals, turn on the igniti and turn the engine slowly. If, when the contacts clo the lamp lights and goes out when they open, circuit is in order. If the lamp fails to light, there is fault in the low-tension circuit. Remove the test la and reconnect the cable to the coil and distributor.

2 If the fault lies in the low-tension circuit, turn the engi until the points are fully open. Using a 0–20 voltmet carry out the following tests when, if the wiring is order, a meter reading of approximately 12 volts be obtained with the ignition switched on. No readi in each case, indicates a faulty cable or loose co nection in the section of wiring being tested.

Note that these tests must be carried out in the or prescribed. The relevance of each test assumes that earlier tests have shown no fault. It is assumed that battery is not discharged.

(a) **Battery to ignition switch.** Connect the me between the brown/white wire connection at ignition switch and earth.

(b) **Ignition switch.** Connect the meter between other, the white wire, connection at the ignition swi and earth. Turn on the ignition when no readi indicates a fault in the switch.

(c) **Ignition switch to fuse No. 3.** Connect the me between the white wire connection at fuse No. 3 a earth.

(d) **Fuse No. 3 to ignition coil terminal 'SW** Connect the meter between terminal 'SW' and ear

(e) **Ignition coil.** Disconnect the cable from the 'C terminal. Connect the meter between this terminal a earth. No reading indicates a fault in the primary c winding and a new coil must be fitted. If the readin correct, reconnect the cable to the coil.

(f) **Ignition coil to distributor.** Disconnect the cal from the side of the distributor. Connect the me between the end of this cable and earth.

(g) **Contact breaker and capacitor.** Connect meter across the contact breaker points. No readi indicates a faulty capacitor.

Capacitor:

The best method of testing a capacitor (condenser) by substitution. Disconnect the original capacitor a connect a new one between the low-tension termi on the side of the distributor and earth for test purpos If a new capacitor is proved to be required, it may then properly fitted. The capacitor is of .2 microfarad ±10 cent capacity.

3:4 Removing, dismantling distributor
Removal:

Provided that the pinch bolt in the clamp plate is r loosened, the distributor can be dismounted and refitt without disturbing the ignition timing. **FIG 1:15** sho the clamp plate, pinch bolt and the single setbolt whi retains the plate to the cylinder block. To dismount t distributor, remove this setbolt, disconnect the low-tensi wire and the vacuum pipe and lift off the unit comple with the clamp plate.

Refitting :

Offer the unit to the housing with the setbolt hole lined up with that in the crankcase. Turn the rotor arm until the driving dog engages with the driving slot. Refit the setbolt.

Dismantling :

To provide a datum, turn the engine until the rotor arm is pointing to the No. 6 cylinder position in the moulded cap. This datum, it will be noted, corresponds with that described in **Chapter 1, Section 1:8** and also in **Section 3:5**

Dismount the distributor as described earlier and refer to **FIG 3:3**.

1 Spring back the clips and remove the moulded cap. Pull off the rotor arm 1. Take careful note of the relative position of parts as they are dismantled.
2 Remove the nut, insulating bush, capacitor lead, low-tension lead, moving contact spring and insulating washer from the spring anchor pin and the moving contact and insulating washer from the pivot pin.
3 Remove screw 3 and lift off the fixed contact plate. Remove the capacitor 9 and earth lead 8. Disconnect the vacuum control and remove the base plate 4.
4 **Before further dismantling, note the relative positions of the rotor arm driving slot above the cam and the driving dog 17 which is offset and can only engage the drive shaft in one position.** Then, when the cam assembly is refitted to the centrifugal weights at reassembly, the timing will not be 180 deg. out.
5 Remove the cam retaining screw 4 in **FIG 3:1** and remove the cam 12. Remove the springs and automatic timing control weights.
6 Remove the circlip at the adjusting nut end to release the vacuum unit. Remove the adjusting nut 15 and spring and withdraw the vacuum unit 6.
7 Check the parts for wear, the moulded cap for 'tracking', the condition of the points and the tension of the moving contact spring which should be 18 to 24 oz. measured at the points. Examine the high-tension leads.
8 If it is necessary to remove the spindle ballbearing, use a mandrel locating on the inner journal to drift it out of the housing. A shouldered mandrel which locates on both the inner and outer journals must be used to fit the new bearing. To change the lower plain bearing the bush must be drifted out using a suitable punch. After allowing the new bush to stand fully immersed in SAE. 30 or 40 engine oil for 24 hours, press it into the housing. Use a shouldered mandrel with a highly polished pilot of the same diameter as the spindle and slightly longer than the bush. To prevent the mandrel from withdrawing the bush, use a stripping washer between the shoulder of the mandrel and the bush.

Reassembly :

This is the reverse of dismantling but note the following points:

1 Lubricate the parts of the automatic timing control, the bearing and cam spigot with thin engine oil.
2 Turn the vacuum control adjustment to mid-position. Engage the cam driving pins with the centrifugal weights so that, when seen from above, the small offset of the driving dog is on the right and the driving slot for the rotor arm is at the 'six o'clock' position.

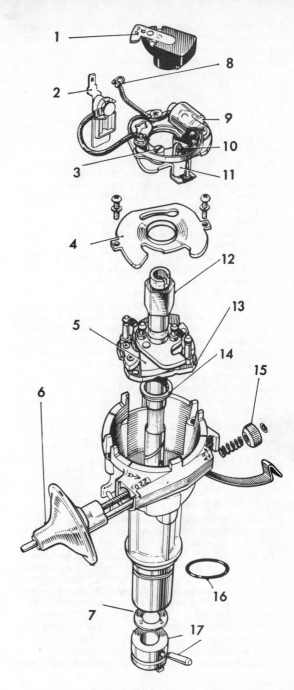

FIG 3:3   Components of the 22D6 distributor

Key to Fig 3:3   1 Rotor arm   2 Low-tension terminal
3 Fixed contact plate securing screw   4 Contact breaker base plate   5 Centrifugal timing control weights
6 Vacuum timing control 7 Thrust washer 8 Contact breaker earth connector   9 Capacitor   10 Contacts   11 Contact breaker moving plate   12 Cam   13 Action plate
14 Distance collar   15 Micrometer adjustment nut
16 Oil seal washer   17 Dog and pin

3 Fit the distributor to its housing and turn the rotor arm to engage the driving dog. If the crankshaft has not been turned, the rotor should be pointing to No. 6 segment. If the clamping plate pinch bolt has been loosened and the clamp plate moved with consequential loss of the timing, refer to the next Section.

3:5 Timing the ignition

The timing scale is marked on the crankshaft damper and is shown in **FIGS 1:11** and **1:12** for S type and 420 type engines respectively. The procedure is as follows:
1 With No. 6 (front) piston on the compression stroke, set the crankshaft to the setting which is appropriate to the particular engine capacity and compression ratio. This information is given at the end of this Section.
2 Check that the distributor micrometer adjustment is in the centre of the scale, that the points are correctly set and that the pinch bolt is loosened. Turn the rotor arm to the No. 6 cylinder segment position, face the vacuum control towards the rear of the engine and engage the driving dog with the distributor drive shaft. Fit the set-bolt and secure the clamp plate to the housing face.
3 Connect a 12-volt test lamp in parallel with the points (one lead to the terminal on the side of the distributor or the 'CB' terminal of the coil and the other to earth) and switch on the ignition. Slowly rotate the distributor body until the test lamp lights up indicating that the points are just breaking. Tighten the clamp plate pinch bolt and fit the vacuum control pipe.

The maximum micrometer adjustment from this setting which is allowed for final tuning to suit fuels of different octane ratings is six clicks towards advance or retard.

Ignition timing information :

Compression ratio	S type	420 type
7:1	TDC	—
8:1	7 deg. BTDC	8 deg. BTDC
9:1	5 deg. BTDC	8 deg. BTDC

3:6 Sparking plugs

Inspect, clean and adjust sparking plugs regularly. When removing sparking plugs, ensure that their recesses are dry and clean so that nothing can fall into the cylinders. Plug gaskets may be re-used provided that they are not less than half of their original thickness. Have sparking plugs cleaned on an abrasive-blasting machine and tested under pressure with the electrode gaps correctly set at .025 inch. The electrodes should be filed until they are bright and parallel. The gaps must always be adjusted by setting the earth electrode. **Do not try to bend the centre electrode.**

Before refitting the plugs, clean the threads with a wire brush. The threads in the cylinder head should be cleared with a tap if the plugs cannot be screwed in by hand. Failing a tap, use an old sparking plug with cross-cuts down the threads. Plugs should be tightened to a torque of 30 lb ft but, in the absence of a torque spanner, tighten with a normal box spanner through half a turn.

Inspection of the deposits on the electrodes can be helpful when tuning. Normally, from mixed periods of high and low speed driving, the deposit should be powdery and range in colour from brown to greyish tan. There will also be slight wear of the electrodes. Long periods of constant-speed driving or low-speed city driving will give white or yellowish deposits. Dry, black, fluffy deposits are due to incomplete combustion and indicate running with a rich mixture, excessive idling and possibly defective ignition. Overheated plugs have a white, blistered look about the centre electrode and the side electrode may be badly eroded. This may be caused by poor cooling, incorrect ignition or sustained high speeds with heavy loads.

Black, wet deposits result from oil in the combustion chamber from worn pistons, rings, valve stems or guides. Sparking plugs which run hotter may alleviate the problem but the cure is an engine overhaul.

Sparking plug leads :

To fit new high-tension cable to the distributor cap and to the ignition coil, thread the cable through the rubber cap and then through the knurled terminal nut. Bare about $\frac{1}{4}$ inch of the wires, fit the brass washer from the old lead and fan out the wires over the face of the washer. Screwing the terminal nuts into their sockets will retain the cables. Push the rubber caps back over the terminal nuts.

3:7 Fault diagnosis

(a) Engine will not fire

1 Battery discharged
2 Distributor contact points dirty, pitted or maladjusted
3 Distributor cap dirty, cracked or 'tracking'
4 Carbon brush inside distributor cap not touching rotor
5 Faulty cable or loose connection in low-tension circuit
6 Distributor rotor arm cracked.
7 Faulty coil
8 Broken contact breaker spring
9 Contact points stuck open

(b) Engine misfires

1 Check 2, 3, 5 and 7 in (a)
2 Weak contact breaker spring
3 High-tension plug and coil leads cracked or perished
4 Sparking plug(s) loose
5 Sparking plug insulation cracked
6 Sparking plug gap incorrectly set
7 Ignition timing too far advanced

CHAPTER 4

THE COOLING SYSTEM

4:1 Description

The cooling system is pressurized at 4 lb/sq in and thermostatically controlled. Coolant circulation is assisted by a centrifugal pump which is mounted at the front of the cylinder block. The pump and fan are belt driven from the crankshaft and the cowled fan, which draws air through the radiator, is fitted (directly on S types, and through a Torquatrol hydraulic unit on 420 models) to the same shaft as the pump impeller.

The pump takes coolant from the bottom of the radiator and delivers it to the cylinder block from which it rises to the cylinder head. At normal operating temperature, the thermostat is open and the coolant returns from the head to the top of the radiator. At lower temperature, the valve is closed and the coolant bypasses the radiator and returns to the pump inlet. This provides a rapid warm-up.

S type cars are provided with integral header tank radiators (see **FIG 4:1**), through which the coolant flow is vertical while those fitted to 420 models have cross-flow radiators (see **FIG 4:2**), fitted with detachable header tanks. 420 type cars fitted with automatic transmission are provided with an oil cooler which is incorporated in the bottom water pipe.

Drain taps are provided at the bottom of the radiator and in the cylinder block. A drain plug is fitted to the bottom water pipe.

4:2 Maintenance

The pump bearing is a permanently sealed and lubricated assembly and requires no maintenance.

The cooling system should periodically be drained, flushed to remove sediment and refilled. If antifreeze is in use, the coolant may be collected for re-use but should be discarded after two winters. Check the tightness of the clips on all hoses including those on the heater inlet and outlet pipes.

Draining:

The radiator tap is operated by the remote control rod which is 11 in **FIG 4:1** and 14 in **FIG 4:2**. The cylinder block drain tap is 25 in **FIG 1:17**.

Remove the filler cap, open both taps and switch the heater to 'Hot'. In the case of 420 models, remove the bottom water pipe drain plug 39 in **FIG 4:2** and arrowed B in **FIG 1:12**.

Flushing:

Use a water hose and allow water to run into the radiator. Adjust the hose rate of flow to balance the rate of draining and, with the header tank full, run the engine at about 1000 rev/min to assist circulation until the drain water runs clear.

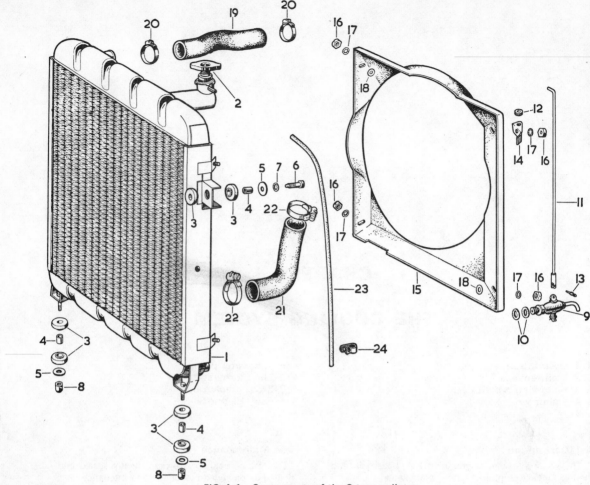

FIG 4:1 Components of the S type radiator

Key to Fig 4:1   1 Radiator block   2 Filler cap   3 Rubber pad   4 Distance tube   5 Special washer   6 Bolt
7 Shakeproof washer   8 Self-locking nut   9 Drain tap   10 Fibre washer   11 Control rod   12 Grommet   13 Splitpin
14 Drain tap control rod bracket   15 Cowl   16 Nut   17 Shakeproof washer   18 Washer   19 Hose   20 Clip   21 Hose
22 Clip   23 Overflow pipe   24 Clip

Filling:

Leave the heater control in the 'Hot' position, close both taps and, on 420 cars, refit the bottom water pipe drain plug. Fill the radiator and top up the coolant level after running the engine.

4:3 Removing the radiator

S type cars:

1 Drain the radiator as described in **Section 4:2** and disconnect the top and bottom hoses.
2 Unscrew the four nuts 16 (see **FIG 4:1**) which secure the fan cowl and rest it on the pump housing behind the fan.
3 Remove the splitpin securing the remote control rod to the drain tap and unscrew the tap from the radiator.
4 Remove the two setscrews 6 which attach the sides of the radiator to the body and the two nuts 8 at the bottom

of the radiator. Collect the pads 3, distance tubes 4 and washers. Carefully lift out the radiator and ensure that the matrix does not get damaged against the fan blades. Remove the fan cowl.

Keep the radiator in an upright position so that any sediment in the bottom tank will not pass into the matrix and cause a blockage.

420 type cars:

If the car is fitted with air conditioning, the system's condenser must be removed before the radiator can be withdrawn. **This requires special tools and knowledge and the operation must be carried out only by Authorized Jaguar Distributors, Dealers or qualified Refrigeration Engineers.**

1 Drain the radiator as described in **Section 4:2**. If an automatic transmission model, refer to **Chapter 7** before removing the oil pipes shown in **FIG 1:12** from

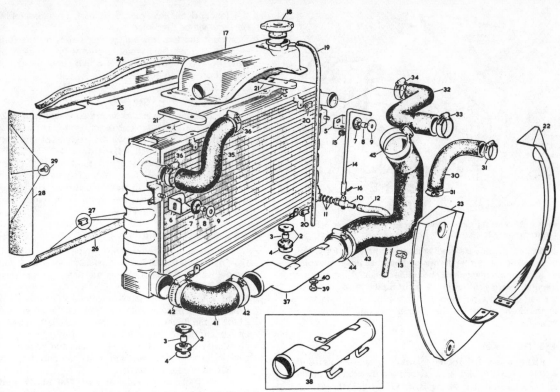

FIG 4:2 Components of the 420 type radiator

Key to Fig 4:2   1 Radiator block assembly   2 Mounting pad (rubber)   3 Distance tube   4 Washer (special)
5 Radiator mounting bracket (righthand)   6 Radiator mounting bracket (lefthand)   7 Grommet   8 Distance tube
9 Washer (special)   10 Drain tap assembly   11 Fibre washer   12 Rubber tube   13 Clip   14 Control rod
15 Grommet   16 Splitpin   17 Header tank   18 Filler cap   19 Overflow pipe   20 Clip   21 Packing piece   22 Fan
cowl (righthand)   23 Fan cowl (lefthand)   24 Rubber seal   25 Support strip   26 Seal   27 Clip   28 Seal
29 Stud   30 Bypass water hose   31 Clip   32 Hose   33 Clip   34 Clip   35 Header tank hose   36 Clip   37 Bottom
water pipe (not automatic transmission)   38 Bottom water pipe (automatic transmission oil cooler)   39 Drain plug   40 Fibre
washer   41 Hose   42 Clip   43 Hose   44 Clip   45 Clip

the cooler 38 in **FIG 4:2**. Disconnect the header tank hose 35, the top hose 32 and the two bottom hoses 41 and 43.

2 Dismount the header tank by removing four setscrews securing it to the radiator and two nuts attaching it to the cowl. Remove the setscrews securing the cowl to the radiator, separate and withdraw the cowl halves after removing the joint bolts.

3 Remove the fan and Torquatrol unit as described in **Section 4:4**. Remove the splitpin securing the remote control rod to the drain tap and unscrew the tap from the radiator.

4 Remove the two lower mounting setscrews and collect the mounting rubbers. On early cars, unscrew the two nuts securing the radiator to the bracket on each wing valance. On later cars, withdraw the two bonnet stop setscrews and collect the mounting straps. Protect the radiator matrix and withdraw it from beneath the car.

Refitting:

This is the reverse of the removal procedure on all models. On S type models, do not forget to rest the cowl behind the fan before lifting the radiator into position.

4:4 Fan drive

A spring-loaded jockey pulley (items 35 to 38 in **FIG 1:7**) on S type models and a similar pulley which is fitted to 420 power assisted steering cars and is shown arrowed in **FIG 10:9**, automatically tensions the fan belt. 420 cars fitted with standard steering are provided with an adjustable jockey pulley. Adjustment is effected by loosening the nut, arrowed in **FIG 4:3**, securing the pulley pivot to its bracket, swinging the pulley upwards until the correct tension is obtained and then retightening the nut. When correctly tensioned, the belt can be depressed by $\frac{1}{2}$ inch between the pulleys. To remove the belt, this pulley is swung downwards until the belt will disengage. On S type cars the fan belt also drives the generator and, to remove the belt, the two generator mounting bolts are loosened and the top link-bolt removed. Swinging generator inwards then allows the belt to be disengaged from the generator pulley. On power assisted 420 models the belt is removed after it is detensioned by swinging the steering pump inwards to the full extent of the slot in its adjuster link.

The Torquatrol unit provides, hydraulically, variable speed drive to the fan on 420 models. When the engine is

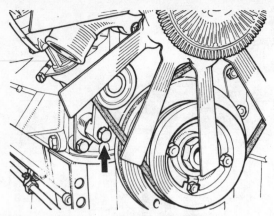

FIG 4:3 Fan belt tensioner fitted to 420 type manual steering models

stationary, the drive is 'free' and this condition should not be mistaken for belt slip.If the unit becomes unserviceable, an exchange replacement should be obtained. To remove the unit, remove the four nuts securing the fan to it. Move the fan onto the pulley hub, remove the four nuts then exposed and dismount the Torquatrol unit. Remove the fan.

4:5 The water pump

FIG 4:4 shows the components of the water pump and 420 type fan, FIG 4:5 shows a section through the pump and S type fan and arrow B in FIG 1:11 shows the balance pieces which are fitted to S type fans.

Pump removal, S type cars:

1 Remove the radiator and fan belt as described in **Sections 4:3** and **4:4**. Mark the relative positions of the fan and balance pieces so that, on reassembly, balance will be preserved.

2 Dismount the fan and pulley after removing the four setbolts and washers which secure them to the hub. Unscrew the setbolts and nuts which retain the pump to the front timing cover.

Pump removal, 420 type cars:

1 Drain the cooling system as described in **Section 4:2**, dismount the header tank as described in instruction 2 of **Section 4:3** and remove the Torquatrol unit, fan and fan belt as described in **Section 4:4**.

2 Disconnect the hoses attached to the pump. If air conditioning is fitted, remove the compressor front mounting bracket but **do not disconnect the compressor hoses.** Unscrew the setbolts which retain the pump to the front timing cover.

Dismantling the pump:

1 Use an extractor to remove the S type hub or the 420 type pulley. Refer to **FIG 4:4**, slacken locknut 4 and remove screw 3 which retains the bearing outer race (see **FIG 4:5**).

2 Using a tube of $1\frac{3}{32}$ inch outside dia. and $\frac{31}{32}$ inch inside dia. to register with the front of the outer race of the pump bearing, drift out the pump shaft, impeller and bearings assembly from the housing. Push the shaft out of the impeller under a press and collect the seal and rubber water thrower. The shaft and bearings cannot be dismantled further.

3 Clean all parts in paraffin **except the shaft and bearings assembly which is a permanently sealed and lubricated unit**. Remove rust and scale but ensure that none enters the bearings. If there is wear or corrosion in the housing bore or face in front of the impeller, a new housing should be fitted.

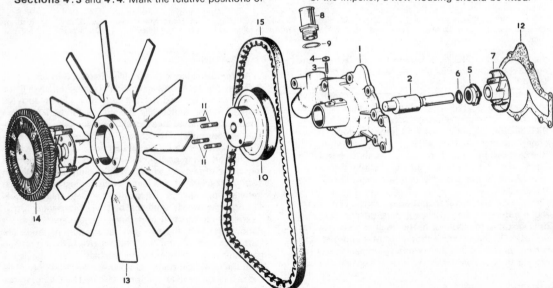

FIG 4:4 Components of the water pump and 420 type fan

Key to Fig 4:4   1 Water pump body   2 Spindle   3 Retaining screw   4 Nut   5 Seal   6 Thrower   7 Impeller
8 Adaptor   9 Copper washer   10 Fan pulley   11 Stud   12 Gasket   13 Fan assembly   14 Torquatrol unit   15 Belt

Reassembly :

Reassembly is the reverse of the dismantling procedure but the following points should be observed:
1 The location hole in the bearings assembly must line-up with the tapped hole in the pump housing.
2 Coat the outside of the brass seal housing with a suitable water resistant jointing compound and ensure that the carbon face is towards the impeller.
3 The rear face of the impeller must be flush with the end of the shaft as shown in **FIG 4 : 5**.

Refitting :

This is the removal procedure in reverse. A new gasket, lightly smeared with grease, should be fitted between the pump and the front timing cover.

4 : 6 The thermostat

Removal :

The thermostat and its location is shown in **FIG 1 : 4**. The S type, item 91, is fitted to the water outlet pipe 87 behind elbow 94. The 420 type, item 101, fits into the forward end of the integral intake manifold and water gallery 96 behind outlet pipe 98. Note that, on both models, a gasket is fitted. If the operation of the thermostat is in doubt, drain sufficient coolant to bring the level below its location and, after removal of the hose, two nuts and spring washers (and, on 420 models, and high-tension lead clip) remove the outlet and withdraw the thermostat.

Testing :

Clean the thermostat and check that the small hole in the valve is clear. Immerse it in a container of cold water together with a zero to 100°C thermometer. Heat the water, keeping it stirred and observe if the operation of the valve is in agreement with the data given in Technical Data.

Refitting :

If the operation is satisfactory, the thermostat may be refitted. Use a new gasket (95 or 100). Should a new unit be required, obtain a replacement that has the same part number and opening temperature stamped on it.

4 : 7 Frost precautions

If antifreeze is to be used, the radiator must first be drained and flushed as described in **Section 4 : 2**. Use only ethylene-glycol-type antifreeze which conforms to Specification BS.3151 or BS.3152. The recommended proportions of water and ethylene-glycol should be measured into a separate container and the system filled from this and not by adding the chemical directly into the radiator. Follow the filling instructions given in **Section 4 : 2**. The proportions of antifreeze for different degrees of frost are:

per cent of antifreeze	Starts freezing at	Absolute safe limit
20	—19°C	—9°C
25	—26°C	—13°C
30	—33°C	—16°C

After the second winter, drain the system and, after flushing thoroughly, refill with fresh solution.

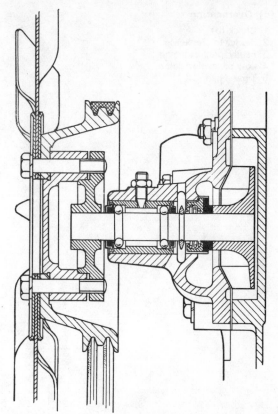

FIG 4 : 5   A section through the water pump and S type fan

If antifreeze is not used, it must be remembered that the action of the thermostat will delay circulation of warm coolant to the radiator which may consequently freeze after the engine has been started.

4 : 8 Fault diagnosis

(a) Internal water leakage

1 Cracked cylinder wall
2 Loose cylinder head nuts
3 Cracked cylinder head
4 Faulty head gasket

(b) Poor circulation

1 Radiator matrix blocked
2 Engine water passages restricted
3 Low water level
4 Slack fan belt
5 Defective thermostat
6 Perished or collapsed radiator or bypass hoses

(c) Corrosion

1 Impurities in the water
2 Infrequent draining and flushing

(d) Overheating

1 Check (b)
2 Sludge in crankcase
3 Faulty ignition timing
4 Low oil level in sump
5 Tight engine
6 Choked exhaust system
7 Binding brakes
8 Slipping clutch
9 Incorrect valve timing
10 Retarded ignition
11 Mixture too weak

CHAPTER 5

THE CLUTCH

5:1 Description

The clutch is a single dry-plate type which operates on the rear face of the flywheel. Early S type cars are fitted with Borg and Beck 10A6.G type clutches which obtain their operational pressure from a multiple of coil springs and this type is shown in section assembled to the flywheel in **FIG 1:2** and its components are illustrated in **FIG 5:1**. Later S type cars (introduced at 3.4 litre engine No. 7B.6572 and 3.8 litre engine No. 7B.60391) and all 420 models are fitted with Borg and Beck BB9/412G type clutches which obtain their operational pressure from a single diaphragm spring. The components of this type are shown in **FIG 5:2**.

When the clutch is engaged, the driven plate which is splined to the gearbox primary shaft and is nipped between the pressure plate and the flywheel, is caused to rotate with the flywheel and transmits torque to the gearbox. The clutch is disengaged when the pressure plate is withdrawn from the driven plate by hydraulically connected leverage between the clutch pedal and the clutch release bearing. The driven plate then ceases to transmit torque.

5:2 Removing and refitting clutch

Remove the engine and gearbox unit as described in **Chapter 1**. Remove the gearbox from the engine as described in **Chapter 6**. Slacken off the six bolts which retain the clutch cover to the flywheel a turn at a time and, working diagonally, release the spring load. Note the balance marks 'B' on the flywheel and cover. Remove the bolts, collect the spring washers and dismount the clutch assembly from the flywheel. Remove the driven plate and ensure that its faces are kept clean.

Examine the driven plate faces. A polished surface is quite normal but the friction linings should be mid-brown in colour and the grain of the material clearly visible. Provided that the linings are not excessively worn, a plate in this condition may be refitted. A highly glazed or a resinous surface results from burned or partially burned-off oil and, as this condition cannot be rectified, a replacement plate will be required. Check the condition of the splines in the hub. Excessive wear, which results from faulty alignment, will dictate the fitment of a new plate.

Refitting:

Place the driven plate onto the flywheel and centralize it by means of a dummy or an actual constant pinion shaft as shown in **FIG 5:3**. Secure the cover assembly with the six securing bolts and their spring washers. Ensure that the balance marks 'B' coincide. Work diagonally and tighten the bolts a turn at a time until they are fully tightened. Remove the centralizing shaft.

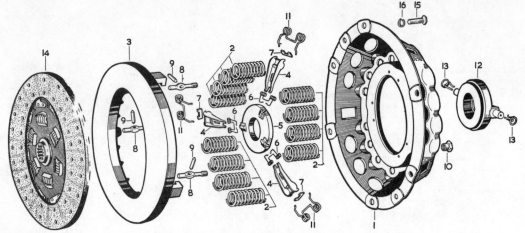

FIG 5:1 Components of coil spring clutch

Key to Fig 5:1   1 Cover   2 Thrust spring   3 Pressure plate   4 Release lever   5 Release lever plate
6 Release lever retainer   7 Release lever strut   8 Release lever eyebolt   9 Eyebolt pin   10 Adjustment nut
11 Anti-rattle spring   12 Release bearing and cup assembly   13 Release bearing retainer   14 Driven plate assembly
15 Securing bolt   16 Spring washer

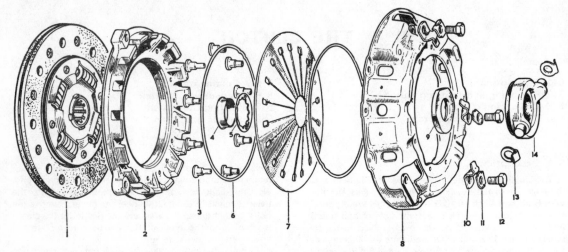

FIG 5:2 Components of diaphragm clutch

Key to Fig 5:2   1 Driven plate   2 Pressure plate   3 Rivet   4 Centre sleeve   5 Belleville washer   6 Fulcrum
ring   7 Diaphragm spring   8 Cover pressing   9 Release plate   10 Retainer   11 Tabwasher   12 Setscrew
13 Retainer   14 Release bearing

5:3 Coil spring clutch

Dismantling:

1 Set the driven plate 14 to one side. Mark the relative position of all major components and proceed to either bolt the cover assembly to a flywheel or to place it on the bed of a press with wooden blocks under the pressure plate so that the cover is free to move downwards when press load is applied to it.

2 With the clutch compressed in either of these ways, unscrew adjusting nuts 10 in **FIG 5:1** and slowly release the clamping pressure. Note that considerable torque is initially needed to break off the squeezed-in portion of each nut. Remove the securing bolts, lift the cover and coil springs off the pressure plate and remove the release lever mechanism.

Examination of the driven plate has been described in **Section 5:2**. Examine the other components now dismantled.

Broken springs and worn release mechanism parts must be renewed. Check that the flange of the cover is not distorted. Inspect the pressure plate face. If this is ridged or pitted, it must be renewed and, as it will then be essential to rebalance the complete cover assembly, the work should be entrusted to a fully-equipped agent. If the graphite bearing is badly worn a new part should be fitted.

Reassembly:

To preserve the balance of the unit, ensure that all major components are refitted in their original positions.

1 Refer to **FIG 5:1**. Fit a pin 9 into an eyebolt 8 and locate them into lever 4. Hold the eyebolt threaded end and the lever 4 inner end closely together and engage a strut 7 within the slots in a lug of the pressure plate. With the other end of the strut, push outwards towards the periphery of the plate. Offer up the lever assembly after engaging the eyebolt within the hole in the plate and locate the strut within the lever groove. Fit the remaining levers in the same way with all contact faces smeared with Lockheed Expander or Duckham's KO12 lubricant.

2 Position the thrust springs 2 onto the bosses of the pressure plate 3. Ensure that the anti-rattle springs 11 are fixed within the cover. Rest the cover onto the thrust springs and align the pressure plate lugs with the slots in the cover.

3 Compress the assembly by reversing instruction 2 of the dismantling procedure. If the securing bolts are being used in a flywheel, they must be turned evenly and a little at a time to avoid distortion of the cover. Screw the adjusting nuts 10 into an approximately correct position.

4 The correct setting of the release levers is essential for the proper operation of the clutch. The following method, although not the most accurate, can be adopted by an owner who does not have access to professional equipment such as a Churchill fixture or a Borg and Beck gauge plate. Mount the clutch onto the flywheel with the new driven plate centralized in its normal position. Fit the securing bolts and their washers and tighten down fully.

5 Refer to **FIG 5:4**. Adjust nuts 10 until dimension A is 1.955 inch. Slacken the securing bolts, turn the plate through a right angle and recheck dimension A. Any lack of parallelism in the driven plate (or variation of dimension C from .330 inch, the gauge thickness) will preclude the 1.955 inch setting from being achieved precisely at every positioning of the driven plate.

6 Finally lock the adjustment nuts by peening the nut into the slot in the release lever eyebolt.

5:4 Diaphragm spring clutch

The Borg and Beck diaphragm spring clutch is normally serviced by fitting a reconditioned exchange unit. Overseas, if exchange units are not available, it will be necessary to obtain spare parts and the necessary special tools. **FIG 5:5** gives the dimensions of the parts of the tool which is required for compressing the diaphragm spring when riveting it to the cover. Except for the spring D, all parts of the tool may be made from mild steel. **FIG 5:6** shows the parts of the special clamping tool and staking guide which is available (part No. SSC.805) from Automotive Products Ltd. of Banbury, England.

Dismantling:

1 Free the release plate 9 in **FIG 5:2** by collapsing the centre sleeve 4 as shown in **FIG 5:7**.

2 Separate the pressure plate 2 from the cover 8 by untabbing and removing the three setscrews 12 which secure the pressure plate to the straps riveted to the cover. Do not detach these straps.

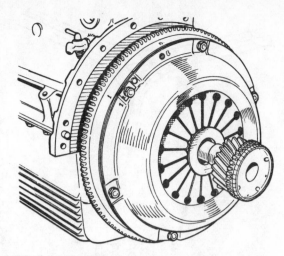

FIG 5:3 Centralizing the driven plate

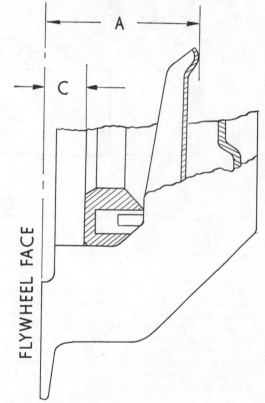

FLYWHEEL FACE

FIG 5:4 Dimensions for release lever setting, for key see text

3 Remove the rivets 3 which secure the diaphragm spring 7 and fulcrum rings to the cover by machining the shank of the rivets with a spotface cutter. Take care not to cut into the cover by more than .005 inch as shown in **FIG 5:8**.

Pin punch out the remains of the rivets.

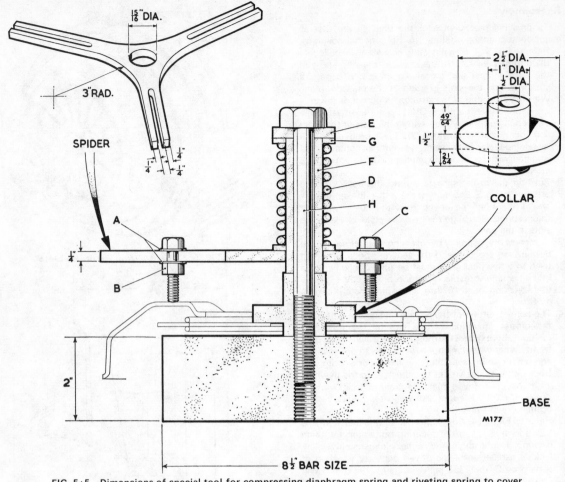

FIG 5:5 Dimensions of special tool for compressing diaphragm spring and riveting spring to cover

Key to Fig 5:5　**A** $\frac{1}{4}$ inch flat washer (6)　　**B** $\frac{1}{4}$ inch nut (3)　　**C** $\frac{1}{4}$ inch diameter screw (3)　　**D** Spring (minimum load of 100 lbs fitted length) (1)　　**E** Washer $\frac{1}{2}$ inch ID x $1\frac{1}{2}$ inch OD x $\frac{1}{4}$ inch thick (1)　　**F** Tube $\frac{1}{2}$ inch ID x $3\frac{1}{4}$ inch long (1)　　**G** Washer $\frac{7}{8}$ ID x $1\frac{1}{2}$ inch OD x $\frac{1}{8}$ inch thick (2)　　**H** Bolt $\frac{1}{2}$ Whit. x 6 inch long (1)

4　Check the condition of the cover by bolting it firmly to a flat surface plate and measure the distance between the underside of the cover pressing flange and the surface plate all round the cover. Variation in this represents flange distortion and must not exceed .007 inch. If it does a replacement cover must be obtained. Should the pressure plate be damaged or excessively scored, it should be renewed. If a new plate is unobtainable, the old one may be salvaged by grinding down to a **minimum thickness** of 1.07 inch.

Reassembly:

1　Refer to **FIG 5:9** and position the fulcrum ring inside the cover. Fit the diaphragm spring and the further fulcrum ring with its location notches diametrically opposite those in the first ring. Line-up the slots in the spring with the small holes in the cover and fit new rivets. Place the base of the special tool which is detailed in **FIG 5:5** onto the rivet heads and then invert the cover and base plate. Fit the remaining parts

of the tool and, as shown in **FIG 5:10**, tighten down until the diaphragm is compressed flat. Rivet securely with a hand punch as shown in **FIG 5:11**.

2　Position the pressure plate inside the cover so that the lugs on the plate engage the slots in the cover. Fit the tabwashers and setscrews, tighten up and lock by retabbing.

3　Grip the flats on the base plate 4 of the special tool shown in **FIG 5:6** in a vice and place the locating boss 3 into the counterbore of the base plate. Place the Belleville washer, concave surface towards the diaphragm spring, onto the centre of the spring and then push the centre sleeve through the spring and into the release plate. Drop the special washer 2 into the sleeve and insert the staking guide 1 into the centre of the assembly. Fit the knurled nut 5 to the thread of the staking guide and tighten down until the whole assembly is solid. Refer to **FIG 5:12** and, using the special punch 6, stake the centre sleeve in six places into the groove in the release plate.

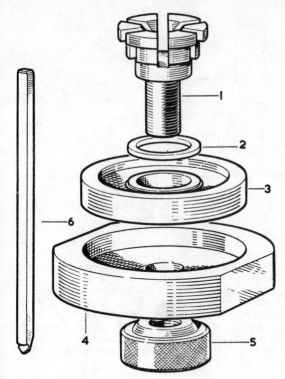

FIG 5:6 Special clamping and staking tool for diaphragm clutch

Key to Fig 5:6   1 Staking guide   2 Washer
3 Locating base   4 Base plate   5 Knurled nut   6 Punch

FIG 5:7 Collapsing the centre sleeve

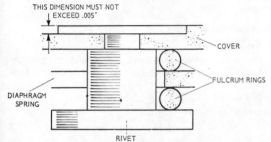

THIS DIMENSION MUST NOT
EXCEED .005"

COVER

FULCRUM RINGS

DIAPHRAGM
SPRING

RIVET

FIG 5:8 Rivet with head machined off

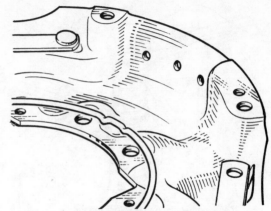

FIG 5:9 Assembly of cover and fulcrum ring

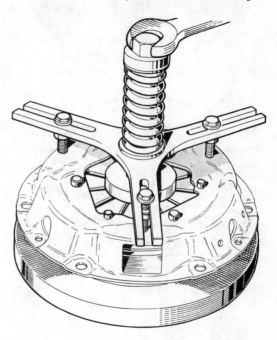

FIG 5:10 Tighten until the diaphragm spring is flat

5:5 Adjustments

FIG 5:13 shows the slave hydraulic cylinder fitted to earlier S type cars. Routine adjustment of the clutch free travel is required and this is effected by slackening off the locknut A and turning the operating rod. Screwing the rod out of the adjuster will decrease the free travel. The free travel is most easily felt, after removal of the return spring, by moving the operating rod towards the slave cylinder and then returning the withdrawal lever to the fullest extent. Ensure that the return spring is refitted.

FIG 5:14 shows the setting dimension for the hydrostatic slave cylinder which is fitted to all 420 cars and was introduced into S type cars commencing at 3.4 litre engine No. 7B.5213 and 3.8 litre engine No. 7B.58367. Normal

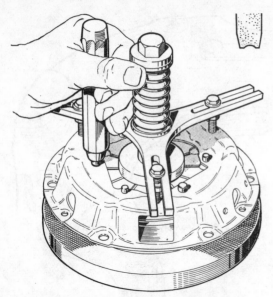

FIG 5:11 Riveting with hand punch

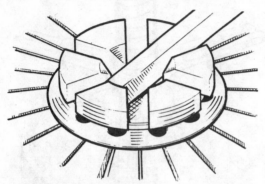

FIG 5:12 Staking centre sleeve to release plate

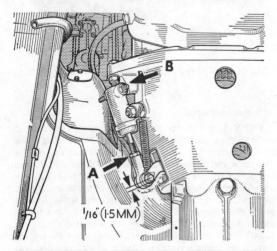

FIG 5:13 Clutch slave cylinder and operating rod

Key to Fig 5:13   **A** Adjustment locknut   **B** Bleed nipple

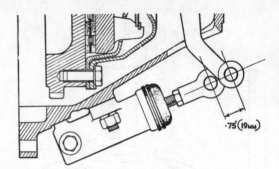

FIG 5:14 Hydrostatic slave cylinder setting dimension

clutch wear is automatically compensated for by this type of cylinder and no clearance adjustment is necessary. If the cylinder has been removed or if a new unit is being fitted, the following procedure must be carried out.

Remove the clevis pin securing the operating rod to the clutch withdrawal lever and release the fork end locknut. Push the clutch lever away from the slave cylinder until resistance is felt and retain the lever in this position. Push the operating rod into the cylinder to the limit of its travel and adjust the fork end to give a dimension of $\frac{3}{4}$ inch between the centres of the fork and the clutch lever as shown in **FIG 5:14**. Tighten the locknut, connect the fork with the clutch lever and refit the clevis pin. Note that no external spring is fitted to the hydrostatic-type of slave cylinder.

5:6 The hydraulic system

The clutch is operated hydraulically and the system is illustrated in **FIG 5:15**. The master cylinder components, 39 to 59, are applicable to S type cars only. This type of master cylinder is the same as that incorporated in the braking system of S type cars and its operation and servicing is consequently covered in **Section 11:4**. The components of the integral reservoir master cylinder which is fitted in the clutch system of 420 models are shown in **FIG 5:16**.

The clutch pedal, 63 in **FIG 5:15**, connects with the master cylinder pushrod (50 in **FIG 5:15**, 9 in **FIG 5:16**) and, when actuated, pushes the piston (48 or 7) along the master cylinder bore. Fluid in the master cylinder is forced through the pipeline to slave cylinder 18 where piston 23, through rod 28, operates the clutch withdrawal fork lever 13.

Scrupulous cleanliness must be observed when servicing the hydraulic system to ensure that dirt does not score the highly-finished bores or cause the rubber cups to seal improperly.

The master cylinder:

S type models:

As mentioned earlier in this Section, the type of master cylinder fitted to S type cars is covered in **Section 11:4**.

420 models:

Removing and refitting:

Disconnect the pedal lever from the pushrod 9 in **FIG 5:16** and the fluid pipe from the plug in the end of the cylinder. Remove the two securing bolts and dismount the

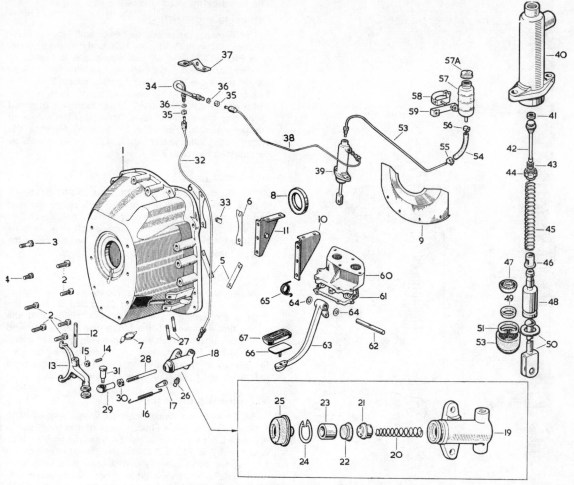

FIG 5:15 Components of clutch operating system

Key to Fig 5:15   1 Clutch housing   2 Bolt   3 Bolt   4 Bolt   5 Plate   6 Plate   7 Cover   8 Oil seal
9 Coverplate   10 Support bracket   11 Support bracket   12 Shaft   13 Fork lever   14 Screw   15 Nut   16 Return spring
17 Plate   18 Slave cylinder   19 Body   20 Spring   21 Cup filler   22 Cup   23 Piston   24 Circlip
25 Rubber boot   26 Bleeder screw   27 Stud   28 Operating rod   29 Adjuster assembly   30 Nut   31 Pivot pin
32 Pipe assembly   33 Clip   34 Flexible hose   35 Nut   36 Washer   37 Bracket   38 Pipe assembly
39 Clutch master cylinder   40 Body   41 Recuperation seal   42 Valve   43 Spring   44 Spring support
45 Main spring   46 Spring support   47 Cup seal   48 Piston   49 Static seal   50 Pushrod   51 Circlip
52 Dust excluder   53 Pipe assembly   54 Low pressure hose   55 Clip   56 Clip   57 Clutch fluid container
58 Clip   59 Clutch mounting bracket   60 Clutch pedal housing   61 Gasket   62 Shaft   63 Clutch pedal   64 Washer
65 Return spring   66 Steel pad   67 Rubber pad

unit. Drain the fluid from the supply tank. Refitting is the reverse of this procedure and must be followed by bleeding the system as described in **Section 5:7**.

Dismantling:

Refer to **FIG 5:16**. Pull back rubber boot 11, remove the circlip 10 and then the pushrod 9 together with its dished washer. Withdraw the internal parts and remove the secondary cup 8 by gently stretching it off piston 7. Use only hydraulic fluid to clean the parts which may then be examined. A new set of rubber cups should be obtained if the unit has seen considerable service.

Reassembly:

Assemble all internal parts wetted with the correct grade of fluid. Stretch the secondary cup 8 over piston 7 and manipulate it to seat correctly. Insert spring 3, large end first, into the cylinder and ensure that retainer 4 is in position. Follow with the main cup 5, lip first. Take care not to turn back or damage the lip. Insert washer 6, piston and secondary cup 7 and 8, pushrod 9 and circlip 10 which must seat correctly in its groove. Refit rubber boot 11. Fill the supply tank with the correct grade of fluid as specified in **Section 5:7**.

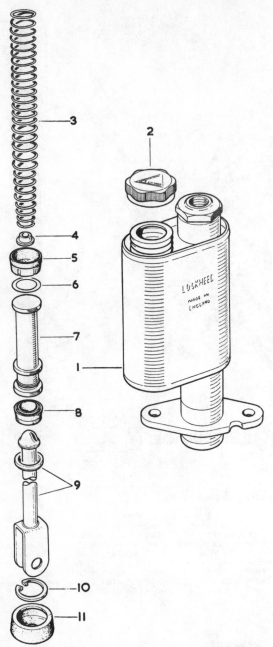

FIG 5:16   Components of master cylinder fitted to 420 models

Key to Fig 5:16

		1 Tank and barrel assembly
2 Filler cap	3 Spring	4 Spring retainer
5 Main cup	6 Piston washer	7 Piston
8 Secondary cup	9 Pushrod	10 Circlip
11 Rubber boot		

Test the unit before refitting it to the car. Push the piston down the cylinder and allow it to return. After one ot two repetitions, fluid should flow from the outlet plug.

The slave cylinder, all models :

Removing and refitting :

The following procedure applies to both types of slave cylinder. Attach a rubber bleed tube to the nipple arrowed B in **FIG 5:13**, unscrew this nipple one turn and, by pumping the clutch pedal, transfer the hydraulic fluid into a clean container. Disconnect the pipe, detach boot 25 in **FIG 5:15** from body 19, remove the two fixing screws and dismount the unit leaving the operating rod attached to the clutch withdrawal lever. Refitting is the reverse of this procedure and must be followed by bleeding the system as described in **Section 5:7** and by adjustment as described in **Section 5:5**

Dismantling :

Thoroughly clean the exterior. Refer to **FIG 5:15** and remove circlip 24. Apply gentle air pressure to the pipe connection to expel the internal parts. Use only the correct grade of fluid to clean the parts which may then be examined. A new rubber cup 22 should be obtained if the unit has seen considerable service.

Reassembly :

Assemble the internal parts wetted with the correct grade of fluid. Attach cup filler 21 in **FIG 5:15** to the small end of spring 20. Insert into the cylinder with the spring first. Follow with the rubber cup 22, lip first and taking care not to turn back or damage the lip. Insert piston 25 with its flat face innermost and fit circlip 24 which must fit correctly in its groove. Note that no external spring 16 is fitted to the hydrostatic-type of slave cylinder.

5:7 Bleeding the system

Fill the master cylinder reservoir with Castrol/Girling Crimson Clutch/Brake Fluid. Ensure that entry of dirt is prevented. Attach a rubber bleed tube to the nipple which is arrowed B in **FIG 5:13**. Immerse the open end of the tube into a small quantity of the same fluid in a clean container. Two operators are required for this procedure. Unscrew the bleed nipple by one turn. Depress the clutch pedal slowly and **retighten the nipple before the pedal reaches the end of its travel**. Allow the pedal to return unassisted. Repeat this cycle until fluid issuing from the bleed tube is entirely free of air bubbles. Replenish the fluid in the reservoir **frequently** during this procedure. If the level is allowed to fall below halfway, air will enter the system and the operation of bleeding will require to be recommenced.

On completion, top up the reservoir to the bottom of the filler neck. It is not advisable to re-use fluid which has been collected in the container unless it is absolutely clean beyond doubt and then it must be de-aerated by being allowed to stand for at least twenty four hours. Do not, under any circumstance, mix different fluids.

5:8 Fault diagnosis

(a) Drag or spin

1 Oil or grease on driven plate linings
2 Misalignment between engine and splined shaft
3 Leaking master cylinder or pipeline
4 Driven plate hub binding on splined shaft
5 Distorted driven plate

6 Warped or damaged pressure plate or clutch cover
7 Broken driven plate linings
8 Dirt of foreign matter in clutch
9 Air in clutch hydraulic system
10 Incorrect operating rod adjustment

(b) Fierceness or snatch

1 Check 1, 2 and 3 in (a)
2 Worn driven plate linings

(c) Slip

1 Check 1, 2 and 10 in (a)
2 Check 2 in (b)
3 Weak thrust spring(s)
4 Seized piston in clutch slave cylinder
5 Port between master cylinder and fluid reservoir choked

(d) Judder

1 Check 1 and 2 in (a)
2 Pressure plate not parallel with flywheel face
3 Contact area of driven plate linings not evenly distributed

4 Bent or worn splined shaft
5 Badly worn splines in driven plate hub
6 Buckled driven plate

(e) Rattle

1 Check 3 in (c)
2 Check 4 and 5 in (d)
3 Broken springs in driven plate
4 Worn release mechanism
5 Excessive backlash in transmission
6 Wear in transmission bearings
7 Release bearing loose on fork

(f) Tick or knock

1 Check 4 and 5 in (d)
2 Release plate out of line
3 Loose flywheel

(g) Driven plate fracture

1 Check 2 in (a)
2 Drag and distortion due to hanging gearbox in driven plate hub

NOTES

CHAPTER 6

THE SYNCHROMESH GEARBOX AND OVERDRIVE

6:1 Description of gearbox

Early S type models which are fitted with manual gearboxes have the type of box which has synchromesh on three of the four forward gears. This type of gearbox is identified by the prefix 'GB' (or 'GBN' if a mainshaft suitable for the attachment of an overdrive is fitted) and its components are illustrated in FIGS 6:1 and 6:2. These gearboxes have the suffix 'JS' after the gearbox number. This suffix distinguishes them from boxes of the same type but of earlier modification standards which are fitted to different types of Jaguar cars. It is essential, when ordering spare parts, to quote the prefix and suffix letters in addition to the gearbox number. The type of overdrive unit which may be fitted to 'GBN' type gearboxes is shown, in cutaway section, in FIG 6:18.

All 420 models and later S type cars (introduced at chassis number 3.4 litre 1B.2192RH and 1B.25301LH and 3.8 litre 1B.52078RH plus 1B.52034RH and 1B.52036RH and 1B.76310LH) are fitted with a box which has synchromesh on all four forward gears. These boxes, which are identified by the prefix letter 'JC' (or 'JCN' if a mainshaft suitable for the attachment of an overdrive is fitted) are not interchangeable with the earlier type. The gears are pressure lubricated from a built-in pump on prefix 'JC' boxes and from the overdrive pump on prefix 'JCN' boxes. The components of

the overdrive which may be fitted to this type of gearbox are shown in FIG 6:19. It is not interchangeable with the earlier type.

Gearbox ratios are tabulated in Technical Data.

6:2 Removing and refitting the gearbox

The following procedure applies to both types of gearbox.

Removal:

1 Remove the engine and gearbox unit as described in **Section 1:2.**
2 Remove the setbolts and nuts which secure the clutch housing to the engine and dismount the clutch housing and gearbox from the engine. **Support the gearbox during this operation to avoid straining the clutch driven plate and constant pinion shaft.**
3 Remove the clutch slave cylinder as described in **Chapter 5, Section 5:6.**
4 Detach the springs and remove the clutch carbon thrust bearing. Refer to **FIG 5:15.** Unscrew the Allen screw 14, push out the fulcrum pin 12 and detach the clutch fork lever 13.
5 Untab the washers, break the locking wire, remove the eight setbolts 2, 3 and 4 and detach the clutch housing from the box.

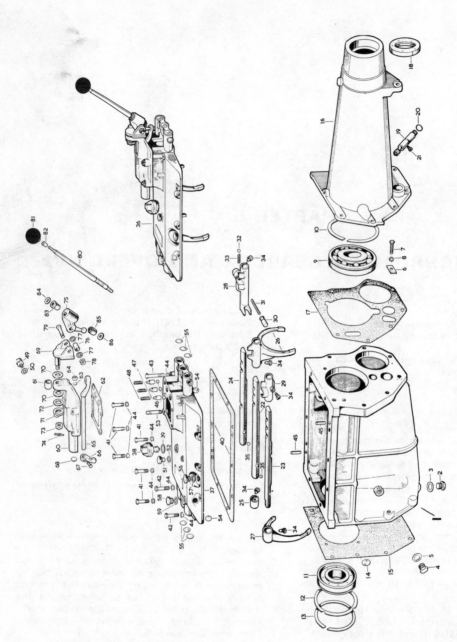

FIG 6:1 Components of the earlier S type gearbox casing

Key to Fig 6:1 1 Gearbox case 2 Drain plug 3 Fibre washer 4 Oil filler plug 5 Fibre washer 6 Locking plate 7 Setscrew 8 Spring washer 9 Ballbearing 10 Circlip 11 Ballbearing 12 Collar 13 Circlip 14 Fibre washer 15 Gasket 16 Gearbox extension 17 Gasket 18 Oil seal 19 Speedometer drive gear 20 O-ring 21 Dowel screw 22 Striking rod, first/second gears 23 Striking rod, third/top gears 24 Striking rod, reverse gear 25 Stop 26 Changespeed fork, first/second gears 27 Changespeed fork, third/top gears 28 Changespeed fork, reverse gear 29 Selector, third/top gears 30 Plunger 31 Spring 32 Locking ball 33 Spring 34 Dowel screw 35 Ball 36 Top cover assembled 37 Top cover 38 Switch 39 Gasket 40 Gasket 41 Bolt 42 Fibre washer 43 Bolt 44 Spring washer 45 Dowel 46 Ball 47 Plunger 48 Spring 49 Breather 50 Fibre washer 51 Plug 52 Fibre washer 53 Stud 54 Welch plug 55 Welch plug 56 Plug 57 Fibre washer 58 Plug 59 Fibre washer 60 Change speed lever housing 61 Pivot jaw bush 62 Gasket 63 O-ring 64 Retaining cap 65 Remote control shaft 66 Slector finger 67 Dowel screw 68 Welch plug 69 Pivot jaw housing 70 Fibre washer 71 Coil spring washer 72 D-washer 73 Slotted nut 74 Splitpin 75 Selector lever 76 Bush 77 Fibre washer 78 Coil spring washer 79 Pivot pin 80 Change speed lever 81 Lever knob 82 Locking cone 83 Rubber bush 84 Washer 85 Rubber bush 86 Washer

60

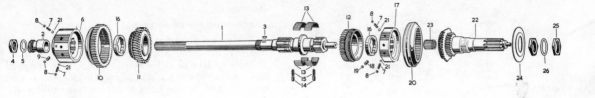

FIG 6 : 2   Components of the earlier S type gearbox

Key to Fig 6 : 2   1 Mainshaft   2 Speedometer driving gear   3 Key   4 Nut   5 Tabwasher   6 Synchronising sleeve second gear   7 Spring   8 Ball   9 Plunger   10 First-speed mainshaft gear   11 Second-speed mainshaft gear 12 Third-speed mainshaft gear   13 Needle roller   14 Plunger   15 Spring   16 Thrust washer   17 Synchronizing sleeve 18 Plunger   19 Ball   20 Operating sleeve   21 Shim   22 Constant pinion shaft   23 Roller bearing   24 Oil thrower 25 Locknut   26 Tabwasher   27 Reverse spindle   28 Reverse gear   29 Lever   30 Fulcrum pin   31 Slotted nut 32 Plain washer   33 Splitpin   34 Reverse slipper   35 Sealing ring   36 Countershaft   37 Gear unit on countershaft 38 Retaining ring   39 Needle roller   40 Thrust washer   41 Thrust washer   42 Retaining ring   43 Thrust washer 44 Thrust washer   45 Sealing ring

Refitting:

Refitting the gearbox to the clutch housing and remounting this unit to the engine is the removal sequence in reverse. **Support the gearbox to avoid straining the clutch driven plate and the constant pinion shaft.**

6:3 Dismantling and reassembling the earlier S type gearbox

The gearboxes covered by this Section are those with prefix letters **'GB'** and **'GBN'**.

Dismantling:

1 Drain the gearbox. Refer to **FIG 6:1**. With the gear-lever in neutral, remove the ten bolts 41, spring washers 44 and top cover 37. Remove and discard gasket 40. Remove screw 21 which retains the speedometer driven gear unit 19 and withdraw it. Remove the fibre washer 14 from the front end of the countershaft.

2 On prefix **'GB'** boxes, remove the setscrews which secure extension 16 to gearbox casing 1. Do not disturb locking plate 6. Withdraw the extension complete with shafts and insert a spare countershaft (or a dummy of .979 inch dia. and 11.125 inch long) into the countershaft bore. Keep these shafts in contact as the countershaft is withdrawn as shown in **FIG 6:3**. On prefix **'GBN'** boxes remove the overdrive as described in **Section 6:6**.

3 Engage top and first gears to lock the box. Refer to **FIG 6:2**. On prefix **'GB'** boxes, untab and remove locknut 4, withdraw speedometer drive gear 2, remove woodruffe key 3, extract the spare or dummy shaft and allow the countershaft gear unit to drop to the bottom of the casing. On **'GBN'** boxes, remove the circlip, washer and shims from behind the gearbox rear bearing.

4 Rotate constant pinion shaft 22 until the cutaway portions of the driving gear face top and bottom of the casing. Tap the mainshaft 1 forwards and knock the constant pinion shaft complete with ballbearing (11 in **FIG 6:1**) out of the casing. Remove the constant pinion shaft and withdraw the bearing from it. Continue to tap the mainshaft forwards until it is free of the rear bearing (9 in **FIG 6:1**) which may then be tapped rearwards and out of the casing.

5 Disengage the reverse gear 28 by pushing it forward to clear first-speed gear 10. Lift the front end of the mainshaft upwards and remove it forwards and out of the casing complete with all mainshaft gears.

6 Draw reverse gear rearwards to clear the countershaft first-gear and lift out the countershaft gear unit. Note the thrust washers which are fitted at both ends of gear unit and collect all the needle rollers 39. Push the reverse gear back into the casing and lift it out.

Dismantling the mainshaft:

1 Refer to **FIG 6:2**. Draw the top/third gear operating and synchronizing sleeves, items 20 and 17, forwards

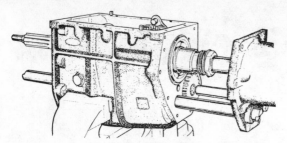

FIG 6:3 Extension removal and dummy shaft insertion

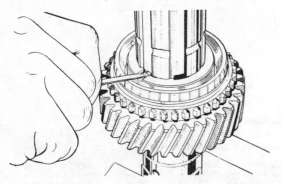

FIG 6:4 Second-speed thrust washer locking plunger

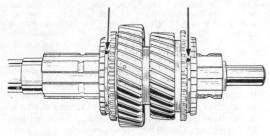

FIG 6:5 Locking plunger depression holes

off the shaft. Press the operating sleeve off the synchronizing sleeve. Remove the six balls 8, springs 7, interlock plungers 18 and balls 19 from the synchronizing sleeve.

2 Draw the second gear synchronizing sleeve 6 complete with the first-speed gear 10 rearwards off the shaft. Press the gear off the sleeve and remove the balls and springs and interlock ball and plunger.

3 Press in plunger 14 which locks the third-speed gear thrust washer 16. Rotate the washer until the splines line up and remove the washer forwards off the shaft followed by the third-speed gear 12. Collect needles 13. Remove locking plunger 14 and spring 15. Refer to **FIG 6:4** and repeat the operation on the second-speed gear thrust washer but, in this case, washer 16 and gear 11 are removed rearwards.

Dismantling the constant pinion shaft:

Untab and remove the two nuts 25 (righthand threads), withdraw the bearing from the shaft and remove the oil thrower 24.

Reassembly:

Assembling the countershaft gear unit:

The reassembly of the countershaft gear unit is the reverse of the dismantling procedure described earlier.

Refer to **FIG 6:2** and fit needle roller retaining rings 38 into the ends of the gear unit 37 and the 29 rollers at each end followed by the outer retaining rings 40 and 42. Apply grease to the needle rollers to facilitate assembly. Offer up the thrust washers to the ends of the gear unit, lower it into the casing and insert the spare or dummy shaft to retain the gear unit in place.

Check the clearance between the bronze thrust washer 41 and the casing. This end float should be .002 to .004 inch. Thrust washers of .152, .156, .159, .162 and .164 inch thickness are available for end float adjustment. A false end float will be obtained if the box is held in a vice during the measurement.

Remove the spare or dummy countershaft and insert a thin rod in its place. Fit the bushed reverse gear in its slipper and draw it rearwards to give clearance for fitting the countershaft gear unit.

Reassembling the mainshaft:

1 Refer to **FIG 6:2**. Apply grease to facilitate assembly, fit the 41 needle rollers 13 behind the mainshaft shoulder and slide second-speed gear 11, with its synchronizing cone to the rear, onto the rollers. Fit the spring and plunger into the plunger hole and slide the thrust washer 16 over the splines.

2 Refer to **FIG 6:5** and align the large hole in the synchronizing cone and, with a steel pin, compress the plunger and rotate the washer into a locked position with the cutaway in line with the plunger.

3 Check the end float of the second-speed gear by inserting a feeler gauge between the thrust washer and the shoulder on the mainshaft. The end float should be .002 to .004 inch and thrust washers in three thicknesses (.471/.472, .473/.474 and .475/.476 inch) are available for adjustment.

4 Repeat instructions 1, 2 and 3 and fit the third-speed gear 12 noting however that its synchronizing cone faces forwards.

5 Fit the springs and balls (and shims 21 if fitted) to the six blind holes in the second-speed synchronizing sleeve 6. Fit the first-speed gear 10 to sleeve 6 with the relieved internal spline tooth in the gear in line with the stop pin in the sleeve.

6 Use a hose clip to compress the springs. Slide the gear over the sleeve and push off the hose clip. The balls will be heard and felt to engage the neutral position groove. 62 to 68 lb axial load should be required to disengage the synchronizing sleeve from the neutral position. This may be adjusted by fitting shims under the springs.

7 Fit this assembly to any spline on the mainshaft and, with no ball and plunger fitted, check that the sleeve slides freely on the mainshaft. Remove the assembly, fit the ball and plunger and refit to the same spline on the mainshaft.

8 Check the interlock plunger by sliding the outer operating sleeve into first gear position as shown in **FIG 6:6**. With slight downwards pressure on the synchronizing assembly, the second-speed gear should rotate without any tendancy for the cones to

rub. If the cones rub, a longer plunger should be fitted.

9 The procedure for assembling the third/top synchronizing sleeve 17 to operating sleeve 20 is similar to instructions 5 and 6. Note that the large boss end of the inner sleeve is fitted to the wide chamfer end of the sleeve and that the relieved splines in the sleeve must line up with the two ball and plunger holes in the sleeve. 52 to 58 lb load should be required to disengage the sleeve from the neutral position. This may be adjusted by fitting shims under the springs.

10 When fitting the assembly to the mainshaft, note that the relieved tooth at the wide chamfer end of the outer operating sleeve must be in line with the **fore-most** groove in the mainshaft. The wide chamfer end of the outer operating sleeve must face forwards. The inner sleeve must slide freely on the mainshaft when the balls and plungers are not fitted. Fit the two balls and plungers, balls first, to the holes in the synchronizing sleeve and refit the assembly.

11 Check the interlock plungers by sliding the third/top operating sleeve over the third-speed dogs as shown in **FIG 6:7**. With the third-gear engaged, lift and lower the synchronizing assembly. Movement of approximately $\frac{3}{32}$ inch should be possible without drag being felt. If the assembly does not move freely, a shorter third-speed plunger should be fitted. This is the plunger which is not opposite the relieved tooth when looking at the wide chamfer end of the outer operating sleeve.

12 Now, as shown in **FIG 6:8,** slide the operating sleeve into the top gear position and lift and lower the synchronizing assembly. Movement of approximately $\frac{3}{16}$ inch should be possible without drag being felt and with slight downwards pressure on the synchronizing assembly, the third-speed gear should rotate without any tendency for the cones to rub. If the synchronizing assembly does not move freely, fit a shorter top gear

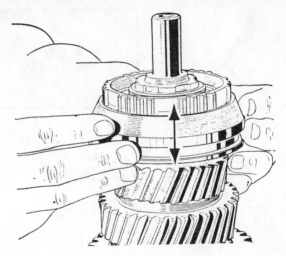

FIG 6:7   Interlock plunger check

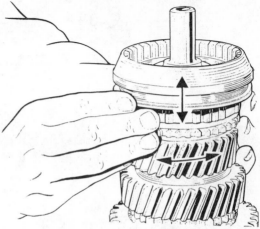

FIG 6:8   Interlock plunger check

plunger. If the cones rub, fit a longer plunger. This plunger is the one in line with the relieved tooth when looking at the wide chamfer end of the outer operating sleeve.

Reassembling the constant pinion shaft:

The procedure is the reverse of the dismantling instructions given earlier.

Reassembling the gearbox:

Fit new gaskets to the front, rear and top faces of the casing.

1 Enter the mainshaft through the top of the casing and pass rearwards through the bearing hole. Offer up the constant pinion shaft at the front of the casing with the cutaway portions facing top and bottom of the casing. Tap this shaft rearwards until the collar and circlip on the bearing butt against the casing and, holding the shaft in position, tap in the rear bearing complete with circlip.

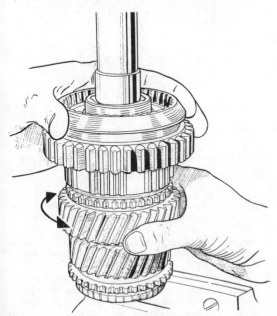

FIG 6:6   Interlock plunger check

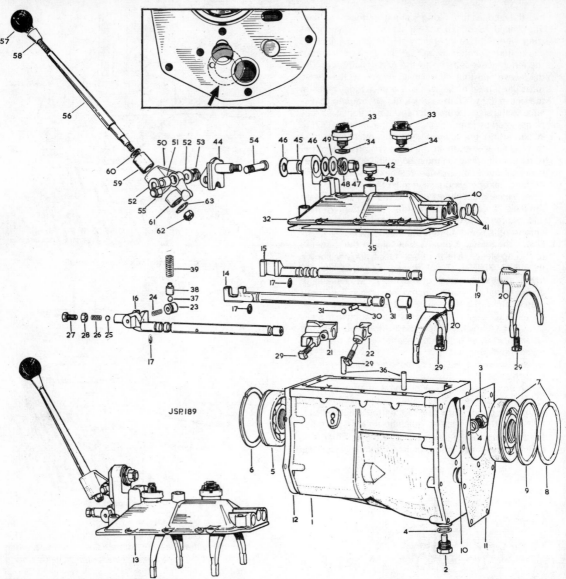

FIG 6:9 Components of 420 and later S type gearbox casing. The countershaft rear washer, arrowed in the inset, is shown in the position referred to in the text

Key to Fig 6:9 1 Gearbox case 2 Oil drain plug 3 Oil filter plug 4 Fibre washer 5 Ballbearing 6 Bearing sleeve 7 Needle roller 8 Circlip 9 Collar 10 Fibre blanking disc 11 Gasket 12 Gasket 13 Remote control assembly 14 Striking rod 15 Striking rod 16 Striking rod 17 O-ring 18 Stop 19 Stop 20 Changespeed fork 21 Changespeed fork 22 Locating arm 23 Plunger 24 Spring 25 Ball 26 Spring 27 Screw 28 Nut 29 Dowel screw 30 Roller 31 Ball 32 Top cover 32 Switch 33 Switch 34 Gasket 35 Gasket 36 Dowel 37 Ball 38 Plunger 39 Spring 40 Welch washer 41 Welch washer 42 Breather 43 Washer 44 Pivot jaw 45 Bush 46 Washer 47 Nut 48 Washer 49 D-washer 50 Selector lever 51 Bush 52 Washer 53 Washer 54 Pivot pin 55 Nut 56 Changespeed lever 57 Knob 58 Locking cone 59 Upper bush 60 Washer 61 Lower bush 62 Nut 63 Washer

2 Lift the countershaft gears into mesh with the thin rod and insert the spare or dummy shaft through the countershaft bore in the front of the casing to replace the thin rod.

3 Engage top and first gears to lock the box. On prefix **'GB'** boxes fit the woodruff key and speedometer drive gear to the mainshaft. Fit the tabwasher and locknut and secure. Disengage into neutral.

4 On prefix **'GBN'** boxes fit as many shims as are needed behind the bearing to eliminate all end float from the mainshaft. Fit the plain washer and circlip.

5 Offer up the extension complete with the counter and reverse shafts and tap into position driving the spare or dummy countershaft forwards and out of the casing. Secure the extension with its setscrews and spring washers.

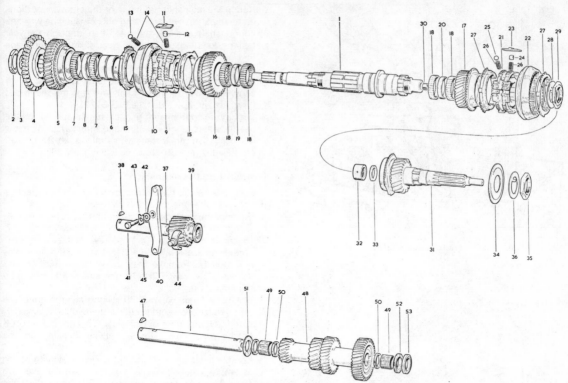

FIG 6:10 Components fitted to the 420 and later S type gearbox

Key to Fig 6:10   1 Mainshaft   2 Nut   3 Tabwasher   4 Reverse gear   5 1st gear   6 Bearing sleeve   7 Needle roller
8 Spacer   9 Synchro hub   10 Operating sleeve   11 Thrust member   12 Plunger   13 Detent ball   14 Spring
15 Synchro ring   16 2nd gear   17 3rd gear   18 Needle roller   19 Spacer   20 Spacer   21 Synchro hub   22 Operating
sleeve   23 Thrust member   24 Plunger   25 Detent ball   26 Spring   27 Synchro ring   28 Nut   29 Tabwasher
30 Plug   31 Constant pinion shaft   32 Roller bearing   33 Spacer   34 Oil thrower   35 Nut   36 Tabwasher
37 Reverse spindle   38 Key   39 Reverse idler gear   40 Lever assembly   41 Setscrew   42 Fibre washer   43 Tabwasher
44 Reverse slipper   45 Splitpin   46 Countershaft   47 Key   48 Cluster gear unit   49 Needle roller   50 Retaining ring
51 Rear thrust washer   52 Front thrust washer   53 Outer thrust washer

6 Fit the top cover noting that the two long bolts fit at
the rear and the two short ones at the front.

7 Fit a new fibre washer at the front end of the countershaft. Fit the speedometer driven gear and bearing to
the extension.

8 On prefix **'GBN'** boxes, fit the overdrive as described
in **Section 6:6**.

6:4 Dismantling and reassembling the 420 and later S type gearbox

The gearboxes covered by this Section are those with
prefix letters **'JC'** and **'JCN'**.

Dismantling:

1 Drain the gearbox and, with the lever in neutral,
remove the eight bolts and two nuts and lift off the top
cover. Engage first and reverse gears to lock the unit.
Untab and remove the flange nut and flange. Withdraw
the setscrews and remove the rear cover. Unscrew the
retaining bolt and remove the speedometer pinion and
bush assembly. Remove the six bolts, withdraw the
extension, collect the distance piece, oil pump driving

pin and filter. On prefix **'JCN'** boxes, remove the
overdrive as described in **Section 6:6**.

2 From inside the extension, break the staking and
withdraw the three countersunk screws securing the oil
pump gear housing. Withdraw the housing by evenly
screwing two of these screws into the tapped holes in
the housing. Mark the gears so that they may be
replaced in the housing the same way up. **FIG 6:16**
shows the pump components.

3 Remove the fibre plug 10 in **FIG 6:9** from the front of
the countershaft and drive it out of the casing forwards.
Ensure that the rear washer drops down clockwise as
shown in the inset to **FIG 6:9** by pushing it with a
piece of wire if necessary.

4 Refer to **FIG 6:10**. Rotate the constant pinion shaft 31
until the cutaway portions of the driving gear face top
and bottom of the casing. With the aid of two levers,
as shown in **FIG 6:11**, ease the constant pinion shaft
and bearing assembly from the casing. Remove roller
bearing 32 and spacer 33 from inside the shaft, untab
and remove nut 35, tabwasher 36, bearing and oil
thrower 34.

FIG 6:11 Constant pinion shaft removal

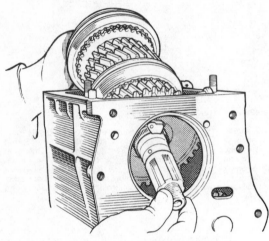

FIG 6:12 Lift out the mainshaft

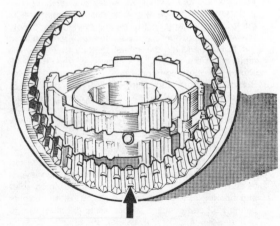

FIG 6:13 The three detent grooves

5 Rotate the mainshaft until one of the cutaway portions in the third/top synchronizing hub 21 is in line with the countershaft and tap the mainshaft through the rear bearing keeping the reverse gear 4 tight against the first gear 5 with a lever. Remove the rear bearing, fit a hose clip to the mainshaft to prevent the reverse gear from sliding off, slacken the reverse lever bolt 41 to allow the lever to move freely, lift out the mainshaft forwards and upwards (see **FIG 6:12**).

6 Lift out the countershaft gear cluster 48 and collect the needle rollers, retaining rings and thrust washers items 49 to 53. Withdraw the reverse idler shaft 37 and lift out the idler gear 39. Note the locking key 38.

Dismantling the mainshaft:

Keep the needle rollers in sets and to their respective positions as they are graded in diameter.

1 Remove the hose clip and withdraw the reverse gear 4, withdraw first gear 5 and collect 120 needle rollers 7, spacer 8 and sleeve 6. Withdraw first/second synchronizing assembly and collect two loose synchronizing rings 15. Remove the second-speed gear 16 and collect 106 needle rollers 18. The spacer 19 remains on the mainshalt.

2 Untab and remove nut 29. Withdraw the third/top synchronizing assembly, collect the two loose rings 27, withdraw the third-speed gear 17 and collect 106 needle rollers 18. The spacer 20 remains on the mainshalt.

3 Completely surround and cover each synchronizing assembly separately with a cloth, push out the hub (9 or 21) from the sleeve (10 or 22) and collect the balls, springs, thrust members, plungers and springs (11, 12, 13 and 14 or 23, 24, 25 and 26).

Reassembly:

The synchronizing assemblies:

Although similar in appearance, the synchronizing hubs are not identical. An identification groove is machined on the edge ol the third/top component. The assembly procedure, however, is the same for both.

1 Assemble the hub to the operating sleeve with (a) the wide boss of the hub away from the wide chamfer end of the sleeve and (b) the three balls and springs must be in line with the teeth having three detent grooves as shown in **FIG 6:13**.

2 Place packing under the hub to bring the holes for the balls and springs exactly level with the top of the sleeve. Use grease and fit the springs, plungers, thrust members, springs and balls. Their relative positions are shown in **FIG 6:14**. Use a large hose clip as shown in **FIG 6:15** to compress the springs and carefully lift the assembly off the packing.

3 Depress the hub slightly and push down the thrust members as shown in **FIG 6:15** until they engage the groove in the sleeve. Finally tap down the hub until the balls are heard and felt to engage the groove.

The cluster gear:

Fit a retaining ring, 50 in **FIG 6:10,** into the front end of the cluster gear 48. Position 29 needle rollers 49 with grease, fit the thrust washer 52 with its peg locating in the groove in the front face of the cluster. Fit a retaining ring, 29 needle rollers and a further retaining ring at the rear of the cluster. Fit the reverse idler gear, lever and shaft. Fit the pegged rear washer 51 to its boss on the casing with grease. Fit the outer thrust washer 53 with grease to the front of the cluster and lower the unit carefully into position. Insert a dummy shaft and check the end float between the rear thrust washer and the cluster gear. This should be .004 to .006 inch. Rear thrust washers of .152, .156, .159, .162 and .164 inch thickness are available so that this may be adjusted. Exchange the dummy shaft for a thin rod.

The constant pinion shaft:

Reassembly is the reverse of the dismantling procedure. Ensure that the bearing is seated squarely on the shaft.

The mainshaft:

Reassembly is the reverse of the dismantling procedure. The end floats should be:—first gear, .005 to .007 inch; second gear, .005 to .008 inch; third gear, .005 to .008 inch. Excessive end float can only be reduced by fitting new parts. The graded needle rollers should be refitted to their original positions. Grades are identified by /1, /2 and /3 after the part number. Fit a hose clip to prevent the reverse gear from sliding off the mainshaft.

Reassembling the gearbox:

Fit new gaskets to the front, rear and top faces of the casing.

1 Enter the mainshaft through the top of the casing and pass it rearwards through the bearing hole. Enter the constant pinion shaft and front bearing assembly through the bearing hole at the front of the casing with the cutaway portions of the driving gear at the top and bottom. Tap the assembly into position and, with a hollow drift, tap the rear bearing into position.

2 Partly withdraw the thin rod from the front of the cluster gear and lever upwards while rotating the mainshaft and constant pinion shaft gently until the cluster gears mesh. Carefully insert the countershaft from the rear and withdraw the thin rod. Fit the key locating the countershaft in the casing.

3 On prefix 'JC' boxes, lubricate the oil pump gears and body and refit the gears the same way up as when removed. Secure the pump to the extension with the three countersunk screws and relock them by staking. Fit the distance piece and driving pin. Fit the extension to the gearbox and secure with the setscrews.

4 Fit the speedometer driving gear to the mainshaft, fit the speedometer driven gear and bush and secure with the retaining bolt. Fit a new oil seal to the rear cover with the lip facing forwards and fit the rear cover to the extension noting that the setscrew holes are offset. Fit the four bolts to the flange. Fit the flange, washer and nut. Tighten up and fit a new splitpin.

5 On prefix 'JCN' gearboxes, refit the overdrive as described in **Section 6:6.**

6 Ensure that the speed change lever and the gearbox are in neutral. Ensure that the reverse idler gear is out of mesh with the reverse gear on the mainshaft by pushing the lever rearwards. Engage the selector forks into the grooves in the synchronizing assemblies and secure the top cover.

After refitting the engine and gearbox unit to the car,

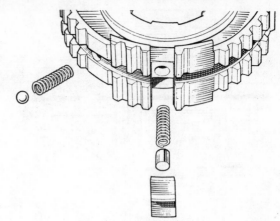

FIG 6:14   The relative positions

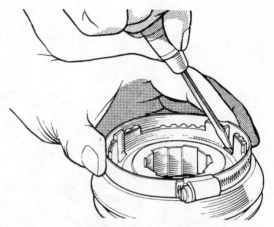

FIG 6:15   Pushing down the thrust members

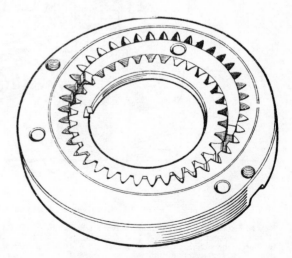

FIG 6:16   The pump components

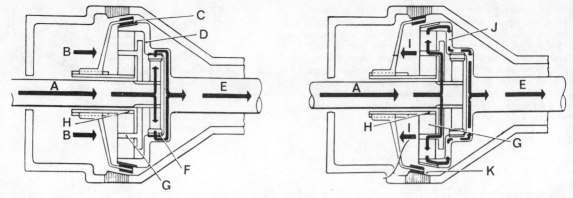

FIG 6:17   The overdrive operation

Key to Fig 6:17   A From gearbox   **B** Spring pressure   **C** Annulus and sunwheel locked   **D** Annulus   **E** To propeller shaft   **F** Uni-directional clutch   **G** Planet wheel and carrier   **H** Sunwheel   **I** Hydraulic pressure   **J** Annulus overdriven by planet wheels   **K** Locked cone clutch holds sunwheel

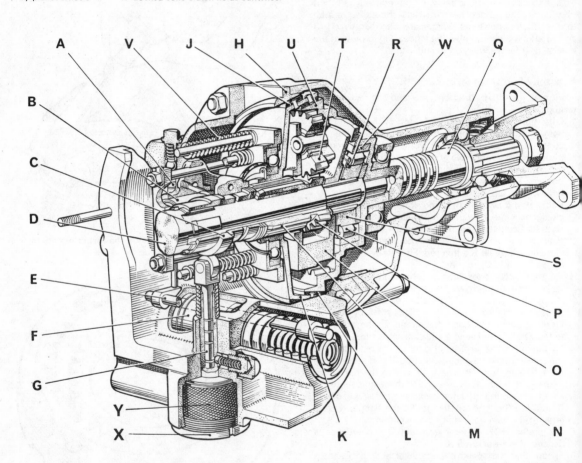

FIG 6:18   Cutaway view of the overdrive fitted to earlier S type cars

Key to Fig 6:18   A Operating valve   **B** Piston   **C** Cam   **D** Shaft   **E** Operating shaft   **F** Spring-loaded piston   **G** Pump plunger   **H** Casing   **J** Outer lining of clutch K   **K** Cone clutch   **L** Inner lining of clutch K   **M** Splined sleeve   **N** Planet wheel carrier   **O** Sun wheel   **P** Uni-directional clutch rollers   **Q** Output shaft   **R** Uni-directional clutch roller ramps   **S** Uni-directional clutch inner member   **T** Planet wheels   **U** Annulus   **V** Spring (cone clutch)   **W** Uni-directional clutch member   **X** Drain plug   **Y** Filter

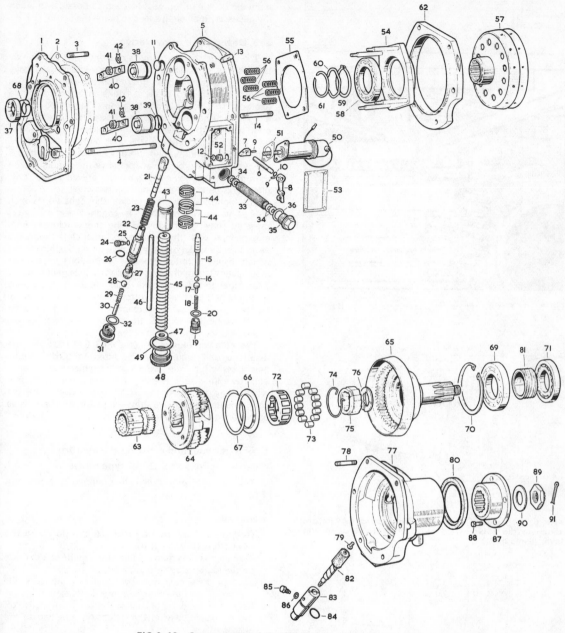

FIG 6:19 Components of the 420 and later S type overdrive

Key to Fig 6:19   1 Adaptor plate   2 Gasket   3 Stud   4 Stud   5 Front casing   6 Shaft   7 Cam   8 Lever
9 Roll-pin   10 O-ring   11 Welch washer   12 Stop   13 Breather   14 Stud   15 Main operating valve   16 Ball
17 Plunger   18 Spring   19 Plug   20 Washer   21 Oil pump plunger assembly   22 Oil pump body   23 Spring
24 Screw   25 Fibre washer   26 O-ring   27 Non-return valve body   28 Ball   29 Spring   30 Support rod   31 Plug
32 Copper washer   33 Oil filter   34 Magnetic ring   35 Plug   36 Washer   37 Cam   38 Operating piston   39 O-ring
40 Bridge piece   41 Nut   42 Tabwasher   43 Accumulator piston   44 Ring   45 Spring   46 Support rod   47 Packing
washer   48 Plug   49 Washer   50 Solenoid   51 Gasket   52 Nut   53 Gasket   54 Thrust ring   55 Retaining plate
56 Spring   57 Clutch sliding member   58 Ballbearing   59 Circlip   60 Corrugated washer   61 Snap ring   62 Brake
ring   63 Sun wheel   64 Planetary carrier assembly   65 Annulus assembly   66 Oil thrower   67 Spring rod   68 Spring
ring   69 Ballbearing   70 Circlip   71 Ballbearing   72 Uni-directional clutch cage   73 Roller   74 Spring   75 Inner
member for clutch   76 Thrust washer   77 Rear casing assembly   78 Stud   79 Thrust button   80 Oil seal
81 Speedometer driving gear   82 Speedometer driven gear   83 Bearing assembly   84 O-ring   85 Retaining screw
86 Copper washer   87 Connecting flange   88 Bolt   89 Nut   90 Washer   91 Splitpin

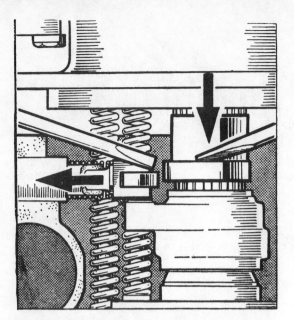

FIG 6:20 Fitting the earlier type gearbox to its over-drive

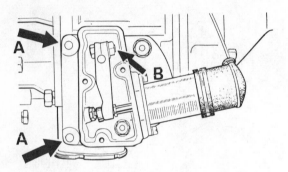

FIG 6:21 Remove the nuts from studs **A** before touching the setscrews (see text) **B** Valve operating lever clamp bolt

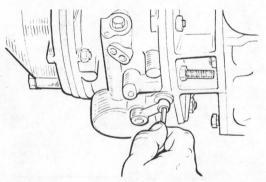

FIG 6:22 The valve setting lever (earlier S type overdrive)

it should be run in top gear as soon as possible to attain the necessary mainshaft speed to prime the pump.

6:5 Description of overdrive

The Laycock de Normanville overdrive unit which may be fitted as an optional extra, comprises a hydraulically controlled epicyclic gear housed in a casing which is directly mounted to a short extension attached to the gearbox. The principle of operation is illustrated in **FIG 6:17**. The lefthand diagram shows the direct drive condition which applies when the overdrive is disengaged and, under spring pressure, the cone clutch locks the sun wheel to the annulus and the drive is taken through the uni-directional clutch. Reverse and overrun torque is taken through the cone clutch which prevents the uni-directional clutch from acting as a freewheel.

The righthand diagram shows the condition which applies when the overdrive is engaged and hydraulic pressure having transferred the cone clutch from engagement with the annulus to engagement with the casing via the brake ring, a step-up gear ratio is introduced which results in reduced engine revolutions for a given road speed. The hydraulic pressure which is generated by a cam operated plunger pump built into the unit, operates on the cone clutch when, in top gear only, the electrical switch which actuates a solenoid is selected. In other gears an inhibitor switch in the gearbox top cover is open and precludes engagement of the overdrive.

The cutaway illustration (see **FIG 6:18**) shows the overdrive unit which may be fitted to **'GBN'** prefix gearboxes which are provided on earlier S type cars. This overdrive unit is not interchangeable with that which may be fitted to **'JCN'** prefix gearboxes the components of which are shown in **FIG 6:19**. Both types of overdrive have a gear ratio of .778.

6:6 Removing and refitting the overdrive

Overdrives fitted to 'GBN'-type boxes:

The following procedure is that referred to in **Section 6:3**.

Removal:

1 **Release the hydraulic pressure by operating the overdrive 10 or 12 times.**
2 Remove the nuts from the five **short** studs before those on the longer studs are touched.
3 Slacken these two nuts by equal amounts until the compression of the clutch springs is released.
4 Remove these two nuts and withdraw the overdrive off the mainshaft leaving the extension attached to the gearbox.

Refitting:

1 Mount the overdrive in a vice, forward end up. Fit the oil pump operating cam **C** in **FIG 6:18** onto the gearbox mainshaft. Align the splines in the clutch inner member **S** and the planet carrier **N**.
2 Engage a gear, turn the gearbox up on end and enter the mainshaft into the overdrive unit. Turn the constant pinion shaft and engage the splines.
3 Ensure that the clutch springs are over their respective bosses on the extension. Fit nuts to the two long studs

and tighten evenly until there is about $\frac{3}{4}$ inch gap. **Ensure that the oil pump cam does not drop down off the mainshaft splines.**

4 Refer to **FIG 6:20.** With one screwdriver, compress the oil pump plunger assembly and, with the other, lever the cam down into alignment with the roller.

5 Tighten the two nuts evenly until the other five nuts can be started. Fully tighten the seven nuts by turning equal amounts.

Overdrives fitted to 'JCN'-type boxes:

The following procedure is that referred to in **Section 6:4.**

Removal:

Remove the nuts from the four short and two long studs and withdraw the overdrive off the mainshaft leaving the extension attached to the gearbox.

Refitting:

1 Fit the oil pump operating cam 37 in **FIG 6:19** and spring clip 68. Rotate the mainshaft so that the cam lobe is uppermost. Engage a gear.

2 Align the splines, in the clutch inner member 75 and planet carrier 64 and carefully fit the overdrive onto the mainshaft. Ensure that the roller of the oil pump plunger 21 aligns with the cam and that the unit pushes easily right up to the adaptor plate 1. If it will not, the splines are misaligned. Realign and refit.

3 Fit and tighten up the nuts on the four short and two long studs.

Dismantling overdrive units:

It is not advisable to attempt to dismantle the overdrive. The large number of special tools and the test equipment required make it essential for the unit to be overhauled or repaired by a fully equipped specialist.

6:7 Servicing the gearbox, adjusting the overdrive

Oil changing:

Change the oil in the gearbox and overdrive (if fitted) every 10,000 miles. The gearbox drain plugs are 2 in **FIG 6:1** and **FIG 6:9.** The overdrive drain plugs are **X** in **FIG 6:18** and 35 in **FIG 6:19** and. when the drain plug is removed, the filter **Y** in **FIG 6:18** or 33 in **FIG 6:19** should be cleaned. The oil for the lubrication and operation of the overdrive is common to that of the gearbox and the overdrive oil level is automatically replenished when the gearbox oil level is topped up to the bottom of the filler plug hole (4 in **FIG 6:1**). Draining the gearbox however does not drain the overdrive unit and it is necessary to remove the overdrive drain plug in addition to that of the gearbox. After refilling through the gearbox filler hole, the level should be rechecked after running the car as some oil will be retained in the overdrive hydraulic system.

Adjusting overdrive valve operating lever:

Overdrives fitted to 'GBN' gearboxes:

Refer to **FIG 6:21.** Removal of the solenoid bracket coverplate gives access to the operating lever clamp bolt which is arrowed **B.** Slacken the clamp bolt securing

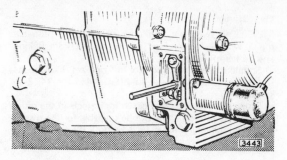

FIG 6:23 The valve setting lever (420 and later S-type overdrive)

nut. On the opposite side of the unit is the valve setting lever and in its outer end there is a $\frac{3}{16}$ inch dia. hole which, **when the solenoid is energized,** should line up with a similar hole in the casing as shown in **FIG 6:22.** Set by rotating the shaft and inserting a $\frac{3}{16}$ inch dia. rod through the lever hole and into the casing hole. Tighten the lever clamp bolt, remove the setting rod and refit the coverplate.

Overdrives fitted to 'JCN' gearboxes:

The operating lever 8 in **FIG 6:19** has a $\frac{3}{16}$ inch dia. hole in it and this should line up with a corresponding hole in the casing when the solenoid is energized. Set by energizing the solenoid, insert a piece of rod as shown in **FIG 6:23** and turn the nut 52 in **FIG 6:19** on the solenoid plunger until it just contacts the fork in the operating lever. Remove the rod and refit the cover.

Pump non-return valve, overdrives fitted to 'GBN' gearboxes:

Access to this valve requires the removal of the solenoid bracket. Refer to **FIG 6:21** and note that **the nuts must be removed from the studs arrowed A before touching the bolts** which may then be slackened off together releasing the accumulator spring load.

6:8 Fault diagnosis

Synchromesh gearbox:

(a) Jumping out of gear

1 Broken spring behind striking rod locating ball
2 Excessively worn locating groove in striking rod
3 Worn coupling dogs
4 Selector fork to striking rod dowel screw loose

(b) Noisy gearbox

1 Insufficient oil
2 Excessive end float in countershaft
3 Worn or damaged bearings or gear teeth

(c) Difficulty in engaging gear

1 Incorrect clutch adjustment
2 Worn synchromesh assemblies

(d) Oil leaks

1 Damaged joint washers
2 Worn or damaged oil seals
3 Damaged top cover face

Overdrive:

When an overdrive unit does not operate properly, top up with fresh oil and test the unit again before making any further investigations.

Should the electrical control not operate, the circuits should be checked. Refer to **FIGS 14:1** or **14:2** in Technical Data.

Faulty units should be checked for defects in the order listed below though it will not be possible for the owner to deal with many of the defects without the support of a fully equipped specialist.

(e) Overdrive does not engage

1 Insufficient oil in gearbox
2 Electrical control or solenoid not operating
3 Leaking operating valve due to foreign matter on ball seat or broken valve spring
4 Pump filter choked
5 Broken pump spring
6 Leaking pump non-return valve due to foreign matter on ball seat or broken valve spring
7 Insufficient hydraulic pressure due to leaks or broken accumulator springs.
8 Damaged gears, bearings or failed internal parts

(f) Overdrive does not release

If the overdrive does not release, do not reverse the car, otherwise extensive internal damage may be caused.
1 Check 2 and 8 in (e)
2 Blocked restrictor in operating valve
3 Sticking clutch

(g) Clutch slip in overdrive

1 Check 1 and 7 in (e)
2 Worn clutch lining

(h) Clutch slip in reverse torque condition or free-wheel on overrun

1 Check 2 in (f) and 2 in (g)
2 Broken clutch springs

CHAPTER 7

THE AUTOMATIC TRANSMISSION

7:1 Description

Automatic transmission, manufactured by Borg Warner, is supplied as an optional extra to take the place of the clutch, synchromesh gearbox and overdrive (if fitted) covered by **Chapters 5** and **6**.

The type of automatic transmission fitted to 420 models differs from that shown in **FIG 7:1**, fitted to S type cars. Both types of automatic gearbox have three forward speeds and reverse and are hydraulically coupled to the engine through a torque converter. Gear ratios are given in Technical Data.

Torque converter:

The action of the torque converter is as follows. The impeller 'A' in **FIG 7:2**, driven by the engine, transmits torque by means of the transmission fluid to the turbine 'B' which drives the automatic gearbox. The stator 'C' redirects the flow of fluid as it leaves the turbine so that it enters the impeller at the most effective angle.

The maximum torque multiplication through the converter is approximately 2.17 in the case of S type cars and 2.0 in 420 models. As the turbine picks up speed and the slip between it and the impeller becomes less, the torque multiplication reduces progressively until, when their speeds become substantially equal, the unit acts as a fluid coupling. In this condition the stator is no longer required to redirect the fluid flow and the free wheel unit 'D' permits it to rotate in the same direction as the impeller and turbine.

S type transmission:

Three forward speeds and reverse are provided and **FIGS 7:9, 7:10, 7:11** and **7:12** illustrate the combinations of two epicyclic sets of gears, three band clutches, one multi-disc clutch and one single-disc clutch which gives these drives. Top gear is a direct drive and the converter is bypassed when the direct drive clutch is engaged. This clutch is integral with the converter assembly. The pressure plate 'A' in **FIG 7:3**, the driven plate 'B' and the backing plate 'C', are locked together when fluid pressure operates on the pressure plate and engine torque is transmitted directly to the main output shaft as shown in **FIG 7:11**.

Cooling of the converter is by means of an integral blower which draws air into the housing through screened

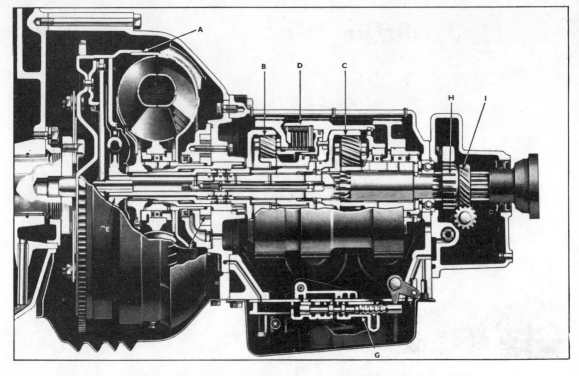

FIG 7:1   Cutaway view of the automatic transmission fitted to S type cars

Key to Fig 7:1   **A** Torque converter   **B** Front planetary gear set   **C** Rear planetary gear set   **D** Multiple disc clutch
E Direct drive clutch   **F** Front pump   **G** Selector valve   **H** Parking gear   **I** Governor and rear oil pump drive gear

FIG 7:2   Components of the torque converter

Key to Fig 7:2   **A** Impeller   **B** Turbine   **C** Stator
D Free wheel unit   **E** Inner race

openings. After passing over the entire surface of the converter it is expelled through louvres in the converter housing coverplate.

Operation is controlled by the position of the selector lever which has five positions. The engine can only be started when **P** (Park) or **N** (Neutral) is selected. In other positions the starter inhibitor switch precludes the starter push button from energizing the starter solenoid. Selection of **D** (Drive) provides a start in first gear and automatic changes to second or intermediate gear and direct drive top. Downward changes are similarly automatic but, should a rapid change-down be required for a burst of acceleration, a kick-down change may be made by depressing the accelerator pedal to its full extent. When, before moving off, **L** (Low) is selected, no upward change will occur. This drive position is used for heavy pulling, steep climbs and maximum braking on descents. **R** (Reverse) provides reverse drive.

An electrical switch 'Intermediate speed hold' allows second or intermediate gear to be held and no automatic change into direct drive will occur or, if already in direct drive a change-down into intermediate will immediately take place.

Anti-creep is a special braking function which prevents the car from creeping forwards when stopped on level ground or slight slopes while the ignition is turned on. Apply the footbrake to stop the car then remove the foot from the brake. The anti-creep solenoid 1 in **FIG 7:4** holds brake pressure on the rear wheels whenever the anti-creep circuit is closed. A pressure control switch 'C' in **FIG 7:6** operated by the transmission rear pump opens the circuit when the car is moving and closes the circuit when the car is stationary or moving in reverse. The anti-creep throttle switch shown arrowed in **FIG 7:5** opens or closes the circuit as the throttle is opened or closed. **FIG 7:4** shows the system diagramatically.

420 type transmission:

Three forward speeds and reverse are provided by combinations of two multi-disc clutches (**A** and **B**), two band clutches (**C** and **D**), a double set of epicyclic gearing (**E**) and a one-way roller clutch (**F**) as shown in **FIGS 7:13, 7:14, 7:15, 7:16** and **7:17**.

The converter casing is aircooled by an integral blower and the transmission fluid is watercooled in a unit positioned below the radiator and shown in **FIGS 1:12** and **4:2** (item 38). Items 20, 21, 22 and 24 in **FIG 7:8** show the piping which connects with this cooler.

Operation is controlled by the manual selector lever which has six positions. The engine can only be started when **P** (Park) or **N** (Neutral) is selected. In other positions the starter inhibitor switch precludes the starter solenoid from being energized. Selection of D1 (Drive 1) provides first gear engagement and automatic gearshifts to second and top. Downshifts are similarly automatic. Selection of D2 (Drive 2) bypasses first gear. Below 63 to 71 miles/hr, when a rapid change-down is required, a kick-down change may be made by depressing the accelerator to its full extent. At approximately 20 miles/hr a kick-down change into first gear from second or top gear may be effected in this way. Selection of **R** (Reverse) engages reverse drive. In first gear when **D1** is selected (see **FIG 7:14**), the one-way roller clutch is operational and this allows freewheeling of the gears. This provides smooth changes from first to second ratio and vice versa. When the car is stationary, selection of **L** (Lockup) provides engagement of first gear without any subsequent gearchange. This drive position is used for heavy pulling, steep climbs and maximum braking on descents. If, when driving in **D1** or **D2** and top gear, **L** is selected, a downshift to second will occur and no automatic upchange will follow. This provides engine braking on demand. In **P**, with the engine running, the rear band **D** is applied and the car is held from rolling on a gradient until forward or reverse drive is operative.

All models:

If the car is to be towed, select **N** and do not exceed 30 mile/hr. If the car has to be push started, select **N**. The car may then be pushed. When a speed of 15 to 20 mile/hr is reached, switch on the ignition and select **L**. **Do not tow the car to start the engine,** it may overtake the tow car. If prolonged idling cannot be avoided, select **P** or **N**. It is inadvisable to select **N** for coasting.

7:2 Maintenance

Transmission fluid, S type cars:

Check the fluid level every 3000 miles. Drain and refill the transmission every 12,000 miles. Use only recommended fluid.

Checking fluid level:

1 With the car on a level floor, set the handbrake firmly and start the engine. With the footbrake applied, select **L** and raise the fluid temperature by running the engine at 800 rev/min for 2 or 3 minutes.
2 Remove the dipstick and wipe it dry. With the footbrake still applied and the selector lever at **L**, run the engine at normal idling speed and check the fluid level. A

FIG 7:3 Components of the direct drive clutch incorporated in the automatic transmission fitted to S type cars

Key to Fig 7:3   **A** Pressure plate   **B** Driven member   **C** Backing plate

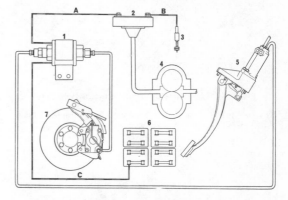

FIG 7:4 Anti-creep system

Key to Fig 7:4   **A** Pressure switch to solenoid cable   **B** Pressure switch to throttle switch cable   **C** Fuse to solenoid cable   1 Solenoid valve   2 Pressure control switch   3 Anti-creep throttle switch   4 Transmission rear pump   5 Brakes system master cylinder   6 Fuses   7 Rear brakes

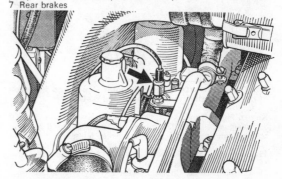

FIG 7:5 The anti-creep throttle switch is arrowed

FIG 7:6 Control levers and anti-creep pressure switch

Key to Fig 7:6   **A** Governor control lever   **B** Selector lever.   **C** Anti-creep pressure switch   **D** Rear pump   **E** Dome nut and locknut (kickdown adjuster disc, clutch pressure take-off plug   **F** Multiple disc, clutch pressure take-off plug   **G** Clutch pressure take-off (driect drive)

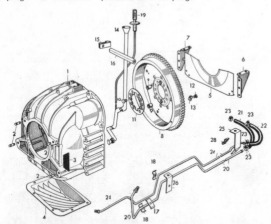

FIG 7:7   Transmission drain plugs, S type cars

Key to Fig 7:7   **A** Oil pan drain plug   **B** Converter drain plug   **C** Converter pressure take-off plug

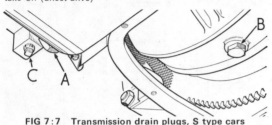

FIG 7:8   Converter housing, cooler piping and flywheel of the automatic transmission fitted to 420 cars

Key to Fig 7:8   **1** Converter housing   **2** Stud   **3** Stoneguard   **4** Bottom cover   **5** Front cover   **6** Support bracket, righthand   **7** Support bracket, lefthand   **8** Drive plate   **9** Dowel   **10** Setscrew   **11** Locking plate   **12** Screw   **13** Tabwasher   **14** Dipstick (filler tube)   **15** Clip   **16** Support bar   **17** Clamp   **18** Clip   **19** Dipstick   **20** Cooler pipe (outlet)   **21** Flexible hose   **22** Flexible hose   **23** Hose clip   **24** Oil return pipe   **25** Bracket   **26** Bracket   **28** Pipe clip

second operator is required for this to be done. Add fluid to bring the level up to the full mark on the dipstick. Approximately one pint will raise the level from 'Low' to 'Full'. **Do not overfill.**

Draining and refilling:

1 Raise the temperature of the fluid by running the engine as described in the fluid level checking procedure.
2 Stop the engine, clean the area round the dipstick, remove the oil pan drain plug 'A' in **FIG 7:7**, remove the converter housing coverplate, rotate the converter to bring the drain plug 'B' to the bottom and remove it.
3 To facilitate draining, remove the converter pressure take-off plug 'C'.
4 After the fluid has drained, refit and tighten the three plugs and refit the housing coverplate.
5 Pour 10 pints of recommended fluid into the transmission through the filler tube.
6 Start the engine and, with the footbrake applied, select **L**. Run the engine at 800 rev/min for 2 or 3 minutes to transfer fluid to the converter.
7 With the footbrake still applied and the selector at **L**, run the engine at normal idling speed and add additional fluid (approximately 5 pints) to bring the level to 'Full' on the dipstick. **Do not overfill.** Check the level as described earlier.

Transmission fluid, 420 models:

Check the fluid level every 3000 miles. Change the fluid every 21,000 miles and whilst doing so, adjust the front clutch band as described later in this chapter.

Checking fluid level:

1 With the transmission at normal operating temperature and the car on a level floor, set the handbrake firmly, select **P** and run the engine at normal idling speed.
2 With the engine running, remove the dipstick, wipe it clean and replace it. Withdraw it immediately and check. Add fluid to bring the level up to the 'Full' mark on the dipstick. Approximately $1\frac{1}{2}$ pints will raise the level from 'Low' to 'Full'. **Do not overfill.**

Draining and refilling:

1 Drain the fluid by disconnecting the bottom of the dipstick/filler tube (item 14 in **FIG 7:8**), the two pipes (21 and 22 in **FIG 7:8**) from the oil cooler and remove and clean out the oil pan. Discard the drained fluid. A few particles in the dregs of the fluid in the oil pan are normal.
2 Adjust the front clutch band **C** as described in **Section 7:7.**
3 Reconnect the dipstick/filler tube and the oil cooler pipes, refit the oil pan using a new gasket and tighten the fourteen setbolts to a torque of 10 to 13 lb ft. Refill the transmission with recommended fluid and check the level as described earlier. The fluid capacity from dry (including the cooler) is 16 pints.

7:3 Power flow (mechanical)

S type cars:

FIGS 7:9, 7:10, 7:11 and **7:12** show how the two forward ratios, the direct drive and reverse are

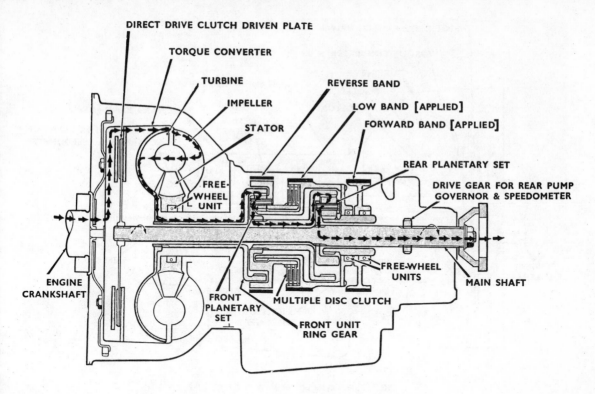

FIG 7:9   S type power flow in first-speed gear

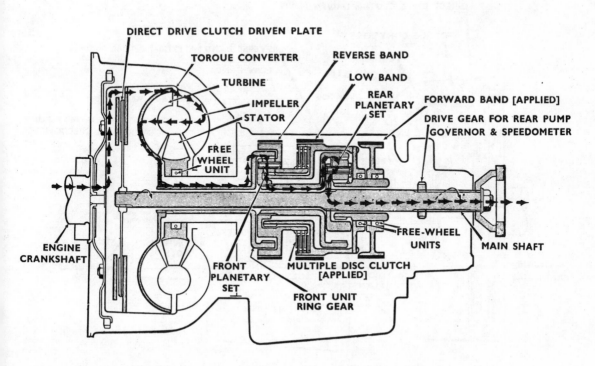

FIG 7:10   S type power flow in second-speed gear (intermediate)

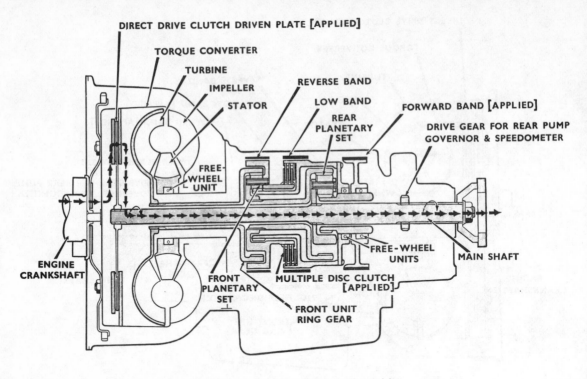

FIG 7:11   S type power flow in direct drive

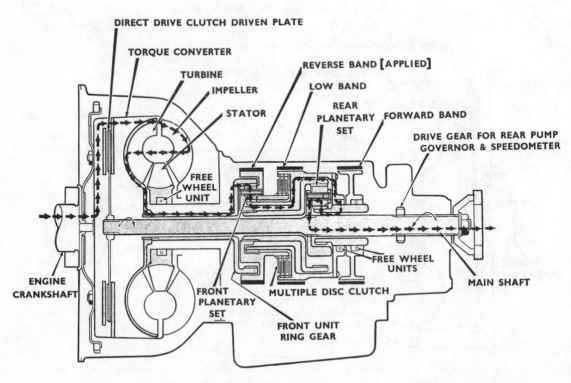

FIG 7:12   S type power flow in reverse

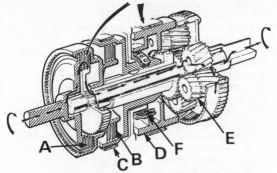

FIG 7:13   420 type power flow in first-speed gear with L selected. The arrowed letters are referred to in the text

obtained from the three band clutches, the multiple disc clutch and the direct drive clutch being applied or free. The line of small arrows shows the power flow from the crankshaft to the output shaft in each case while the captions indicate which clutch or clutches are engaged. In **N** (Neutral) and **P** (Park) positions, all clutches are free, but in **P** the parking gear pawl is engaged.

420 models:

FIGS **7:13, 7:14, 7:15, 7:16** and **7:17** show how the three forward ratios and reverse are obtained from the two multi-disc clutches **A** and **B** in **FIG 7:13,** the two band clutches **C** and **D,** the double set of epicyclic gearing **E** and the one-way roller clutch **F.** In the illustrations. the line of small arrows shows the power flow from the torque converter to the output shaft while the two larger arrows indicate which clutches are engaged in each case except **FIG 7:14** where, in **D1,** it should be noted that the one-way roller clutch **F** may freewheel.

7:4 Removing and refitting

S type cars:

The automatic gearbox can be removed leaving the converter and housing in position.

Removing the automatic gearbox:

1 Drain off the fluid as described in **Section 7:2.**
2 Refer to **Section 8:2** and remove the propeller shaft.
3 Refer to **FIG 7:6.** Uncouple the control rods from the governor control lever 'A', the selector lever 'B' and disconnect the two cables from the anti-creep pressure switch 'C'. Disconnect the speedometer drive.
4 Remove the two lower nuts which secure the automatic gearbox to the converter housing, place a lift under the gearbox and prepare it to take the weight of the unit. Remove the two upper nuts and dismount the gearbox by sliding it rearwards until the mainshaft is clear of the converter. Remove the oil transfer tube from the centre of the converter with a pair of long-nosed pliers if it did not come away with the mainshaft.

Refitting the automatic gearbox:

1 Use an alignment fixture (Tool No. J4283) to position the splines on the transmission shafts and the internal splines in the converter.

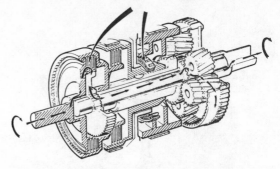

FIG 7:14   420 type power flow in first-speed gear with D1 selected

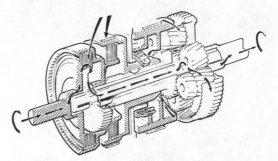

FIG 7:15   420 power flow in second-speed (intermediate) gear with L or D2 selected

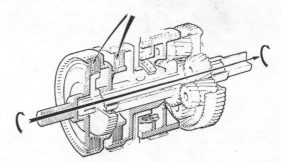

FIG 7:16   420 type power flow in third-speed gear with D1 selected

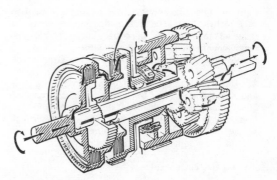

FIG 7:17   420 type power flow in reverse gear (R selected)

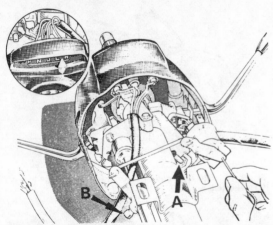

FIG 7:18 Setting the starter/reverse inhibitor switch on S type cars

Key to Fig 7:18 A Switch securing bolt B Control lever securing screw

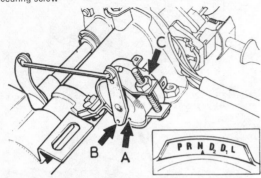

FIG 7:19 Setting the starter/reverse inhibitor switch on 420 type cars

Key to Fig 7:19 A Indent in switch B Hole in lever C Clamp ring bolt

2 Fit the oil transfer tube into the mainshaft.
3 The remaining operations are the removal procedure in reverse. Refill the transmission with recommended fluid as described in **Section 7:2**.

Removing the converter:

1 Remove the engine and transmission unit as described in **Section 1:2**. The automatic gearbox may be removed separately as described earlier or may be removed with the engine and converter.
2 Remove the starter motor. Note the earth strap which is attached to the top bolt. Remove the coverplate from the front face of the converter. Remove the bolts and nuts which secure the converter housing to the engine crankcase and dismount the housing.
3 Remove the six self-locking nuts and washers which secure the converter to the engine drive plate and withdraw the converter assembly.

Refitting the converter:

1 The alignment mark 'O' on the converter must align with the similar mark on the engine drive plate.

2 Install the converter to the engine drive plate and **loosely** fit the washers and nuts.
3 Clean the mating faces of the engine crankcase and the converter housing. Fit the housing, noting that it is located by dowels. Install the starter motor ensuring that the earth strap is fitted to the top bolt.
4 Position the converter alignment flange (Tool No. J4286) into the bore of the converter housing and over the pump drive fingers on the converter. Fit the two top gearbox securing nuts to hold the alignment flange in position. Rotate the converter through two complete revolutions to centre it and tighten fully the nuts which attach the converter to the engine drive plate and which were left loose in instruction 2. Remove the alignment flange.
5 Refit the coverplate to the front face of the housing and refit the gearbox as described earlier in this section.

420 models:

If no transmission hoist is available, remove the complete engine and transmission unit as described in **Section 1:2**. If a hoist is available, the gearbox can be removed after raising the front of the engine until the unit is at an angle of approximately 45 deg. The whole of the engine removal procedure must still be carried out when using this method but the unit is finally tilted instead of being lifted out.

Removing the automatic gearbox:

1 Remove the engine and transmission unit as described in **Section 1:2** or, instead of lifting out the unit, tilt it to an angle of approximately 45 deg. as explained earlier.
2 Disconnect the cooler feed and return pipes (20 and 24 in **FIG 7:8**) from the gearbox. Place a tray beneath the torque converter to catch the fluid which will drain from the unit.
3 Remove the four nuts and washers which secure the gearbox to the converter housing and withdraw the unit.

Refitting the automatic gearbox:

This is the removal procedure in reverse but ensure that the converter lugs are properly aligned with the front pump driving gear so that parts are not damaged by forcing the impeller hub drive tangs against the pump drive gear lugs.

Removing the converter:

1 Remove the setbolts which secure the converter housing to the crankcase and dismount the housing.
2 Mark the converter and flywheel so that the converter may be refitted in its original position.
3 Untab and remove the four setbolts (12 in **FIG 7:8**) which attach the converter to the flywheel and dismount the assembly.

Refitting the converter:

This is the reverse of the removal procedure. When installing the converter housing, check the bore and face dial indicator runout relative to the crankshaft centre line. Preferably this should be less than .006 inch in each case and should not exceed .010 inch.

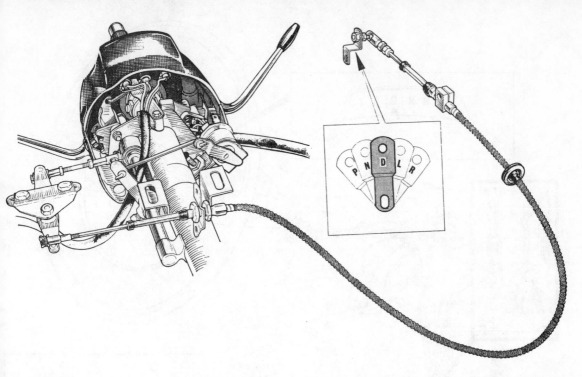

FIG 7:20 Selector cable adjustment on S type cars

7:5 Faulty performance

Those tests and adjustments which can be made by a reasonably competent owner are given in **Sections 7:6** and **7:7**. More serious performance faults which require pressure takeoff points to be opened and pressure measurements taken to diagnose the fault, adjustment of the governor, renewal of clutch bands, partial or complete dismantling to replace worn or failed internal components, dictate that the services of a fully equipped specialist should be enlisted. Quite apart from the specialized knowledge which is required, test equipment and a large number of special tools are mandatory and **it is consequently advised that the automatic transmission should not be dismantled except by a Service Station.**

The internal parts of the converter assembly are not supplied separately. A replacement torque converter, if one is required, is obtainable as a complete assembly.

7:6 Testing

Stationary tests:

Starter inhibitor switch, all models:

The starter switch should operate only when **P** or **N** is selected. If the switch will operate when any other position is selected, the starter inhibitor switch should be adjusted as described in **Section 7:7**.

Selector linkage, S type cars:

Set the handbrake firmly, start the engine and select **D**. Apply slight throttle so that the sound of the engine is clearly noticeable and slowly select **N**. Just before the **N** position is reached, a sudden increase in engine speed should occur. Select **L** and move the lever slowly towards **R**. The change out of first gear should be accompanied by an increase in engine speed then, close to **R**, as reverse engages, the engine speed should decrease.

Selector linkage, 420 models:

Apply the brakes and, with the engine running at normal idling speed, move the selector from **N** to **D2**, to **D1** to **L** and to **R**. Engagement should be felt as each position is selected.

Converter stall speed tests, all models:

The stall speed is the maximum rev/min at which the engine can drive the converter impeller while the turbine is held stationary. Set the handbrake and start the engine. With the footbrake applied, select **L** and open the throttle fully. Note the engine rev/min and release the throttle. Repeat in **R**. Do not hold full throttle in any driving position with the rear wheels held stationary for more than 10 seconds at a time or for a total time of more than one minute in any half hour period.

With an engine in good condition and operating at sea level, the normal stall speed for an **S type** is 2000 rev/min. A stall speed of 1400 to 1500 rev/min, if the engine is normal, indicates slip of the converter stator freewheel unit while a stall speed higher than normal indicates slip in the automatic gearbox.

The normal stall speed for a **420 model** with an engine

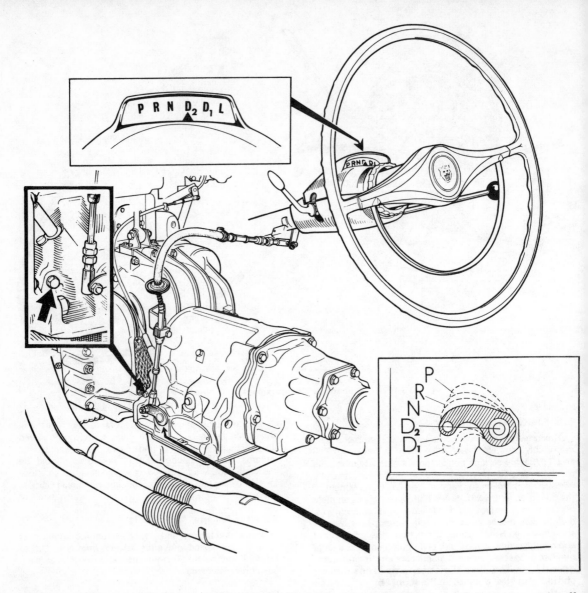

FIG 7:21 Selector cable adjustment on 420 type cars. The lefthand inset shows the transmission pressure take-off point

in good condition is 1600 to 1700 rev/min. A stall speed of under 1000 rev/min indicates slip of the converter stator freewheel unit while a stall speed of over 2100 rev/min indicates slip in the transmission gearbox.

Road tests:

Gearchange speeds, S type cars:

The following tabulation gives the normal speeds at which gearchanges should occur. Select **D** and, by testing on a level road, check the actual gearchange speeds.

Change	Throttle	Road speed, mile/hr.
1 to 2	Light	11
2 to direct	Light	23
1 to 2	Full	40
2 to direct	Full	64
2 to direct	After 'kick-down'	78
Direct to 2	Closed	16
2 to 1	Closed	4
Direct to 2	'Kick-down'	Up to 68

Avoid manual change from **D** to **L** above 45 mile/hr.

Gearchange speeds, 420 models:

The following tabulation gives the normal road speeds at which gearchanges should occur.

Selector Position	Throttle Position	Upshifts 1 to 2	2 to 3	
D1	Minimum	6.5 to 7.5	11 to 13	
	Full	33 to 38.5	58 to 62	
	Kickdown	45 to 49	70.5 to 77.5	
D2	Minimum	—	11 to 13	
	Full	—	58 to 62	
	Kickdown	—	70.5 to 77.5	

		Downshifts 3 to 2	3 to 1	2 to 1
D1	Minimum	6.5 to 12.5	—	3.5 to 6.5
	Full	19.5 to 32.5	—	—
	Kickdown	63 to 71	17 to 21	17 to 21
D2	Minimum	7 to 13	—	—
	Full	19.5 to 32.5	—	—
	Kickdown	63 to 71	—	—
L	Zero	ANY	—	10 to 18

Engine braking, all models:

While driving at about 30 mile/hr in **D**, release the throttle and select **L**. This should result in rapid decelleration and an increase in engine speed.

Parking pawl, all models:

Brake to a stop on a gradient and select **P**. The parking pawl should hold the car when the brakes are released.

Anti-creep, S type cars:

On level ground, release the throttle pedal, apply the footbrake and stop the car. Now, with the car stationary on level ground, the engine idling, one of the driving positions selected and the anti-creep preventing the car from creeping, touch the throttle pedal lightly and then release it. This should release the anti-creep hold and the car should creep slowly from a standstill. The system is illustrated diagramatically in **FIG 7:4**.

7:7 Adjustments

Starter inhibitor switch, S type cars:

To adjust for correct operation, refer to **FIG 7:18** and slacken the securing nut shown arrowed at **A**. Move the selector lever halfway between **L** and **R** and have an assistant hold it there. Adjust the position of the switch until the hole in the lever is in line with the hole in the switch base plate. Hold this position by inserting a piece of wire through the two holes. Retighten nut **A** and remove the wire. Check that the starter will only operate when **P** or **N** is selected and that the reversing light operates only when **R** is selected.

Starter inhibitor switch, 420 models:

Refer to **FIG 7:19** and slacken the securing nut shown arrowed at **C**. Select **N** and position the switch so that the hole **B** in the lever lines up with the indent **A** in the switch body. Hold this position by inserting a piece of wire through the hole and into the indent and tighten nut **C**. Check that the starter will only operate when **P** or **N** is selected and that the reverse light operates only when **R** is selected.

Selector linkage:

S type cars:

Adjustment of the selector linkage will normally only be required if the gearbox or the linkage has been removed from the car. Check correct reassembly and ensure that the flat on the control shaft aligns with the securing screw **B** arrowed in **FIG 7:18**. Before refitting the linkage to the selector valve lever, place it in the **D** position, that is the centre position of the five possible positions. Select D and adjust the linkage length so that the ballpin slips easily into the hole in the selector valve lever. Connect the linkage, check in all five positions and tighten the locknut.

Adjustment of the linkage length is effected by screwing the cable rod in or out of the ballpin end. Tighten the lock after adjusting.

420 models:

The procedure is as described for S type cars but **D2** is selected and, as shown in the inset to **FIG 7:21**, the gearbox lever is positioned in the corresponding position. Finally check the linkage in all six positions and tighten locknuts.

Accelerator to governor lever linkage, S type cars:

Before adjusting the linkage, shown for a righthand model in **FIG 7:22**, between the accelerator pedal and the governor lever, the idling speed should be checked and, if necessary, adjusted. Proceed as follows:

1 Disconnect the control rod from the governor control lever.
2 Refer to **FIG 7:5**, slacken the locknut which retains the anti-creep throttle switch (arrowed) to its bracket and screw the switch so that the plunger in the centre of the switch is out of contact with the operating lever.
3 Check that the carburetter slow-running screws are on their stops and that the idling speed is 500 rev/min.
4 Reset the anti-creep throttle switch as described later in this section.
5 Depress the accelerator pedal to the full throttle position at the carburetters. **Do not compress the pedal sufficiently hard as to compress the 'kick-down' overtravel spring.**
6 Turn the governor control lever to the full throttle position where solid resistance is felt before overcoming the cam detent. Adjust the length of the control rod at the large knurled nut so that the ballpin slips easily into the hole in the lever.

Anti-creep throttle switch adjustment, S type cars:

1 Refer to the accelerator to governor lever linkage adjustment instructions given earlier in this section and carry out instructions 2 and 3.
2 Adjust the position of the anti-creep switch in its bracket so that the plunger is fully depressed by the operating lever when the carburetter throttles are in the normal idling position. Tighten the locknut.
3 Check the operation of the anti-creep system by road testing as described in **Section 7:6**.

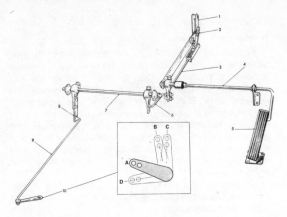

FIG 7:22 Governor control lever linkage on S type righthand cars

Key to Fig 7:22   **A** Full throttle   **B** Maximum free travel
C Maximum closed throttle   **D** Full throttle overtravel
(kick-down)   1 Pivot lever   2 Throttle connection
3 Throttle rod and overtravel spring (kick-down)   4 Shaft
5 Throttle pedal   6 Connecting link   7 Shaft   8 Lever
9 Governor lever control rod   10 Governor lever

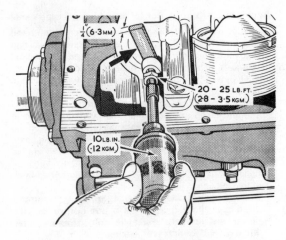

FIG 7:23   420 type front band adjustment

Kick-down adjustment, S type cars:

Adjust the loading of the overtravel spring to overcome the tension of the throttle return spring and to compress only after the full throttle position (obtained by depressing the accelerator pedal) has been reached. Check the operation on road test.

Kick-down adjustment, 420 models:

Gearshift quality and correct shift positions are controlled by precise movement of the kick-down cable in relation to the carburetter throttle shaft movement. On a flat road in **D1** or **D2** and at minimum throttle opening, the 2 to 3 upshift should occur at 1100 to 1200 rev/min.

A 'runup' of 200 to 400 rev/min at the change point indicates **low** pressure. At full throttle opening, a jerky 2 to 3 upshift or a sharp 2 to 1 downshift in **D1** when stopping the car indicates **high** pressure.

Connect a 0 to 200 lb/sq in pressure gauge (Tool No. CBW.1A) to the pressure take-off point shown arrowed in an inset in **FIG 7:21** (use adaptor No. CBW.1A-5A). Run the engine until normal operating temperature is reached, with the handbrake applied firmly, select **D1** and **D2** and increase the engine speed to exactly 1250 rev/min. The pressure gauge reading should be 70 to 75 lb/sq in. If the pressure is outside this range the kick-down cable requires adjustment. This adjustment **must only be made at the fork end** shown arrowed in **FIG 7:25** access to which requires the removal of the battery. Proceed as follows:

1 Remove the bonnet as described in instruction 1, **Section 1:2,** place the battery on the floor and reconnect it with suitable temporary leads.
2 Release the fork end locknut and remove the splitpin and clevis pin.
3 To **lower** the pressure turn the fork end clockwise; to **raise** the pressure turn anticlockwise. One full turn of the fork end will alter the pressure by approximately 9 lb/sq in.
4 Refit the fork end, tighten the locknut, restart the engine and recheck the pressure at 1250 rev/min.

Slight adjustment only should be required and excess will result in loss of kickdown or increase in shift speeds. If the pressure is unstable when checked and rechecked, the inner cable may be kinked or binding and it should be renewed as follows.

1 Remove the jackshaft bracket from the inlet manifold studs, disconnect the cable at the fork end and remove the cable retaining clip after withdrawing the setscrew.
2 Lift the carpeting from below the radio speaker in the console at the lefthand side, remove six screws and detach the coverplate now exposed.
3 Remove the Allen screw and washer which retains the outer cable. Withdraw the outer cable.
4 Locate the spring clip which secures the inner cable to the control rod operating the kick-down cam. Spring the clip open with a small screwdriver and withdraw the cable.

Refitting is the reverse of this procedure. Adjust the length of the cable to $3\frac{5}{16}$ inch between the centre of the clevis pin and the end of the outer cable. Check that the carburetter butterfly valves are closed. Adjust the pressure as described earlier.

Front band adjustment, 420 models:

Every 20,000 miles the front band should be adjusted when the transmission fluid is being changed. With the fluid drained off and the oil pan removed, refer to **FIG 7:23.**

1 Loosen the adjusting screw locknut. Fit a $\frac{1}{4}$ inch thick gauge block between the servo piston pin and the servo adjusting screw as shown arrowed in **FIG 7:23**.
2 Tighten the adjusting screw with a torque screwdriver (official tools are: setting gauge CBW.34, adaptor CBW.548-2 used with a torque screwdriver as illustrated) to 10 lb in.
3 Tighten the adjusting screw locknut to 20 to 25 lb ft and remove the $\frac{1}{4}$ inch setting gauge.

Rear band adjustment, 420 models:

Every 20,000 miles adjust the rear band. Access is external through the grommeted hole shown arrowed in **FIG 7:24** which is exposed after removing the console as described in **Section 13:10.**

1 Loosen and back off the adjusting screw locknut by three or four turns and check that the adjusting screw works freely.
2 Turn the adjusting screw in with a torque screwdriver (official adaptor is CBW.547A-50-2) to 10 lb ft then back off the adjusting screw by exactly 1½ turns.
3 Tighten the locknut to 35 to 40 lb ft, refit the grommet and console.

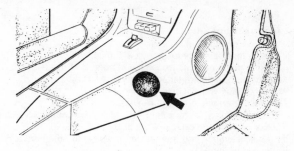

FIG 7:24   Access to the 420 type rear band adjuster

7:8 Fault diagnosis

This section indicates the rectification action relevant to an extensive list of possible faults. Although the owner will be in a position to deal with only a few of these himself, the list will assist him to consult knowledgeably with the specialist whose services will have to be enlisted to deal with the majority of these possible faults. Before any attempt is made at diagnosis, the fluid level must be checked as described in **Section 7:2** and the selector, kick-down and governor linkages must be correctly adjusted as described in **Section 7:7.**

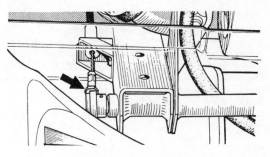

FIG 7:25   420 type kick-down cable adjustment

Indirect gears, S type cars:

FAULT	ACTION
Slip or ineffective drive:	
Inoperative in D, L and R	1, 2, 3, 4, 5, 6, 7
Excessive slip on take-off in D, L and R	2, 3, 4, 5
	4, 5,
Excessive slip on take-off in D only	2, 3, 12
	8, 11,
	4, 5.
Excessive slip on take-off in R only	2, 3, 12
	10, 11,
	14, 15, 16
Excessive slip on change from low to intermediate	2, 3, 13
	12, 17, 18
	14, 15, 16, 22, 21
Excessive slip on change from intermediate to direct drive	2, 3, 19 4, 17
	12, 20
	21
Drag or engine labouring:	
Drag on down-change from intermediate to low (HT models only)	13, 14, 18
Drag in R	7, 8, 9, 11
Drag in D and L	7, 10, 11
Drag in D, L and R	7
Engine stalls when selecting D or when coming to rest in D	19, 14, 22, 21
Judder on engagement of direct drive	21
Drag on change from low to intermediate (HT models only)	4
Poor hill-climbing, lack of acceleration in indirect ranges	7, 23
Judder while cruising in direct drive	7, 6
NOTE: HT model indicates a transmission with an operative relay valve	
Incorrect operation:	
Will not change up in D	13, 19, 20, 14, 32
Will not kick-down at speeds below 45 mile/hr.	24, 14
Over-sensitive on kick-down, "hunts" between direct and intermediate	24, 14
Starts in intermediate	24, 14, 13, 18
Will only move off in L	1, 6

FAULT	ACTION

Incorrect operation:

Will only move off in R	1, 6
Selects reverse at speeds above 3-5 mile/hr.	25, 4
Parking pawl attempts to engage at speeds above 3-5 mile/hr.	25, 26, 31
Car cannot be push-started	1, 2, 25
Parking pawl will not engage	1, 26, 31
Ineffective engine braking on overrun in L	1, 9, 11
Excessive jerk when selecting D, L or R (Accumulator valve sticking)	7, 2, 8, 10, 4
Delay in taking up drive in D, L or R	2, 4, 7, 6
Poor acceleration and low maximum speed in direct drive, normal in indirect ranges (Stall speed normal)	7, 21
Car creeps or drives in N	1, 8, 10, 21

Noisy operation:

Rattling noise, more noticeable at idling speeds	1, 7, 24
Whine in direct drive at 30-40 mile/hr (Do not confuse with axle or tyre noise) ..	28, 32
Whine at fast idling speed in all selector positions	29
Gear noise at low speed in indirect ranges	30
Knocking, scraping or grating noise in all selector positions	7, 27, 29, 6
Excessive swishing noise on take-off from rest	2, 24, 20, 23
Barking noise when selecting D, L or R	2, 4

Action key, S type cars:

Where the 'Action' line is divided, if the preceding pressure reading is incorrect, follow the upper line. If the pressure reading is correct, follow the lower line.

1 Check selector linkage.
2 Check fluid level.
3 Check front pump pressure.
4 Clean or overhaul valve block and clean filter.
5 Check front pump and drive tangs on converter hub.
6 Check freewheels and/or races.
7 Check external features (e.g. engine performance, carburetter linkage, idling speed, brakes, anti-creep and halfshafts.
8 Check forward band adjustment, and/or condition of band and adjuster.
9 Check low band adjustment, and/or condition of band and adjuster.
10 Check reverse band adjustment, and/or condition of band and adjuster.
11 Check relevant servo pressure, and/or correct functioning of servo piston.
12 Check for blocked fluid passage, and/or damaged casting.
13 Check multi-disc clutch pressure.
14 Check action of governor, governor valve, hydraulic detent, and booster spring (if used).
15 Check oil rings, O-rings and oil seals in gear train.
16 Check gaskets on extension case, valve block and collector ring.
17 Check for tightness and correct position of lubrication valve and tube in mainshaft.
18 Check mechanical condition of multi-disc clutch pack, piston and retractor springs.
19 Check direct drive clutch pressure.
20 Check converter pressure.

21 Change torque converter and direct drive clutch assembly.
22 Check that transfer tube is correctly fitted, and has grooved front end.
23 Check stall speed. If low, change torque converter assembly.
24 Check governor linkage and second speed hold (if fitted).
25 Check rear pump pressure. If incorrect see 4 and 32.
26 Check action of parking pawl, interlock piston and spring.
27 Check for converter fouling housing, gearbox or adjacent parts.
28 Change rear pump assembly.
29 Inspect and if necessary replace front pump.
30 Inspect and if necessary replace gear train components.
31 Check adjustment of pawl actuating rod.
32 Check rear pump drive.

Direct drive, S type cars:

Difficulty may be experienced in obtaining direct drive (top gear) although the transmission operates normally in indirect ranges. Direct drive may be unobtainable or may only be obtainable when the accelerator is momentarily eased.

Ensure that Intermediate Speed Hold is not engaged and carry out the following pressure checks.
1 Check direct drive clutch pressure at 30 mile/hr.
2 Check torque converter pressure at 30 mile/hr.

Compare the pressure obtained with the normal nominal figures in the following tabulation to locate the fault and rectification action.

	Direct Drive Clutch		Torque converter			Action
	At 30 mile/hr	Low	Inter-mediate	Direct at 30 mile/hr	Reverse	
Normal pressures:						
Normal nominal pressures	80	60	30	30	60	If normal pressure readings are obtained and direct drive does not engage correctly, replace Torque converter Assembly for suspected fault in Direct Drive Clutch
Incorrect pressures:						
Faulty Governor, Governor Valve or Bushing	0	60	30	30	60	Service Extension Case
Lubrication valve blocked or twisted in mainshaft..	80	80	80	80	200	Replace mainshaft
Converter shuttle valve seized in open position	80	60	60	60	140	Service Valve Block
Faulty direct drive clutch oil seals ..	80	60	30	60–80 (rises slowly)	60	Replace Torque Converter Assembly
Transfer tube missing	65	80	30	45	60	Install transfer tube

420 models, fault chart:

	Check (in car)	Check (on bench)
Engagement:		
Harsh	B, D, c, d	2, 4
Delayed	A, C, D, E, F, a, c, d	b
None	A, C, a, c, d	b, 9, 10, 11, 13
No forward	A, C, a, c, d	B, 1, 4, 7
No reverse	A, C, F, a, c, j, k, h	b, 2, 3, 6
Jumps in forward	C, D, E, F	4, 7, 8
Jumps in reverse	C, D, E	2
No neutral	C, c	2
Upshifts:		
No. 1-2	C, E, a, c, d, f, g, h, j	b, 5, 17
No. 2-3	C, a, c, d, f, g, h, k, l	b, 3, 17
Shift points too high	B, C, c, d, f, g, h, j, k, l	b
Shift points too low	B, c, f, g, h, l	B
Upshift quality:		
1-2 slips or runs up	A, B, C, E, a, c, d, f, g, k	b, 1, 5
2-3 slips or runs up	C, a, c, d, f, g, h, k, l	b, 3, 5
1-2 harsh	B, C, E, c, d, f, g, h	1, 7, 8
2-3 harsh	B, C, E, s, d, f	4
1-2 Ties up or grabs	F, c	4, 7, 8
2-3 Ties up or grabs	E, F, C	4
Downshifts:		
No. 2-1	B, C, c, h, j	7
No. 3-2	B, c, h, k	4
Shift points too high	B, C, c, f, h, j, k, l	b
Shift points too low	B, C, c, f, h, j, k, l	b

420 models, fault chart:

	Check (in car)	Check (on bench)
Downshift quality:		
2-1 Slides		7
3-2 Slides	B, C, E, a, c, d, f, g	b, 3, 5
2-1 Harsh		b, 1, 7
3-2 Harsh	B, E, c, d, f, g, 5	3, 4, 5
Reverse:		
Slips or chatters	A, B, F, d, c, g	b, 2, 3, 6
Line pressure:		
Low idle pressure	A, C, D, a, c, d	b, 11
High idle pressure	B, c, d, e, f, g	
Low stall pressure	A, B, a, c, d, f, g, h	b, 11
High stall pressure	B, c, d, f, g	
Stall speed:		
Too low (200 rev/min or more)		13
Too high (200 rev/min or more)	A, B, C, F, a, c, d, f	b, 1, 3, 6, 7, 9. 1.
Others:		
No push starts	A, C, E, F, c	12
Transmission overheats	E, F, e	1, 2, 3, 4, 5, 6, 13, 18
Poor acceleration		13
Noisy in neutral	m	2, 4
Noisy in park	m	14
Noisy in all gears..	m	2, 4, 14, 16
Noisy during coast (30-20 mile/hr)		16, 19
Park brake does not hold	C, 15	15

420 models, key to fault chart:

1 Preliminary checks in car

A Low fluid level
B Throttle cable incorrectly assembled or adjusted
C Manual linkage incorrectly assembled or adjusted
D Engine idle speed
E Front band adjustment
F Rear band adjustment

2 Hydraulic faults

a Oil tubes missing or broken
b Sealing rings missing or broken
c Valve body screws missing or not correctly tightened
d Primary valve sticking
e Secondary valve sticking
f Throttle valve sticking
g Compensator or modulator valve sticking
h Governor valve sticking, leaking or incorrectly assembled
i Orifice control valve sticking
j 1-2 shift valve sticking
k 2-3 shift valve sticking
l 2-3 shift valve plunger sticking
m Regulator

3 Mechanical faults

1 Front clutch slipping due to worn plates or faulty parts
2 Front clutch seized or plates distorted
3 Rear clutch slipping due to worn or faulty parts
4 Rear clutch seized or plates distorted
5 Front band slipping due to faulty servo, broken or worn band
6 Rear band slipping due to faulty servo, broken or worn band
7 One-way clutch slipping or incorrectly installed
8 One-way clutch seized
9 Broken input shaft
10 Front pump drive tangs on converter hub broken
11 Front pump worn
12 Rear pump worn or drive key broken
13 Converter blading and/or one-way clutch failed
14 Front pump
15 Parking linkage
16 Planetary assembly
17 Fluid distributor sleeve in output shaft
18 Oil cooler connections
19 Rear pump

CHAPTER 8

THE PROPELLER SHAFT, FINAL DRIVE UNIT AND REAR SUSPENSION

8:1 The propeller shaft

Two types of open propeller shafts with needle roller universal joints are fitted. The forward end of the fixed length shaft which is fitted to S type cars with the early (synchromesh on three speeds) manual gearbox without overdrive is shown in **FIG 8:1** above the type of shaft which is fitted to all other models. The rear end of both types of shaft is of common design. Axial movement is accommodated by a sleeve 7 which slides on the early type gearbox mainshaft or by a sleeve yoke 3 sliding on the splines of the forward end of the propeller shaft. This joint is shown assembled in **FIG 8:1** (bottom right).

Sliding and universal joints require no routine maintenance.

8:2 Shaft removal and refitment

1 Chock one rear wheel and jack up the other so that the propeller shaft can be rotated.
2 Remove the nuts and washers which secure the shaft to the final drive flange.

3 On the upper **FIG 8:1** type shaft, separate these flanges, withdraw sliding yoke 7 from the splines on the gearbox mainshaft and remove the shaft.
4 On 420 models and later S type cars, remove the rear mounting as described in **Section 1:15**. Remove the nuts and washers from the front flange, compress the sliding joint and remove the **lower FIG 8:1** type shaft.

Refitting:

Refitting is the reverse of the removal procedure in each case.

8:3 Shaft dismantling and reassembly

On the later type shaft, release gaiter 4, rings 5 and remove sleeve yoke 3 from the splined shaft. Clean thoroughly. Remove all circlips 2. Bearings are removed by tapping the yoke with a hide hammer as shown in **FIG 8:2** and, if stubborn, by using a small diameter aluminium drift on the inside. Repeat this on the opposite bearing and remove the yoke. The remaining bearings

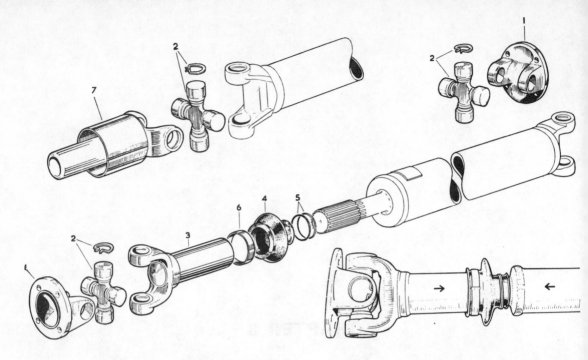

FIG 8:1 Propeller shafts. The difference in the forward ends is explained in the text. Note the arrows at the sliding joint

Key to Fig 8:1   1 Flange yoke   2 Journal assembly   3 Sleeve yoke assembly   4 Gaiter   5 Rubber ring   6 Steel ring
7 Sliding yoke (S type standard transmission)

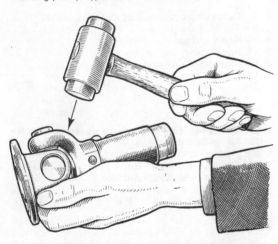

FIG 8:2   Removing a journal bearing

are similarly removed. Wash all parts in petrol. Check the condition of the gaiter, bearings and spiders and renew if necessary.

Before reassembly, fill each journal trunnion reservoir and half fill each bearing with grease. Fit the rubber seals to the inner end of each bearing, insert the spider journals into the yoke holes and tap the bearings into position using an aluminium drift. Fit new circlips and ensure that

they seat correctly in their grooves. When reassembling the sliding joint, ensure that the yokes are in the same plane with the arrows which are stamped on the two parts in line as shown in **FIG 8:1**.

8:4 The final drive unit

FIG 8:3 shows a cross-section through the final drive assembly. It is mounted independently from the hubs which are connected by halfshafts (with universal joints at each end) to the final drive output shafts through the rear brake discs. The pinion and crown wheel are a matched pair. All bearings are taper roller type. Shims provide adjustment of bearing preload and drive gear meshing. Drive ratios are given in Technical Data.

A Thornton 'Powr-Lok' limited slip differential is fitted as standard to all 4.2 litre and 3.8 litre models and as an optional extra to 3.4 litre cars. These cars must not be run in gear with only one rear wheel lifted as, due to the action of the differential, the car may drive itself off the jack or stand. It is safe to run with both rear wheels lifted. The operation of this differential is shown in **FIG 8:4**. The upper drawing illustrates the straight-ahead condition and the lower shows the corner turning condition. This type of differential, the components of which are included in **FIG 8:8,** has two pinion shafts and two mates on each. These shafts 49 do not make contact at their intersection. Double ramps with flat surfaces at each end of the pinion shafts, mate with similar ramps in the differential case halves 42. Resistance to turning at the wheels causes the pinion shafts to slide up the ramps,

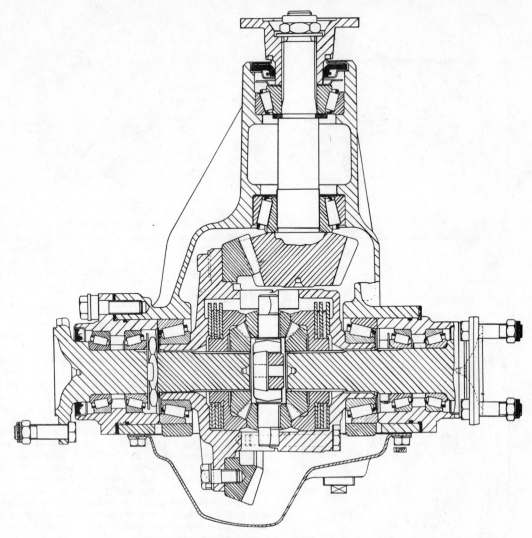

FIG 8:3 A section through the final drive assembly

force the shafts apart and apply load to the clutch plates so restricting turning between the axle shafts and the differential case. The axle shafts are now clutched to the differential case to a degree dependent upon the torque transmitted. This, in effect, locks the axle shafts to the case in the normal straight-ahead driving position and prevents spinning of either rear wheel should it encounter a poor traction surface. In cornering, the load is relieved from the clutch plates and normal differential action occurs.

Every 3000 miles, check that the oil level is up to the bottom of the filler plug hole. Change the oil every 12,000 miles. Use only hypoid oil of the correct grade. New or overhauled final drive units should, for the first 6000 miles, be run with special limited slip differential oil (Jaguar Part No. 9991).

Section 8:8 gives the procedure for dismantling and reassembling the drive unit. Intricate settings have to be made and special tools are required. The alternative of obtaining an exchange replacement (less hubs, halfshafts and brake details) should be considered.

8:5 Hub removal

Remove the appropriate road wheel, withdraw the splitpin and remove the nut and washer from the halfshaft. Refer to **FIG 8:5,** use extractor Tool No. JIC and withdraw the hub and hub carrier from splined end of the halfshaft retaining the inner oil seal track and end float spacer. Remove the lower wishbone fulcrum shaft as described in **Section 8:11** and remove the hub and hub

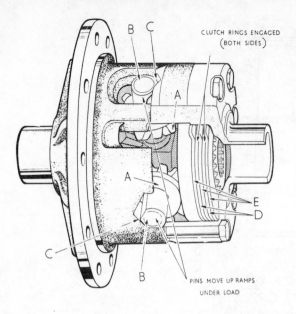

CLUTCH RINGS ENGAGED
(BOTH SIDES)

PINS MOVE UP RAMPS
UNDER LOAD

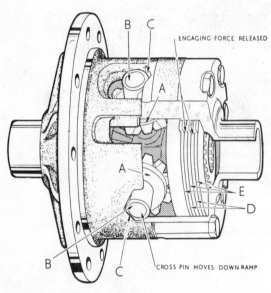

ENGAGING FORCE RELEASED

CROSS PIN MOVES DOWN RAMP

FIG 8:4 Operation of limited slip differential. Upper, straight driving. Lower, cornering

Key to Fig 8:4   A Pinion mate gear   B Pinion mate cross-shaft   C Ramps in differential case   D Friction discs   E Friction plates

carrier. Remove the halfshaft as described in **Section 8:6.**

Dismantling:

Refer to **FIG 8:6** and press out the hub with the outer bearing inner race and outer oil seal track in place. Discard the outer oil seal. Remove three screws and

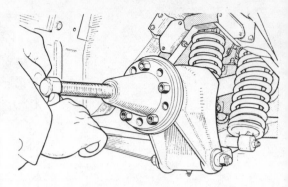

FIG 8:5   Removing a rear hub

withdraw the water deflector. Prise out the inner oil seal and remove the inner bearing inner race. If necessary, drift out the outer races of both bearings and withdraw the outer bearing inner race with a suitable extractor (Churchill Tool No. SL.14 with adaptor J.16A).

Reassembly:

If bearings have been renewed, use Churchill Tool No. J.20A with adaptors J.20A-1 to fit the outer races. Place the outer bearing inner race in position and press the outer oil seal into its recess. Fit the water deflector and press the hub with the outer oil seal track in position into the outer bearing inner race until the hub is fully home. Hold the hub and carrier as shown in **FIG 8:6.** Place the inner bearing inner race on the hub, fit the master spacer (Churchill Tool No. J.15) and press the race into the hub. Measure the end float and subtract .004 inch. Subtract this from .150 inch (the master spacer thickness) and fit a spacer the thickness of which is nearest to this. Spacers are available in .003 inch steps from **A** at .109 to **R** at .151 inch. Place the inner oil seal track and end float spacer onto the halfshaft. Apply a drop or two of 'Loctite' (Jaguar Part No. 9035) to the clean splines at the thread end, introduce the halfshaft into the hub and engage the splines. Press the hub onto the halfshaft, fit the washer and nut and torque tighten to 140 lb ft. Fit a new splitpin.

Refitting:

This is the same as refitting a halfshaft and is described in **Section 8:6.**

8:6 Halfshaft removal

Proceed as described in **Section 8:5** until the hub assembly can be withdrawn. Refer to **Section 8:10** and remove the forward hydraulic damper and spring unit. Remove the four all-metal self-locking nuts which secure the inner universal joint to the final drive output flange and brake disc. Withdraw the halfshaft as shown in **FIG 8:7.** Note the number of camber shims 41 in **FIG 8:13.**

Dismantling:

Removal of the halfshaft from the hub and hub carrier is described in **Section 8:5.** Dismantling of universal joints is as described in **Section 8:3.**

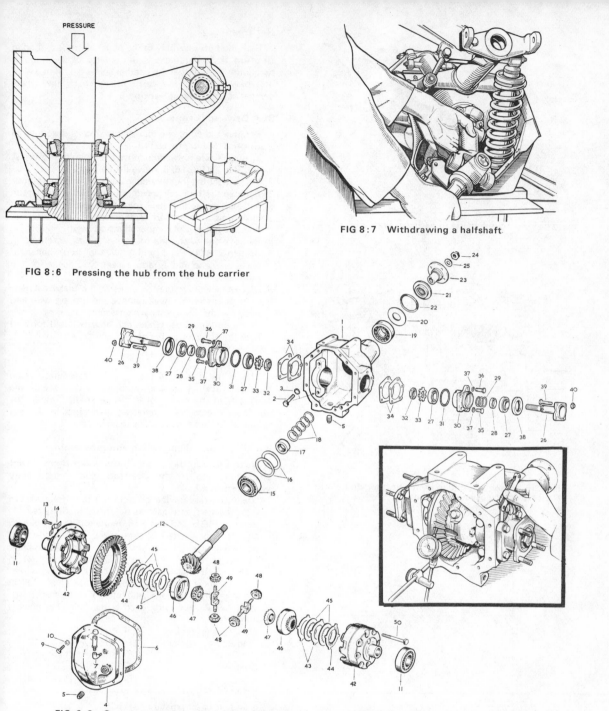

PRESSURE

FIG 8:6   Pressing the hub from the hub carrier

FIG 8:7   Withdrawing a halfshaft.

FIG 8:8   Components of the final drive. 420 and later S type. The inset is referred to in the text

Key to Fig 8:8   1 Gear carrier   2 Screw   3 Lockwasher   4 Cover   5 Plug   6 Gasket   7 Elboe   9 Setscrew   10 Lockwasher   11 Roller bearing   12 Crownwheel and pinion   13 Setscrew   14 Lock strap   15 Roller bearing   16 Shim   17 Distance washer   18 Shim   19 Roller bearing   20 Oil slinger   21 Oil seal   22 Gasket   23 Companion flange   24 Nut   25 Washer   26 Drive shaft and flange   27 Roller bearing   28 Spacing collar   29 Shim   30 Drive shaft bearing housing   31 O-ring   32 Nut   33 Lockwasher   34 Shim   35 Screw   36 Screw   37 Washer   38 Oil seal   39 Bolt   40 Nut   41 Breather   42 Differential case   43 Friction plate   44 Friction plate   45 Friction disc   46 Ring   47 Side gear   48 Pinion mate gear   49 Shaft   50 Bolt

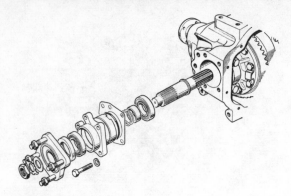

FIG 8:9 Components of earlier S type drive shaft

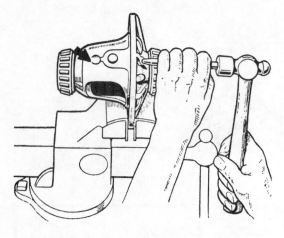

FIG 8:10 Removing pinion mate shaft locking pin (3.4 litre S type conventional differential)

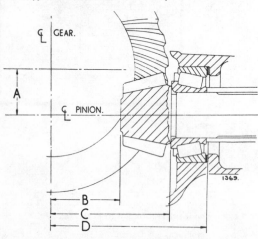

FIG 8:11 Pinion setting distances

Key to Fig 8:11   **A** Pinion drop, 1.5 inch (38.1 mm)
B Zero cone setting 2.625 inch (66.67 mm)   **C** Mounting distance, 4.312 inch (108.52 mm)   **D** Centre line to bearing housing, 5.495 inch (139.57 mm) to 5.505 inch (139.83 mm)

Refitment:

Refit the hub assembly to the halfshaft as described in **Section 8:5**. Refitment is the reverse of the removal procedure. Ensure that the camber shims are refitted and, if a new halfshaft has been fitted, check the wheel camber as described in **Section 8:12**.

8:7 Drive unit removal

Remove the complete rear suspension as described in **Section 8:9** and proceed to:
1 Invert the assembly and remove the 14 bolts arrowed **A** and **B** in **FIG 8:15**. Remove the tie plate.
2 Disconnect the four hydraulic damper and spring units.
3 Remove the four self-locking nuts which secure each halfshaft inner universal joint to the brake disc and drive unit output shaft. Withdraw the halfshafts and note the number of camber shims on each.
4 Remove the wishbone fulcrum shaft as described in **Section 8:11** and withdraw the hub, halfshaft, wishbone and radius arm assembly. Repeat for the other side.
5 Disconnect the hydraulic pipes at the brake calipers.
6 Turn the assembly over, remove the locking wire and unscrew the four bolts which secure the gear carrier to the crossmember which can now be tilted forward over the companion flange and withdrawn.

Refitting:

This is the reverse of the removal procedure. Ensure that **all-metal** self-locking nuts are used to secure the halfshafts to the output shaft flange studs. Tighten the four gear carrier bolts (removed in instruction 6) to a torque of 75 lb ft and wire lock them in pairs.

8:8 Drive unit dismantling and reassembly

Note the number of all shims, keep them intact and identified to the position from which they were removed.
1 Drain and discard the oil from the unit. Remove the brake calipers and discs as described in **Chapter 11**.
2 Refer to **FIGS 8:3** and **8:8,** remove the five bolts 35 and 36 and washers 37 from each side, remove the bearing housings 30 and drive shaft assemblies. Collect shims 34. (On **early S type** cars, refer to **FIG 8:9**, untab and remove the nuts, tabwashers, plain washers, flanges and bearing housings. Collect the shims.) Drive shafts with integral flanges as shown in **FIG 8:8** were introduced at the following chassis numbers.

Transmission type	3.4 litre	
Standard or automatic	1B.3576	1B.25511
	(Righthand)	(Lefthand)
Overdrive	1B.3686	1B.25517
	(Righthand)	(Lefthand)
	3.8 litre	
Standard or automatic	1B.53892	1B.77577
	(Righthand)	(Lefthand)
Overdrive	1B.53983	1B.77649
	(Righthand)	(Lefthand)

3 Untab and remove nut 32. Press shaft 26 through housing 30 and collect the inner bearing inner race, spacing collar 28 and shims 29. The outer bearing inner race and oil seal 38 will remain on the shaft. If

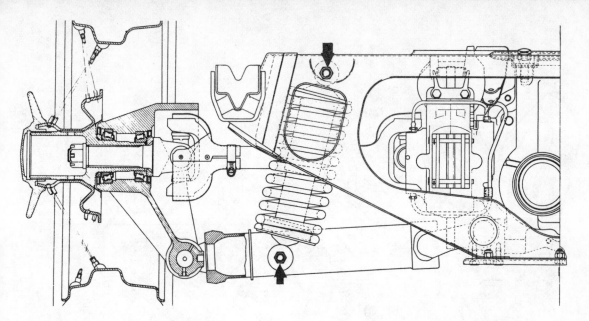

FIG 8:12 The rear suspension with a section through a wire spoke wheel hub. The hydraulic damper mounting points are arrowed

the outer bearing is to be renewed, the oil seal must also be renewed as withdrawing one scraps the other. The bearing outer races may be drifted from the housing 30.

4 Remove cover 4 and discard gasket 6. Withdraw the four bolts 2, lockwasher 3 and the bearing caps. Use a stretching fixture (Churchill Tool No. SL.1) with extreme caution **(do not exceed half a turn with a spanner on the turn-buckle)** and prise out the differential assembly. Alternatively, lever out the differential taking care not to wedge it by tilting. Use protective packing between the levers and drive case.

5 Differential bearings 11 may be withdrawn using Churchill Tool No. SL.14 with adaptor SL.14-3.

6 Untab and remove bolts 13 and, with a soft hammer, tap the crown wheel off the differential case. Scribe a line across casings 42 to facilitate reassembly in the original relative position before removing the eight bolts 50.

7 Split the casing, remove the friction plates and discs 43, 44 and 45 from one side. Remove ring 46, pinion side gear 47 and pinion mate shafts 49 complete with mate gears 48. Separate the shafts. Repeat on the other side. **(On 3.4 litre conventional differential models,** untab and remove the drive gear screws and remove the drive gear from the differential by tapping with a hide mallet. Discard the lockstraps. Use a small punch break the peening and drive out the shaft locking pin as shown in **FIG 8:10.** Remove the shaft and spacer. Rotate the side gears until the mate gears are opposite openings in the differential case and remove the mate gears. Collect the thrust washers. If the differential bearings are to be removed, use Tool No. SL.14 with SL.14-3).

8 Remove the pinion nut 24 and washer 25. Pull off

flange 23, **press** the pinion 12 out of bearing 19 and remove it from the housing. Remove oil seal 21, slinger 20 and, if the bearing is to be replaced, extract bearing outer race 19 using Tool No. SL.14 with SL.14-1. **Collect the shims.** If it is to be replaced, remove the pinion inner bearing 15 outer race with the same tools as for removal of the outer bearing.

Reassembly:

Ensure that all shims are replaced in their identified positions. Depending upon which parts may have been replaced, shims may require to be added to or subtracted from when the final adjustments are made.

Pinion drive:

Refit the pinion drive by reversing the dismantling procedure. Use Tool No. 550 with adaptor SL.550-4 to fit the outer bearing outer race. Press the inner bearing inner race onto the pinion using a length of tube the diameter of which only contacts the inner portion of the race and not the roller retainer. The oil slinger and oil seal are not fitted until after checking and, if necessary, adjusting the pinion cone setting and preload as follows:

FIG 8:11 gives the pinion setting dimensions. Dimension 'B' in the tabulation is for a zero correction pinion. All pinions have a + or a — amount etched on the face and this must be added or subtracted from the zero cone setting dimension. Shims 18 in **FIG 8:8** allow the specific setting dimension to be achieved. It is then checked by using gauge SL.3. Shims 20 allow the preload to be adjusted so that it requires 8 to 12 lb inch torque to turn the assembled pinion drive. **Dimension 'B' must be set before the preload is adjusted** and not the other way round.

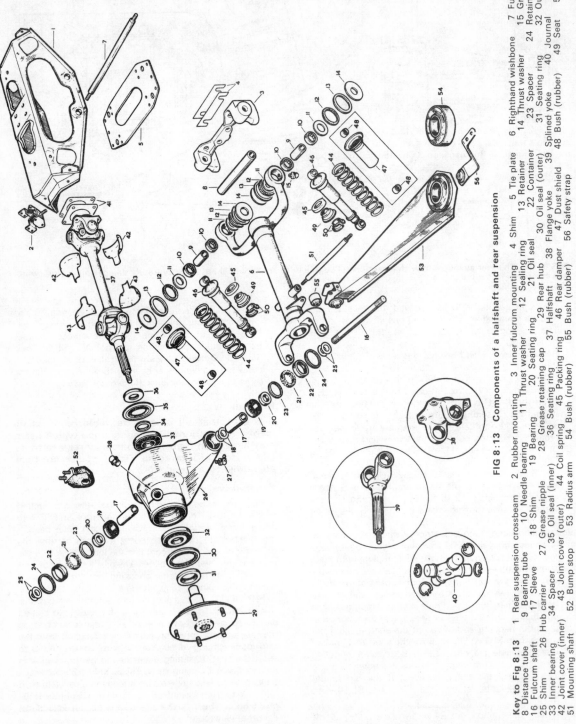

FIG 8:13   Components of a halfshaft and rear suspension

Key to Fig 8:13   1 Rear suspension crossbeam   2 Rubber mounting   3 Inner fulcrum mounting   4 Shim   5 Tie plate   6 Righthand wishbone   7 Fulcrum shaft
8 Distance tube   9 Bearing tube   10 Needle bearing   11 Thrust washer   12 Sealing ring   13 Retainer   14 Thrust washer   15 Grease nipple
16 Fulcrum shaft   17 Sleeve   18 Shim   19 Bearing   20 Seating ring   21 Oil seal   22 Container   23 Spacer   24 Retaining washer
25 Shim   26 Hub carrier   27 Grease nipple   28 Grease retaining cap   29 Rear hub   30 Oil seal (outer)   31 Seating ring   32 Outer bearing
33 Inner bearing   34 Spacer   35 Oil seal (inner)   36 Seating ring   37 Halfshaft   38 Flange yoke   39 Splined yoke   40 Journal   41 Shim
42 Joint cover (inner)   43 Joint cover (outer)   44 Coil spring   45 Packing ring   46 Rear damper   47 Dust shield   48 Bush (rubber)   49 Seat   50 Retainer
51 Mounting shaft   52 Bump stop   53 Radius arm   54 Bush (rubber)   55 Bush (rubber)   56 Safety strap

96

Differential:

Reassembly of the differential is the dismantling procedure in reverse. Ensure that the shafts are assembled to the ramps in the case. Ensure that the splines in the side gear 47 are in line with those in the rings 46 by inserting the drive shafts temporarily and torque tightening the eight bolts 50 to 40 to 45 lb ft with the drive shafts in position. Check that the driving gear and differential case mating faces are clean and free of burrs and that the bolt holes are lined up before tapping the gear home with a hide hammer. Use new lock straps 14 and tighten bolts 13 evenly and finally to 70 to 80 lb ft torque before retabbing. Use Churchill Tool No. 550 with adaptor SL.550-1 and press on bearings 11. Ensure that the bearing caps are refitted in their identified positions and tighten the cap bolts to a torque of 60 to 65 lb ft. Dial check the runout of the drive gear. If this exceeds .005 inch, dirt or a burr between the faces of the gear and case is indicated. **(On 3.4 litre conventional differential models,** refer to **FIG 8:10** and lock the pin by peening differential case metal over the end arrowed).

Drive shafts:

Reassemble the drive shafts into their housings but, before locking nut 32, check that the shaft end float is within .001 to .003 inch (adjust if necessary by shims 29) then adjust the drive gear meshing and differential preload as described later in this section. Renew O-rings 31, temporarily install the drive shaft without any shims 34 being fitted. Fit only three bolts 35 and 36 on each side, set up a dial indicator as shown in the inset to **FIG 8:8** and move the crownwheel by hand to obtain a backlash reading. This must be adjusted to match the backlash figure which is etched on the sloping face of the wheel by tightening the three drive shaft housing bolts on one side and slackening the bolts on the other. When correct meshing is achieved, measure the gap between the housing and the carrier on each side with a set of feeler gauges as shown in the inset to **FIG 8:8**. Note the gaps after checking that they are even all round and make up shim packs to fill each gap **less .003 inch for preload.** Finally fit the drive shaft assemblies with these shims in position, fit the five bolts and tighten up.

Tooth contact:

Use marking raddle and check the tooth contact. If correction is required, it is carried out by adjusting the pinion setting and the backlash. Note that the minimum backlash requirement is .004 inch however.

Final assembly:

Remove the temporarily fitted companion flange, fit the oil thrower 20, the oil seal gasket 22 and oil seal 21 with the lip inwards. Use Tool No. SL.4 to drive the seal home. Fit the companion flange, washer and nut and tighten to a torque of 120 to 130 lb ft. Check that the drain plug is tight, fit a new gasket 6 and refit the cover. Refit the brake calipers as described in **Chapter 11.**

8:9 The rear suspension

FIG 8:12 shows how the wheels are transversely located by two links of which the top link is the halfshaft universally jointed at each end. The lower link (the wish-

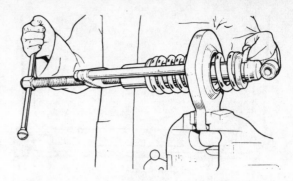

FIG 8:14   Removing a rear road spring from a hydraulic damper

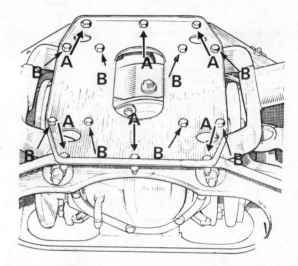

FIG 8:15   The underside of the rear suspension crossmember and tie plate. The arrowed setbolts are referred to in the text

bone) is pivoted at the hub carrier and at the crossbeam adjacent to the differential carrier. Radius arms attached between the body structure and each wishbone provide fore and aft location. The suspension medium is provided by four coil springs which each enclose a telescopic damper. The complete assembly is carried in the steel crossbeam 1 in **FIG 8:13** which illustrates the components of the rear suspension. The crossbeam is attached to the body by four rubber mountings 2.

Removal:

Remove the silencers as described in **Section 13:12** and the radius arms as described in **Section 8:11**. Jack up, place chassis stands under the body forward of the radius arm posts and remove the road wheels. Refer to **Section 11:8** and disconnect the flexible brake pipe at the connection on the body. Disconnect the handbrake cable as described in **Section 11:9**. Refer to **Section 8:2** and uncouple the propeller shaft from the final drive unit. Place a jack under the tie plate 5 in **FIG 8:13** (interpose a wooden bolster) and support the suspension

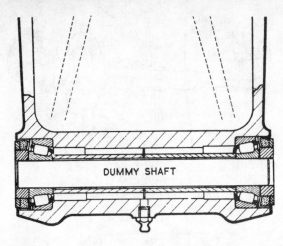

FIG 8:16 Showing a dummy shaft in position in a hub carrier

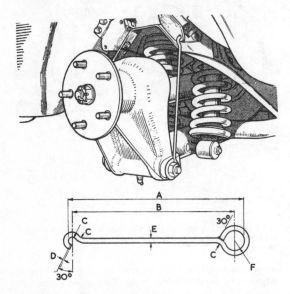

FIG 8:17 The setting links used when checking the rear camber angle

Key to Fig 8:17   A $9\frac{1}{32}$ B $8\frac{3}{16}$ C $\frac{1}{4}$ rad.   D $\frac{1}{16}$
E $\frac{9}{32}$ dia. steel bar   F $\frac{13}{32}$ rad.

unit. Remove the bolts and self-locking nuts which attach the four rubber mountings to the body frame, lower the unit on the jack and withdraw it from under the car.

Refitment:

This is the reverse of the removal procedure. Refer to **Section 11:7** and bleed the brakes.

8:10 The road springs and dampers

These may be removed with the suspension assembly in position. Remove the two self-locking nuts and washers which secure the dampers to the wishbone

(lower arrow in **FIG 8:12**), support the wishbone and drift out shaft 51 in **FIG 8:13**. Remove the nut and bolt from the other end of each damper (upper arrow in **FIG 8:12**) and withdraw the spring and damper assemblies. Use Churchill Tool No. J.11A and SL.14 as shown in **FIG 8:14** to compress the spring until the split retainer 50 in **FIG 8:13** can be removed, decompress the spring and withdraw the damper.

The telescopic hydraulic dampers are the sealed type and require no replenishment. Should a damper become unserviceable a replacement must be fitted. **FIG 9:7** shows a section through a damper.

Bleeding a damper:

Before fitting a damper, bleed any air which may have accumulated during storage by holding it vertically with the shroud uppermost and making several short strokes until there is no lost motion. Finish by extending it to full length once or twice but only after the short strokes have been made. After bleeding, keep it in a vertical position until fitted to the car.

8:11 Radius arms and wishbones

Radius arm removal:

Refer to **FIG 8:13**, remove the locking wire and unscrew the two bolts which secure the safety strap 56 to the frame. Remove the radius arm securing bolt and spring washer, remove the safety strap and withdraw the arm from its mounting post. Drift out the wishbone fulcrum shaft 16 as described later in this section. Remove the self-locking nut and special thin-headed bolt securing the radius arm to the wishbone.

Refitting is the reverse of this procedure. Torque tighten the radius arm securing bolt to 46 lb ft. Wire lock the safety strap bolts. Refit the wishbone fulcrum shaft as described later in this section.

Wishbone removal:

Remove the road springs and dampers as described in **Section 8:10**. Refer to **FIG 8:15**, remove the six self-locking nuts and bolts arrowed **A** which secure the tie plate to the crossbeam and the eight self-locking nuts and bolts arrowed **B** which secure the tie plate to the inner fulcrum wishbone brackets (3 in **FIG 8:13**). Remove the tie plate. Remove one of the self-locking nuts securing the fulcrum shaft 16 in **FIG 8:13**, drift out the shaft, separate the wishbone from the hub carrier and note the number and position of any shims 25 fitted between the wishbone and the hub carrier. Slip a dummy shaft (Churchill Tool No. J.14) into the hub carrier as shown in **FIG 8:16**. Use sticky tape to prevent seating rings 20 from becoming displaced. Disconnect the radius arm from the wishbone. Remove the self-locking nut securing the wishbone fulcrum shaft 7 to the crossbeam, drift out the shaft, withdraw the wishbone and collect thrust washers 11 and 14, oil seals 12 and retainers 13. Remove the two bearing tubes. Unless the bracket 3 is being renewed, there is no need to remove the distance tube 8. To remove the needle roller bearings 10, use a suitable drift, gently tap the needle cages out of the wishbone and remove the needle roller spacers.

Refitment is this procedure in reverse. Use grease to retain the needle rollers. Offer up the wishbone to the mounting, align the holes and insert dummy shafts (Churchill Tool No. J.14) through **both sides** of the wishbone to locate it together with the thrust washers, the crossbeam and bracket. Smear the fulcrum shaft with grease and tap it into position displacing the two dummy shafts as it enters completely. Ensure that the dummy shafts are kept in contact with the shaft so precluding any of the loose items from becoming displaced. Similarly displace the dummy shaft from the hub carrier when the other fulcrum shaft is fitted. Torque tighten the self-locking nuts on both fulcrum shafts to 55 lb ft.

8:12 Adjustment of rear suspension

If a new halfshaft has been fitted, check and adjust the rear wheel **camber angle** as follows:

1 Lock the front suspension in the mid-laden position as described in **Section 9:6.** Lock the rear by means of two setting links (Churchill Tool No. J.25 or make up to the dimensions given) as shown in **FIG 8:17.** To fit these links, insert the hook end into the lower hole in the rear mounting, depress the body and slide the other end over the hub carrier fulcrum nut. Repeat on the other side.

2 Use an approved gauge and check the camber angle. With the suspension locked as described, the angle should be $\frac{1}{2}$ deg. to 1 deg. negative and the two rear wheels should be within $\frac{1}{4}$ deg. of each other.

3 If adjustment is necessary, add or subtract shims 41 in **FIG 8:13.** One .020 inch shim will alter the angle by approximately $\frac{1}{4}$ deg. Refer to **Section 8:6,** remove the four all-metal self-locking nuts which secure the inner universal joint to the final drive output flange and brake disc (do not disturb the hub end) and pull the halfshaft away from the studs. Add or subtract shimming. Reassemble, recheck the camber angle and **remove the suspension locking** from both the the front and rear.

8:13 Fault diagnosis

(a) Noisy final drive

1 Insufficient or incorrect lubricant

2 Worn bearings
3 Worn gears

(b) Excessive backlash

1 Worn gears or bearings
2 Worn drive shaft splines
3 Worn side gear splines
4 Worn halfshaft universal joints
5 Worn propeller shaft universal joints
6 Worn or broken wheel studs (disc wheel models)
7 Worn sliding joint

(c) Oil leakage

1 Defective seals in drive shaft housing
2 Defective pinion drive seal
3 Loose drain plug

(d) Vibration

1 Propeller shaft out of balance
2 Halfshaft out of balance
3 Worn universal joint

(e) Rattles

1 Wishbone bearing worn
2 Radius arm bushes worn
3 Worn damper attachment
4 Broken coil spring
5 Dampers loose

(f) 'Settling'

1 Weak or broken coil spring
2 Loose or broken damper mounting

(g) 'Bottoming' of suspension

1 Check 1 in (f)
2 Bump stops worn or missing
3 Damper ineffective

NOTES

CHAPTER 9

THE FRONT SUSPENSION AND HUBS

9:1 Description

FIG 9:1 shows a section through a disc wheel hub and the coil spring independent suspension assembly. FIG 9:2 illustrates the components of the front suspension, hubs (the wire spoke wheel type) and steering linkage.

The assembly comprises a fabricated steel crossmember 2, wishbones 7 and 23, stub axle carrier 53, coil spring 28, hydraulic damper 34 and their associated details. The steering unit 82, idler assembly 83, track and tie rods are mounted on the crossmember. Each coil spring, which has a damper fitted inside it, is mounted between a turret at each end of the crossmember and, at the lower end, a seat pan 27 which is bolted to the lower wishbone 23. Pivoted between the upper and lower wishbones is the stub axle carrier 53 to which, through tie rod lever 65, the steering linkage is attached. Item 1 in FIG 9:2 shows these components assembled. The wheel hub is mounted on two taper roller bearings to the stub axle 55. An anti-roll bar 72 is fitted between the lower wishbones and is attached to the chassis by rubber insulated brackets 73. A rubber bump stop 5 and rebound stop 19 are provided on each side. The whole assembly is attached to the body underframe at four points through the rubber bonded mountings 4 and 6 as shown in FIG 9:3.

9:2 Maintenance

Wheel swivels:

Every 6000 miles, grease the ball joint nipples 16 and 48 in FIG 9:2. Each ball joint incorporates a nylon washer which lifts and allows grease to escape when sufficient has been applied.

Front wheel bearings:

Every 12,000 miles, lubricate the wheel bearings by applying grease sparingly to nipples 61 in FIG 9:2. Access, on wire spoke wheel models, requires removal of the wheel and, on disc wheel models, removal of the nave plate only.

9:3 Hub removal

Remove the road wheel, refer to Chapter 11 and dismount the brake caliper. Remove the splitpin (wire spoke wheel hubs have a withdrawal hole), retaining nut

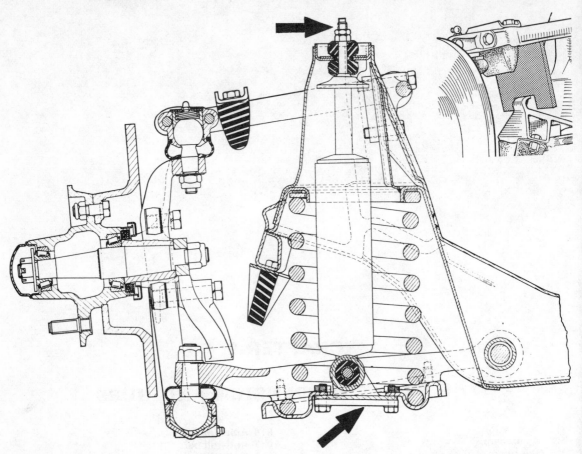

FIG 9:1 Section through a disc wheel hub and front suspension unit. The hydraulic damper mounting points are arrowed and a distance piece which is referred to in the text is shown in the inset

and plain washer (on disc wheel hubs, prise off the end cap) and withdraw the hub by hand. Extract the grease seal and withdraw the inner races. If new bearings are to be fitted, drift out the outer races. Drift grooves are provided.

Refitting:

This is the reverse of the removal procedure. Relubricate the bearings as described in **Section 9:2** and adjust the end float. Bleed the brakes as described in **Chapter 11.**

Bearing end float adjustment:

The correct end float is .003 to .005 inch. If no dial indicator gauge is available, tighten the hub until there is no end float and rotation feels 'sticky' and then slacken off by between one and two flats depending upon the position of the splitpin hole in relation to a slot in the nut. Temporarily fit the road wheel and check that it spins freely. If satisfactory, fit a new splitpin and lock.

9:4 Removing suspension assembly

Jack up under the suspension crossmember and remove the road wheels. Support the car under the front jacking sockets on stands not less than 16 inch in height. Leave the jack under the crossmember, refer to **FIG 9:2** and proceed to:

1 Remove the two bolts which secure the rear mountings 6 and the four nuts and bolts which secure the front mountings 4 to the chassis.
2 Refer to **Section 9:7** and disconnect the anti-roll bar from the chassis.
3 Refer to **Section 11:8** and disconnect the flexible brake hoses from the body brackets.
4 Refer to **Section 10:2** and disconnect the steering column universal joint from the steering box shaft. If power-assisted steering is fitted, drain off the fluid as described in **Section 10:6** and disconnect the hoses from the steering box.
5 Lower the assembly on the jack until it can be drawn forward from under the car.

Refitting:

Refitting the suspension assembly to the car is the reverse of the removal procedure. Ensure that the road wheels and steering wheel are both in the straight-ahead position before refitting the lower steering column

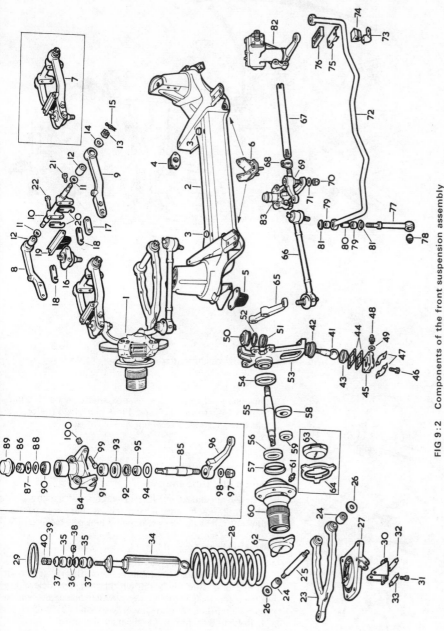

FIG 9:2   Components of the front suspension assembly

Key to Fig 9:2   1 Suspension assembly   2 Crossmember assembly   3 Rubber plug   4 Mounting rubber   5 Rubber bump stop   6 Mounting rubber   7 Upper wishbone assembly   8 Upper wishbone lever—front   9 Upper wishbone lever—rear   10 Fulcrum shaft   11 Distance washer   12 Rubber bush   13 Slotted nut   14 Washer   15 Splitpin   16 Upper ball joint assembly   17 Distance piece   18 Shim—adjusting castor angle   19 Rebound stop   20 Shim—adjusting camber angle   21 Bolt   22 Bolt   23 Lower wishbone lever   24 Rubber bush   25 Fulcrum shaft   26 Washer   27 Coil spring seat   28 Coil spring   29 Packing ring   30 Bracket   31 Setscrew   32 Tabwasher   33 Tabwasher   34 Shock absorber   35 Rubber buffer   36 Inner washer   37 Outer washer   38 Spacing collar   39 Nut   40 Locknut   41 Ballpin   42 Spigot   43 Railko socket   44 Shim   45 Cap   46 Bolt   47 Tab washer   48 Grease nipple   49 Nylon washer   50 Gaiter assembly   51 Insert   52 Ring   53 Stub axle carrier   54 Water deflector   55 Stub axle shaft   56 Oil seal   57 Water deflector   58 Inner bearing   59 Outer bearing   60 Front hub   61 Grease nipple   62 Hub cap   63 Hub cap (Continental)   64 Tool (for removing and refitting Continental hub cap)   65 Tie rod lever   66 Outer tie rod assembly   67 Tie rod tube   68 Clamp   69 End assembly   70 Nut   71 Washer   72 Anti-roll bar   73 Bracket   74 Rubber bush   75 Rubber lever   76 Packing block   77 Link   78 Rubber bush   79 Tabwasher   80 Distance piece   81 Retaining washer   82 Steering box assembly   83 Steering idler assembly   84 Bracket   85 Idler spindle   86 Nut   87 Tabwasher   88 D-washer   89 End cap   90 Bearing   91 Bearing   92 Felt seal   93 Retainer   94 Abutment   95 Abutment ring   96 Idler lever   97 Nut   98 Washer   99 Setscrew   100 Nut

JS420

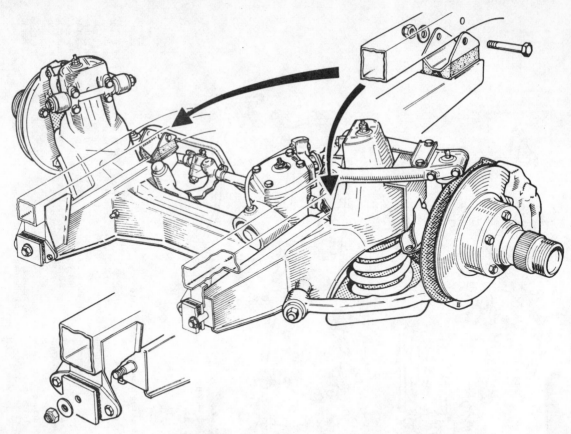

FIG 9:3   The front suspension assembly attachment points

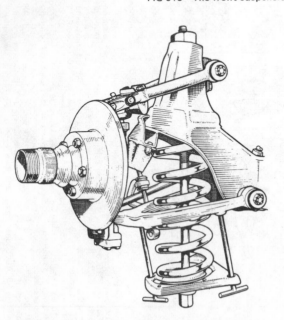

FIG 9:4   Refitting a spring. Note the pilot studs

universal joint to the steering box shaft. On completion, refer to **Sections 10:9** and **11:7** and bleed the brakes and power-assisted steering system if fitted.

9:5 Dismantling and reassembly

Bump and rebound stops:

These are shown in **FIG 9:1** and are items 5 and 19 in **FIG 9:2.** Each stop is secured to the crossmember turret or to the upper wishbone by two self-locking nuts.

Coil spring:

Remove the damper as described in **Section 9:8.** The spring compressor (Churchill Tool No. JD.16) is shown in **FIG 9:4.** Run the nut down the thread sufficiently to relieve the load on the screws which attach the spring pan 27 in **FIG 9:2** to the lower wishbone 23. Proceed to:

1 Refer to **Section 9:7** and detach the anti-roll bar.
2 Remove the six setscrews and spring washers which secure the spring seat pan to the lower wishbone.
3 Release and remove the spring compressor tool completely when the seat pan and coil spring can be removed. Collect the packing ring, if fitted, from the top of the spring.

Refitting:

FIG 9:4 shows the coil spring, seat pan and the spring compressor tool in position ready to compress the spring. Also shown are the two 8 inch long, threaded $\frac{3}{8}$ inch UNF, pilot studs fitted through two of the seat pan attachment holes which facilitate alignment of the seat pan holes. Refitting is the reverse of the spring removal procedure.

Coil spring packing rings:

A packing ring, 29 in **FIG 9:2**, may be fitted above the coil spring to compensate for spring manufacturing variations and, depending upon the model, to equalize the car standing height. The three grades of springs are identified by a colour patch in the middle of the coils (disregard any stripe of paint along its length) and the following tabulations give the thickness of rings which are applicable to different models and spring grades.

S type cars:

Commencing at Chassis No. 1B.4000 (3.4 litre) and 1B.54357 (3.8 litre).

	Packing ring thickness (inch)	
Spring colour	Lefthand spring	Righthand spring
Red	$\frac{1}{4}$	$\frac{3}{8}$
Yellow	$\frac{1}{8}$	$\frac{1}{4}$
Purple	None	$\frac{1}{8}$

Lefthand spring thickness rings are fitted to both sides on early cars.

420 models, righthand drive cars:

	Packing ring thickness (inch)	
Spring colour	Lefthand spring	Righthand spring
Red	$\frac{1}{4}$	$\frac{3}{8}$
Yellow	$\frac{1}{8}$	$\frac{1}{4}$
Purple	None	$\frac{1}{8}$

420 models, lefthand drive cars:

Lefthand spring thickness rings are fitted to both sides.

Air conditioned models:

Purple colour coded springs **only** may be fitted to cars which have air conditioning equipment and these have packing rings as follows:

Side of drive	Packing ring thickness (inch)	
	Lefthand spring	Righthand spring
Lefthand	$\frac{1}{4}$	$\frac{1}{4}$
Righthand	$\frac{1}{4}$	$\frac{3}{8}$

Stub axle carrier:

Jack up under the lower wishbone and remove the road wheel. Refer to **Section 9:3** and remove the wheel hub.

Remove the self-locking nut and plain washer securing the upper ball joint to the stub axle carrier. Drift out the ballpin which is a taper fit in the axle carier or use extractor Churchill Tool No. JD.24.

The stub axle itself is retained in the taper bore of the carrier by a self-locking nut and plain washer.

Refitting is the reverse of this procedure.

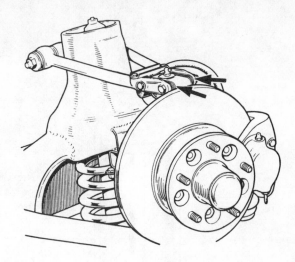

FIG 9:5 The castor angle adjustment shims are shown arrowed

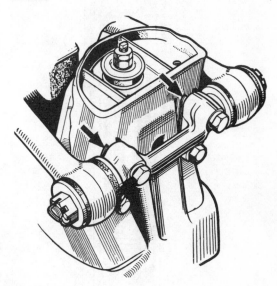

FIG 9:6 The camber angle adjustment shims are shown arrowed

Lower wishbone:

Remove the coil spring and stub axle carrier as described earlier in this section. Refer to **FIG 9:2** and remove the splitpin, nut and washer from one end of the fulcrum shaft 25 which can then be drifted out and the wishbone removed from the crossmember. Bushes 24 are a press-fit in the wishbone.

Refitting is the reverse of this procedure but the car must be in the normal riding position before the fulcrum shaft is fully tightened and locked with a new splitpin.

Upper wishbone:

Jack up under the lower wishbone and remove the road wheel. Remove the self-locking nut and washer

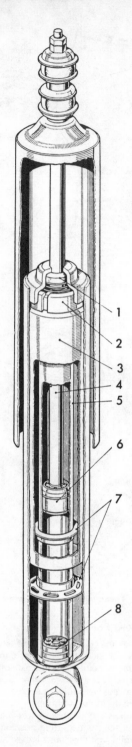

FIG 9:7 Cutaway view of a telescopic hydraulic damper

Key to Fig 9:7   1 Cone seal   2 Piston rod guide
3 Drain sleeve   4 Piston rod   5 Pressure tube   6 Piston
assembly   7 Fluid baffles   8 Base valve

securing the upper ball joint to the stub axle carrier and
drift out the ballpin 16 in **FIG 9:2** which is a taper fit in
the axle carrier. Tie up the carrier so that the flexible brake
pipe is not strained.

Remove the two short bolts 21 and two long bolts 22
which secure the fulcrum shaft 10 to the crossmember
turret. Collect and carefully note the relative positions of
the shims 20 which control the camber angle.

Remove the rebound stop 19 and the bolts, nuts and
washers which secure the ball joint 16 between the
wishbone levers 8 and 9. Collect and carefully note the
relative positions of the distance piece 17 and shims 18
which control the castor angle. Remove the splitpins 15,
nuts 13 and washers 14 and remove the levers from the
fulcrum shaft. The bushes 12 are a press-fit in the wishbone levers.

Refitting is the reverse of the removal procedure but
the car must be in the normal riding position before the
nuts 13 are fully tightened and locked with new splitpins.

9:6 Adjustments

Compress and lock the front suspension in the mid-
laden position by inserting $3\frac{3}{8}$ inch distance pieces
between the upper wishbones and the brackets on the
turrets as shown in the inset to **FIG 9:1**. Lock the rear
suspension as described in **Section 8:12**. On completion
of checks and adjustments, **remove the front distance
pieces and rear links.**

Castor angle:

Use an approved gauge and check the castor angle
which should be $-\frac{1}{2}$ deg. to $+\frac{1}{2}$ deg. Adjustment is
effected by either transposing shims 18 in **FIG 9:2** from
the rear of the upper wishbone ball joint to the front or
transposing the packing piece 17 and shim(s). To
decrease negative castor, transpose shimming from the
rear to the front. The two wheels must be within $\frac{1}{2}$ deg.
of each other. As the holes in the shims are slotted it is
only necessary to slacken the two through bolts to
enable shims to be removed or fitted. If the packing piece,
which does not have slotted holes, has to be removed it
will be necessary to place a support under the lower
wishbone and to remove the two through-bolts. To
increase negative castor or to decrease positive castor,
transfer in the opposite direction. Shims are $\frac{1}{16}$ inch thick
and this thickness will alter the castor angle by approximately $\frac{1}{4}$ deg. The shims are arrowed in **FIG 9:5**.

Camber angle:

Adjustment is effected by removing or adding equal
thicknesses of shims 20 in **FIG 9:2** and are arrowed in
FIG 9:6. Line up the wheel being checked parallel to the
centre line of the car. Using an approved gauge, check
the camber angle. Rotate the wheel through 180 deg. and
recheck. The angle should be zero to 1 deg. positive.
Inserting shims decreases the positive camber; removing
shims increases positive camber or decreases negative
camber. $\frac{1}{16}$ inch of shimming alters the camber angle by
approximately $\frac{1}{4}$ deg. and shims are available in thick-
nesses of $\frac{1}{32}$, $\frac{1}{16}$ and $\frac{3}{64}$ inch. After the camber angle has
been checked on both wheels and if any adjustment was

made to the camber angle, the front wheel alignment should be checked and reset as described in **Section 10:4** if necessary.

9:7 Anti-roll bar

Raise the car on a lift, refer to **FIG 9:2,** remove the four bracket bolts which attach the support brackets 73 to the chassis and collect the spring washers. Remove the self-locking nuts and the bolts which attach the link arms 77 to the coil spring seat pans 27. The anti-roll bar is separated from the link arms by removing the self-locking nut, cup washers 81, rubber buffers 79 and spacers 80. The bushes 78 are a press-fit in the eyes of the link arms. The rubber pads 74 are split to enable them to be removed from the anti-roll bar.

Refitting is the reverse of this procedure. Ensure that the spacers 78 are refitted. The full weight of the car must be on the road wheels when attaching the support brackets to the chassis.

9:8 Dampers

FIG 9:7 is a cutaway view of a damper which is of the sealed type and requires no maintenance. Should a damper become unserviceable, a replacement must be fitted.

Removal:

Jack up the car under the suspension crossmember and remove the road wheel. Place a support under the lower wishbone and partly lower the jack so that the wishbones are approximately horizontal. Remove the locknut 40 and nut 39 in **FIG 9:2** (upper arrow in **FIG 9:1**) and withdraw outer washer 37, rubber buffer 35 and inner washer 36. Untab and remove bolts 31 which attach bracket 30 to spring seat pan 27 (lower arrow in **FIG 9:1**), remove the damper and collect spacing collar 38.

Refitting:

This is the reverse of the removal procedure. Ensure that spacer 38 is refitted and that bolts 31 are locked by tabbing.

Before fitting a damper, bleed it as described in **Section 8:10.**

9:9 Fault diagnosis

(a) Wheel wobble

1 Worn hub bearings
2 Broken or weak front springs
3 Uneven tyre wear
4 Worn suspension linkage
5 Loose wheel fixings
6 Incorrect tracking

(b) 'Bottoming' of suspension

1 Check 2 in (a)
2 Rebound rubbers worn or missing
3 Damper(s) not working

(c) Heavy steering

1 Neglected lubrication of wheel swivels
2 Wrong suspension geometry

(d) Excessive tyre wear

1 Check 4 and 6 in (a) and 2 in (c)

(e) Rattles

1 Check 2 in (a) and 1 in (c)
2 Worn bushes
3 Damper attachments loose
4 Anti-roll bar mountings loose or bushes worn

(f) Excessive rolling

1 Check 2 in (a) and 3 in (b)
2 Anti-roll bar broken, mountings loose or bushes worn

NOTES

CHAPTER 10

THE STEERING GEAR

10:1 The standard steering

The components of the standard steering box are shown in **FIG 10:1**. The idler unit components are shown in **FIG 9:2**. The unit is item 83 and the steering box is item 82. **FIG 9:2** also illustrates the components of the steering linkage. The linkage, which is basically the same on standard and power assisted models, is shown assembled in **FIG 10:5**. Lefthand and righthand drive models have the same components but the steering box and idler units are interchanged on the front crossmember.

The steering box is a recirculating ball type. Steering column motion is transmitted from the inner column worm 3 in **FIG 10:1**, which is supported in loose ball races 6 and 7, to the rocker shaft 18 by means of the main nut 4 which runs on a continuous train of steel balls 6. The drop arm 21 is taper splined to the rocker shaft. Shown in **FIG 9:2** is the adjustable track rod 67 which connects the drop arm and idler lever. Extensions from these attach to the two steering tie rods 66 which are connected to the tie rod levers 65. These levers, or steering arms, are rigidly bolted to the stub axle carriers 53.

10:2 The steering box
Removal:
1 On **S type** cars, refer to **Section 10:11** and disconnect the upper column from the lower column.
2 On **420 models**, remove the pinch bolt from the upper universal joint and pull back the steering wheel until the column splines are clear of the socket. Detach the universal joint from the steering box and remove the lower steering column.
3 Remove the self-locking nut and washer securing the taper fitting track rod end into the drop arm 21 in **FIG 10:1** and drift it out. Untab and remove the four bolts 34 and 35 which attach the steering box to the suspension crossmember. Dismount the box.

Dismantling:
1 Remove setscrews 26, washers 27, coverplate 24 and gasket 25. Remove roller 5 from the top of the main nut 4 and take care not to dislodge spring 30 from adjusting screw 28. Drain the oil into a clean container.
2 Remove nut 22, collect spring washer 23, note for correct assembly the line scribed across the drop arm

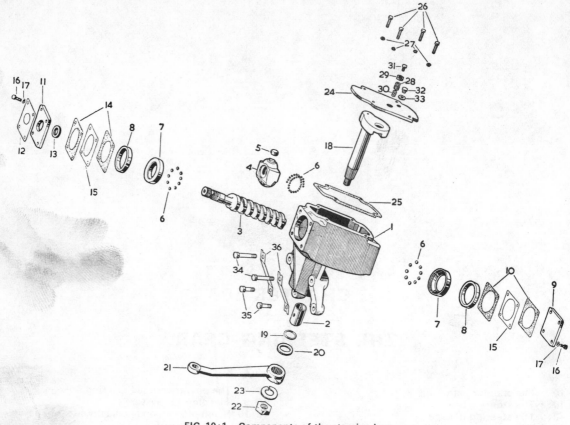

FIG 10:1   Components of the steering box

Key to Fig 10:1   1 Steering box   2 Trunnion bush   3 Inner column worm   4 Main nut   5 Roller   6 Steel balls
7 Ballrace   8 Distance piece   9 Bottom end plate   10 Gasket   11 Top end plate   12 Oil seal retainer plate
13 Oil seal   14 Gaskets   15 Shims   16 Setscrew   17 Spring washer   18 Rocker shaft
20 Washer   21 Drop arm   22 Nut   23 Spring washer   24 Coverplate   25 Gasket   26 Setscrews
27 Spring washer   28 Rocker shaft adjustment screw   29 Locking nut   30 Spring   31 Spring tension bolt
32 Oil filler plug   33 Washer   34 Long bolt   35 Short bolt   36 Tabwasher

21 and rocker shaft 18 (see **FIG 10:2**) and, **using a suitable extractor** and not a hammer, draw the arm off the rocker shaft. Remove the O-ring 19 from the steering box.

3 Remove the four setscrews 16 and washers 17 and detach the plates 11 and 12, gasket 14, shims 15, further gasket 14 and distance piece 8.

4 Push the wormshaft outwards, withdraw the outer race 7 and collect the ten balls 6. Unscrew the wormshaft 3 through the main nut 4 and withdraw it from the box.

5 Remove the bolts, washers, gaskets, shims, distance piece, outer race and bearing balls from the outer side of the box.

6 Untab and remove the two setscrews retaining the ball transfer tube to the main nut. Remove the clip, tube and thirty-one balls.

Wormshaft end float:

By means of gaskets 10 and 14 and selection of shims 15, the wormshaft bearings should be given a preload of .002 to .003 inch. The shims are .005 and the gaskets .003 inch thick. Unscrew the rocker shaft adjustment screw 28 so that there is no load on the shaft. Eliminate, or reduce to a minimum, the end float of the wormshaft by removing shims as necessary. Check that the wormshaft turns freely. Remove a shim and/or gasket to obtain the prescribed preload but maintain a gasket at each side of the shim pack at both ends of the box.

Rocker shaft end float:

Set the rocker shaft in the centre of its travel, that is half way between 'lock to lock'. Unscrew bolt 31 and remove spring 30. Slacken the adjustment screw locknut 29 and screw down adjustment screw 28 until it contacts the rocker shaft and eliminates all end float. Hold the adjustment screw and tighten the locknut. Test the freedom of the wormshaft. If it is tight in the centre of its travel, readjust the rocker shaft end float. Refit spring 30 and bolt 31.

Reassembly:

This is the reverse of the dismantling procedure but the following points should be noted.

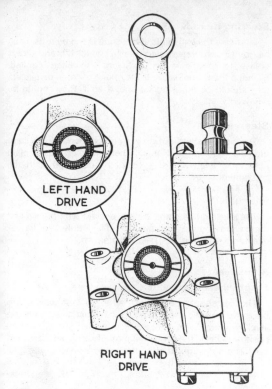

FIG 10:2 Drop arm/rocker shaft alignment marks

When reassembling, adjust the preload on the worm-shaft bearing and eliminate the end float on the rocker shaft as described earlier. To protect the bore of oil seal 13, cover the wormshaft serrations with Sellotape when sliding the end plate over the serrations. Ensure that the tape is then removed completely. Use grease to retain the balls in position when reassembling them to the main nut and wormshaft bearings.

Refitting:

Fit the drop arm to the rocker shaft with its scribed line matching the appropriate line on the rocker shaft according to whether the steering is for righthand or lefthand drive. **FIG 10:2** illustrates the positioning for righthand drive while the inset shows the positioning for lefthand drive.

10:3 The steering linkage

Idler unit:

The components of the standard steering idler unit are shown in **FIG 9:2** (items 84 to 100). The taper roller bearings are prepacked with grease and require no routine maintenace. The lockstops are accommodated in the idler unit bracket and are shown in **FIG 10:4**. The unit is similar to that fitted to power assisted models but is not identical.

Removal:

Remove the self-locking nut and washer securing the taper fitting track rod end to the idler lever and drift it out.

On **S type cars,** remove the four bolts and washers and, on **420 models,** the two setbolts and one long bolt which attach the idler bracket to the crossmember. Dismount the unit and note the location of any packing washers which may be inserted between the crossmember and the bracket.

Refitting:

This is the reverse of the removal procedure.

Steering arm:

Removal:

1 Jack-up under the suspension crossmember and remove the road wheel.
2 Remove the self-locking nut and plain washer securing the tie rod to the steering arm and drift out the taper fitting tie rod ballpin from the arm.
3 Unscrew the centre self-locking nut which secures both the stub axle and steering arm to the carrier. Remove the wired bolt attaching the end of the arm to the carrier. Dismount the steering arm. Note any shims fitted between the steering arm and the brake caliper lower mounting point.

Refitting:

This is the reverse of the removal procedure.

Tie rod:

Tie rod ball joints cannot be dismantled and, if worn, a complete tie rod assembly must be fitted. Remove the self-locking nuts and washers securing the tie rod to the steering arm and to the track rod end. Tap out the taper fitting pins. Refitting is the reverse of this procedure.

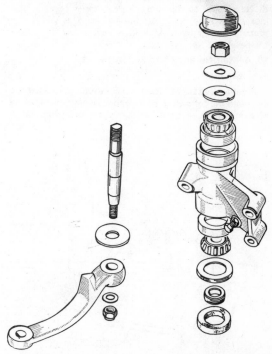

FIG 10:3 Components of the idler unit

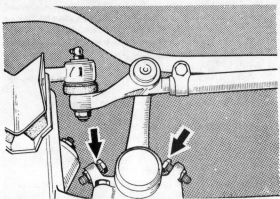

Track rod:

The track rod ends incorporate rubber/steel-bonded bushes. Remove the self-locking nuts and washers from the inner ball joint of each tie rod and tap out the taper fitting pins. Similarly, uncouple the track rod from the idler lever and the drop arm and dismount the track rod. Slacken the clamp at each end of the rod and unscrew the track rod ends noting that **one has a lefthand thread.**

When refitting track rod ends to the centre tube, **screw in each end an equal number of turns.** Final setting is described in **Section 10:4** under the heading of wheel alignment.

Refitting is the reverse of the removal procedure but before fitting the track rod, check that the drop arm and idler lever are in the straight-ahead position and tap in the taper pins so that they do not turn when the self-locking securing nuts are tightened up. This will ensure that no undue torsional load is placed on the rubber bushes.

10:4 Maintenance and adjustments

Maintenance:

Refer to **Section 9:2.** It will be found convenient to deal with the following maintenance operations when, at 6000 mile intervals, the wheel swivels are being lubricated.

Steering tie rods:

Lubricate the ball joints at the ends of the tie rods. Each ball joint incorporates a nylon washer which lifts and allows grease to escape when sufficient has been applied. Examine the rubber seals. If they have become displaced, they should be repositioned and, if split, they should be renewed.

Steering unit:

Top up the steering box with recommended lubricant until no more oil will enter. The filler plug has a plain hexagonal head and should not be confused with the adjustment screw.

Idler unit:

The idler unit bearings are pre-packed with grease and require no routine maintenance. They only require re-packing if the unit has been dismantled.

Adjustments:

Front wheel alignment:

The car should be full of petrol, oil and water; tyre pressures must be correct and the car must be standing on level ground. With the wheels in the straight-ahead position, check the wheel alignment using an approved track setting gauge. They should be parallel to $\frac{1}{8}$ inch total 'toe-in' measured at the wheel rims. Push the car forward until the wheels have turned through 180 deg. and recheck.

If adjustment is required, slacken the clamp bolt at each end of the track rod and rotate the rod one way or the other until the alignment is correct. Tighten the clamp bolts and recheck the alignment.

Lockstops:

The hexagonal headed lockstop bolts are shown in **FIG 10:4.** They are factory set to allow 38 deg. of idler lever and drop arm travel each side of the central position. The stops should not normally require adjustment. If adjustment is necessary, slacken the locknuts and screw in the stop bolts as far as possible. Turn the steering to full

FIG 10:5   Steering layout. A lefthand drive S type power assisted model is illustrated. The lockstops are arrowed

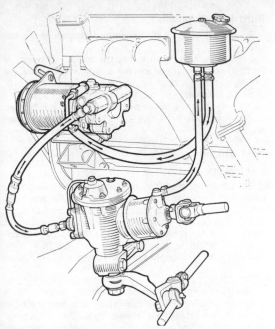

FIG 10:6 Power assisted system. A lefthand drive S type is illustrated

lock in one direction, screw out the stop bolt until the head contacts the idler lever. Screw out by a further two turns and tighten the locknut. Repeat for the other lock.

Castor and camber angles:

Adjustment is described in **Section 9:6**.

10:5 The power assisted steering

The layout of the linkage on a lefthand drive S type car is shown in **FIG 10:5**. This is similar for all models but, on 420 power assisted models only, the tie rods are adjustable for length. The idler unit has taper roller bearings and is similar to, but not the same as, units fitted to standard steering cars. The pump supplies a continuous flow of oil while the engine is running and the steering is in the straight-ahead position. Pressure, which is only generated when the steering column is rotated, is proportional to the effort applied to the steering wheel.

S type cars:

Burman hydraulically assisted worm and recirculating ball-type steering is fitted as an optional extra to S type cars.

FIG 10:6 shows the hydraulic layout of earlier cars which are fitted with eccentric rotor pumps. Later cars have pumps with roller type rotors and a modified worm and valve type of steering box. A flexible hose supplies oil from the reservoir to the inlet of the pump which is driven off the rear of the generator. The outlet of the pump is fed to the forward end of the steering box and the oil outlet from the rear of the box is connected with the reservoir. **FIG 10:7** is a cutaway view of the steering box. Hydraulic assistance is applied to one side or the other of the piston which forms part of the main nut 14 depending

on which steering lock is applied. The piston operates in a cast iron sleeved cylinder in the steering box casing. Admission of oil to the appropriate side of the piston is controlled by selector valve 8 integral with which is the splined shaft which is connected to the steering column universal joint in the same manner as standard steering. Rotary movement of the valve relative to the wormshaft 17 opens and closes ports in the wormshaft and directs oil to that side of the piston which is appropriate to the lock selected by the rotation of the selector valve. When steering effort is at a minimum, centralization of the valve is effected by the action of a torsion bar 10 which is keyed to the valve by a serrated operating ring 9 and locked to the wormshaft by a retaining pin. An interrupted flange is formed on the outside of the selector valve. This limits the rotary movement of the valve within the wormshaft, prevents overloading of the valve and, in the event of no hydraulic pressure being available, allows normal unassisted steering.

A grooved recess in rocker arm 1 engages with a spherical boss formed on the main nut 14. The preload, which is applied by shims fitted under adjusting screw 4 (and by spring load on earlier type boxes), is augmented by hydraulic pressure fed to the rocker shaft coverplate from the inlet by a small-bore rigid pipe.

420 models:

Marles Varamatic cam and roller power assisted steering is fitted as an optional extra to 420 models. A hydraulic control valve is embodied in the input shaft of the cam and hydraulic assistance is provided from a servo piston operating in a cylinder which is integral with the steering box. **FIG 10:8** shows a cutaway view of this type of box. The power assistance is transferred from the piston through a rack which transmits servo piston movement to a quadrant of pinion which is integral with the steering shaft.

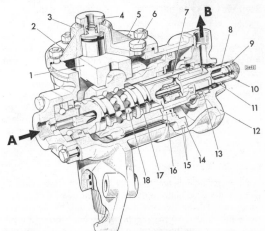

FIG 10:7 Cutaway view of an S type power assisted steering box. Lefthand drive illustrated

Key to Fig 10:7 1 Rocker shaft 2 Dowel 3 Top cover 4 Adjusting screw 5 Dowel 6 Air bleed plug 7 Sealing sleeve 8 Selector valve 9 Operating ring 10 Torsion bar 11 Seal 12 Top end plate 13 Roller race 14 Main nut 15 Piston rings 16 Sealing rings 17 Inner column or wormshaft 18 Recirculating balls **A** Inlet **B** Outlet

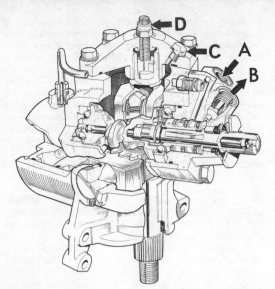

FIG 10:8 Cutaway view of the 420 type power assisted steering box

Key to Fig 10:8   **A** Pressure oil from pump
B Return to pump   **C** Air bleed plug   **D** Steering shaft
adjuster

The hydraulic pump is a vaned rotor type and the fluid reservoir is incorporated in its end cover. The pump is belt driven and is mounted independently from other units. A flexible feed and a return hose connect with the steering box. No external lockstops are provided as they are incorporated in the steering box.

10:6 The power assisted steering box

Removal, S type cars:

Remove the return hose from the steering box top end plate and drain the oil into a clean container. Remove the feed hose from the steering box and blank off the pipes and box unions to preclude entry of dirt. Refer to **Section 10:11** and disconnect the lower steering column from the upper steering column. Remove the self-locking nut, drift out the taper fitting pin from the drop arm, remove the three setscrews and one long bolt securing the box to the suspension crossmember and dismount the box. Collect the spacer (if fitted) from between the box and the cross-member.

Removal, 420 models:

The steering box can only be removed from beneath with the car on a ramp or over a pit. Remove the feed and return hoses from the box and collect the oil in a clean container. Blank off the pipes and steering box connections to preclude the entry of dirt. Remove the nut and washer and disconnect the ball joint from the drop arm using a suitable extractor. Disconnect the upper steering column from the lower column as described in **Section 10:11**, remove three bolts and two nuts securing the unit to the crossmember and withdraw the steering box complete with lower column and drop arm from beneath the car.

Refitting, all models:

This is the reverse of the removal procedure in each case.

On S type cars, ensure that the spacer (if fitted) is refitted between the box and the crossmember. Check the setting of the lockstops as described in **Section 10:10**.

Bleed the system as described in **Section 10:9**.

If the drop arm was removed, ensure that it is refitted in the same position relative to the steering shaft as it had originally.

10:7 The pump

S type cars:

The power assisted steering pump fitted to early S type cars is an eccentric rotor type. Later models are fitted with a roller type, the components of which are illustrated in **FIG 10:10**. The pressure generated by the eccentric rotor type pump is as high as 800 to 850 lb/sq in at full lock and 1000 lb/sq in by the roller rotor type. Their overhaul or repair should only be undertaken by a specialist.

Removal:

The following procedure is applicable to both types of pump. Clean the exterior of the pump and the hose connections to the pump thoroughly so that dirt cannot contaminate the oil when it is drained nor enter the pump inlet or outlet when the hoses are removed. Disconnect the hoses from the pump and drain the oil into a clean container. Remove the nuts and spring washers and dismount the pump from the generator. Collect the coupling and driving dogs.

Refitting:

Assemble the driving dogs to the coupling and fit the unit to the generator. Align the slot in the pump driving shaft with the driving dog, push the pump home onto the mounting studs, secure with nuts and spring washers and connect the hoses. Refer to **Section 10:9** and bleed the system.

420 models:

The components of the vaned type pump are shown in **FIG 10:11**. The oil reservoir is integral with the end cover.

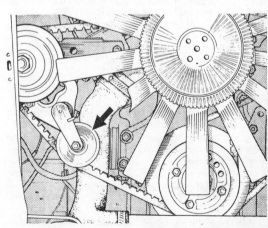

FIG 10:9 Pump drive jockey pulley. 420 type illustrated

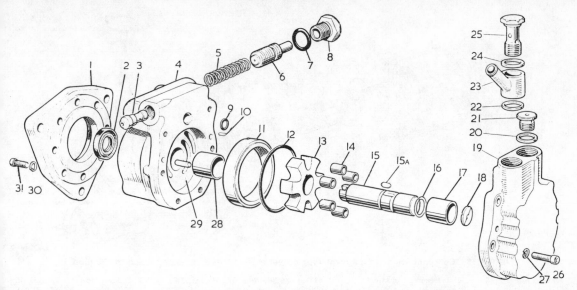

FIG 10:10 Components of roller rotor type power assisted steering pump fitted to S type cars

Key to Fig 10:10   1 End plate   2 Oil seal   3 Orifice tube   4 Pump body   5 Flow control spring   6 Flow control valve
7 Valve seal   8 Valve cap   9 Sealing ring   10 Cam locking peg   11 Cam   12 Sealing ring   13 Roller carrier
14 Rollers   15 Drive shaft   15a Drive pin   16 Snap ring   17 Drive shaft bush   18 Thrust washer   19 Pump cover
20 Plug seal   21 Plug   22 Gasket   23 Adaptor   24 Fibre washer   25 Adaptor screw   26 Cover screw
27 Spring washer   28 Drive shaft bush   29 Dowel pin (two off)   30 Spring washer   31 End plate screw

The pump is mounted independently from other units and the shaft is fitted with a pulley for the belt drive. The pressure generated at full lock is 1100 to 1250 lb/sq in. Pump overhaul or repair should be undertaken by a specialist.

Removal:

Release the bottom pump mounting bracket bolt, remove the setscrew and washer securing the adjusting link to the water pump, swing the pump towards the engine, lift the jockey pulley (arrowed in **FIG 10:9**) against the spring pressure and remove the belt from the pump pulley. Release the hose clip, disconnect the low pressure pipe and collect the oil in a clean container. Disconnect the high pressure hose from the pump and blank off the pipes and pump unions. Remove the two nuts and washers from the mounting studs and withdraw the unit from the bracket. Note the location and number of any spacing washers between the pump and the mounting bracket.

Refitting:

This is the reverse of the removal procedure. Refit the spacing washers in their original positions between the pump and the bracket. Fill the reservoir to the FULL mark on the dipstick and prime the pump by turning the pulley anticlockwise for several turns. After refitting the belt, swing the pump away from the engine to the full extent of the elongated hole in the adjusting link and tighten the setscrew and bottom mounting bracket bolt.

Bleed the system as described in **Section 10:9.**

10:8 The power assisted steering linkage

Except for the following points, **Section 10:3** is applicable and should be referred to.

S type cars:

The lockstops are shown arrowed in **FIG 10:5.**

420 models:

Lockstops are incorporated in the power assisted steering box. The tie rods are adjustable for length and, as described in **Section 10:10**, are used for adjustment of wheel alignment. The track rod, on power assisted models, must be set to the fixed length of $16\frac{7}{16}$ inch and **must never be adjusted for wheel alignment setting.**

10:9 Bleeding the system

Bleeding is required if any part of the steering hydraulic system has been dismantled. Proceed as follows:

S type cars:

1 Fill the reservoir to the top of the filter element with recommended oil. Start the engine and allow it to idle. While the engine is idling, pour more oil into the reservoir to bring the level to the top of the filter element. Check the hose connections for leaks.
2 Increase the engine speed to 1000 rev/min and turn the wheels from lock to lock five or six times.
3 Recheck for leaks and top up the oil level after road test.

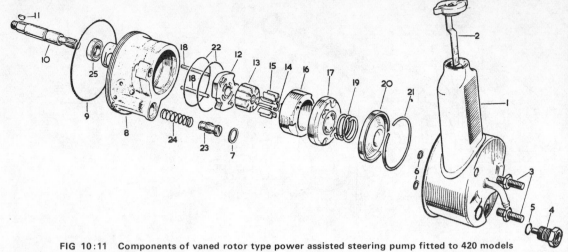

FIG 10:11   Components of vaned rotor type power assisted steering pump fitted to 420 models

Key to Fig 10:11   1 Reservoir assembly   2 Filler cap assembly   3 Stud   4 Outlet union   5 O-ring
6 Seal (small)   7 Seal (large)   8 Pump body assembly   9 O-ring   10 Shaft   11 Key   12 Thrust plate
13 Rotor   14 Clip   15 Pump vane   16 Pump ring   17 Pressure plate   18 Pin   19 Spring   20 End plate
21 Clip   22 O-ring   23 Flow control   24 Spring   25 Oil seal

If stiffness is felt on either lock, slacken the bleed screw 6 in **FIG 10:7** by half a turn or more with the engine running and release air from the unit. Retighten the bleed screw securely.

420 models:

1 Fill the reservoir to the FULL mark on the dipstick with recommended oil. Release the plug arrowed **C** in **FIG 10:8** and start the engine. Close the plug when all air has been expelled.
2 With the engine running, turn the steering from lock to lock five or six times.
3 Check for leaks and top up the reservoir after road test.

10:10 Maintenance and adjustment of power assisted steering

Maintenance, all models:

Steering idler unit:

The unit is prepacked with grease and only requires replenishment if it is dismantled.

Steering tie rods:

Every 6000 miles, these should be lubricated as described in **Section 10:4.**

Maintenance, S type cars:

Reservoir oil level:

Every 3000 miles, check the level of oil in the reservoir. Clean the area round the filler cap before removing it. The level of the oil must be just above the filter element which is located in the reservoir.

Oil reservoir filter:

Every 12.000 miles renew the paper element in the reservoir. Unscrew the bolt securing the reservoir cover,

lift off the cover, collect the spring and retainer plate. Ensure that the new element is located in the support plate at the bottom of the reservoir. Refit the retainer plate, spring and cover. Tighten the central bolt.

Maintenance, 420 models:

Reservoir oil level:

Every 3000 miles, check the level of the oil in the reservoir. Clean the area round the filler cap before removing it. The level of oil must be up to the FULL mark **when the oil is warm.**

Adjustments, S type cars:

Front wheel alignment:

Refer to **Section 10:4.** Alignment and method of adjustment is as described for standard steering models.

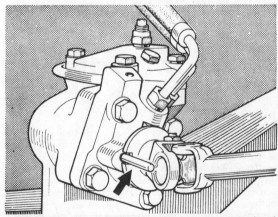

FIG 10:12   Centralizing the 420 type power assisted steering

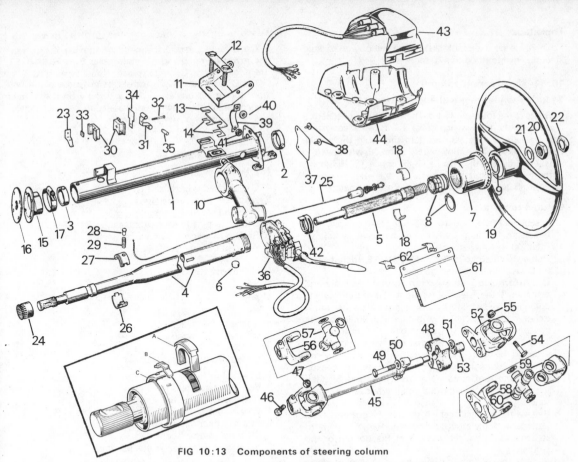

FIG 10:13 Components of steering column

Key to Fig 10:13   **A** Thrust bearing   **B** Spring clip   **C** Retaining ring   1 Outer assembly   2 Top bearing
3 Bottom bearing   4 Inner column   5 Inner column shaft   6 Stop button   7 Locknut   8 Split collet and circlip assembly
9 Circlip only   10 Steering column lock (when fitted)   11 Upper mounting bracket   12 Screw plate assembly   13 Spacer
14 Shims   15 Lower mounting bracket   16 Gasket   17 Clip   18 Split cone   19 Steering wheel   20 Steering wheel nut
21 Washer   22 Locknut   23 Earth contact   24 Slip ring   25 Horn switch cable   26 Rotor (bottom half)
27 Rotor (top half)   28 Cable contact   29 Contact spring   30 Contact holder   31 Contact   32 Contact securing bolt
33 Nut   34 Insulating strip   35 Dowel   36 Direction indicator switch   37 Insulating strip   38 Studs for insulating strip
39 Direction indication switch clamp   40 Spacer   41 Locking nut   42 Striker ring   43 Switch cover (upper)
44 Switch cover (lower)   45 Lower column   46 Bolt   47 Locknut   48 Rubber coupling   49 Bolt   50 Plain washer
51 Locknut   52 Upper universal joint   53 Rubber steady bush   54 Bolt   55 Locknut   56 End yoke, lower universal joint
57 Journal assembly   58 Flange yoke, upper universal joint   59 End yoke, upper universal joint   60 Journal assembly
61 Shield assembly   62 Shield bracket

Lockstops:

The lockstop bolts are shown arrowed in **FIG 10:5**.
Although their location is different, the procedure for
their adjustment is as for standard steering models and is
described in **Section 10:4**.

Adjustments, 420 models:

Front wheel alignment:

Centralize the steering by turning the steering wheel
until the hole in the centralizing plate on the input shaft
aligns with the hole in the steering box. Hold this setting
by inserting a piece of $\frac{1}{4}$ inch dia. rod as shown arrowed
in **FIG 10:12**.

Refer to **FIG 10:4** but note that, as stated in **Section
10:8**, adjustable tie rods are fitted to power assisted 420
models and **the track rod must remain set at the**

fixed length of $16\frac{7}{16}$ inch. The wheels should be
parallel to $\frac{1}{8}$ inch total 'toe-in' as for standard steering but
**each wheel must be individually adjusted by its
tie rod to give half this total 'toe-in'.** On completion,
remove the $\frac{1}{4}$ inch dia. rod.

Steering box backlash:

If, after high mileage, there is lost motion in the steering
box, proceed as follows:
1 Centralize the steering as described earlier in this
   section and disconnect the track rod from the drop
   arm as described in **Section 10:3**
2 Release the adjuster locknut (arrowed **D** in **FIG 10:8**).
   Rock the drop arm and screw in the adjuster until only
   slight backlash can be felt at the drop arm. Retighten
   the locknut.
3 Remove the centralizing rod and refit the track rod.

Lockstops:

There are no external lockstops on the power assisted steering linkage fitted to 420 models.

10:11 The steering column

Steering wheel removal and refitment:

Remove the four screws from beneath the wheel centre and detach the horn switch cover. Remove the setscrews and washers and detach the horn ring from the wheel. Refer to **FIG 10:13**, remove nuts 22 and 20, withdraw the wheel and collect the two half split cones 18. Refitment is the reverse of this procedure. Set the road wheels at straight-ahead and fit the steering wheel to match.

Column removal:

1 Disconnect the battery. Disconnect the indicator/ headlamp flashing switch and overdrive switch (if fitted) at the snap connectors.
2 Remove switch cover 43 in **FIG 10:13**. Identify and withdraw the three bulb holders.
3 **On automatic transmission models,** identify and disconnect the four cables from the starter/reverse light inhibitor switch. On **S type cars,** if a **righthand drive** model, unscrew the ratchet adjustment on the adjustment rod and lift out the ball joint on the crank lever. If a **lefthand drive** car, remove the four bolts securing the bracket to the bulkhead as the control rod which operates the cable passes through the bracket.
4 **On 420 models,** remove the four cap nuts and detach the trim panels covering the column above the parcel tray.
5 Release the hose clip which secures the bottom of the outer tube to the mounting bracket. Remove the horn switch cable from the contact at the bottom of the column.
6 Remove the pinch bolt securing the lower column top universal joint to the upper column and identify the relative position of the upper column and the universal joint socket.
7 Remove the two bolts, nuts and washers which secure the outer tube to the upper mounting bracket, collect any shims fitted and withdraw the steering column assembly.

Refitting:

In each case, refitting is the reverse of the removal procedure. Ensure that the road wheels are pointing straight-ahead and fit the column with the steering wheel positioned to match. On **automatic transmission** cars, ensure that the starter/reverse light inhibitor switch is correctly set as described in **Section 7:7**.

Disconnect the upper column from the lower:

On **S type cars,** disconnect the upper column from the lower by removing the spring clip **B** in **FIG 10:13**, the retaining ring **C** and the plastic thrust bearing **A**.

On **S type and 420 models,** remove the pinch bolt from the upper universal joint and draw back the inner upper column by pulling on the steering wheel until its splines are clear of the joint socket.

10:12 Fault diagnosis

(a) Wheel wobble

1 Unbalanced wheels and tyres
2 Slack steering connections
3 Incorrect steering geometry
4 Excessive play in steering gear
5 Broken or weak front springs
6 Worn hub bearings

(b) Wander

1 Check 2, 3 and 4 in (a)
2 Front and rear suspension out of line
3 Uneven tyre pressures
4 Uneven tyre wear
5 Ineffective dampers

(c) Heavy steering

1 Check 3 in (a)
2 Very low tyre pressures
3 Neglected lubrication
4 Wheels out of track
5 Steering gear maladjusted
6 Steering columns bent
7 Upper steering column bushes tight

(d) Lost motion

1 Loose steering wheel, worn splines
2 Worn universal joints or flexible coupling
3 Worn steering box and idler unit
4 Worn ball joints
5 Worn suspension system and wheel swivels

(e) Power assisted steering stiff or ineffective

1 Low oil level in reservoir
2 System requires bleeding
3 Reservoir filter on S type cars requires renewal
4 Pump drive belt slipping or broken
5 Worn pump, leaking valves
6 Worn steering box seals or broken piston rings
7 Blocked hose

CHAPTER 11

THE BRAKING SYSTEM

11:1 Description

S type cars and 420 models have vacuum servo assisted hydraulically operated disc brakes. Each front wheel has a rigidly mounted caliper which straddles a brake disc attached to the hub. The inboard brake discs which serve the rear wheels are attached to the final drive output shafts and their main calipers also carry the independent handbrake calipers which are cable operated. The hydraulic load applied to the front friction pads is greater than that applied to the rear pads. This gives a differential braking effect in favour of the front wheels. Adjustment for friction pad wear is automatic both in the main calipers and the handbrake units.

A $6\frac{7}{8}$ inch type servo unit is fitted to earlier S type cars while later models have an 8 inch type. S type units operate a single-line hydraulic system in which the front and rear brakes are served by a slave cylinder which has a single piston. When the brake footpedal, which is connected to the hydraulic master cylinder, is depressed fluid pressure is generated in the master cylinder. This pressure is boosted by the vacuum servo unit which is activated by depression in the engine inlet manifold. The boosted hydraulic pressure is transmitted to the brakes through a system of metal and flexible pipes. This system is covered in **Section 11:4**.

420 models have a dual-line system. The slave cylinder incorporates two pistons in tandem and either, in the event of failure, will operate independently. One hydraulic line serves the front brakes and a second line serves the rear. This system is covered in **Section 11:6**.

11:2 Maintenance

Brake fluid level:

On S type cars, the single reservoir is attached to the wing valance on the driver's side. On 420 righthand drive models, one reservoir is attached to each valance while on lefthand drive cars, both are fitted to the lefthand valance.

Every 3000 miles top up to the mark 'Fluid Level' above the fixing strap. The level can be seen through the plastic reservoir. **Do not overfill.** Disconnect the two cables and unscrew the filler cap. Top up and insert the combined filler and float slowly. Screw down the cap and reconnect the cables. A fluid level indicator pin is provided between the two terminals. Press this down and allow it to return to its normal position. If it can then be lifted between finger and thumb, the reservoir requires topping up. Use only recommended fluid (Castrol/Girling Crimson Clutch/Brake fluid).

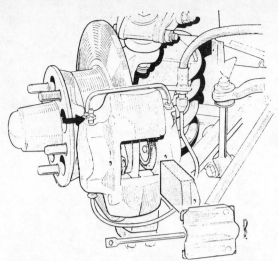

FIG 11:1 Friction pad removal. The bleed screw is arrowed

Brake servo air filter:

Service the air filter on **S type cars** every 6000 miles. On $6\frac{7}{8}$ inch type servos the air filter, which is attached to the righthand wing valance adjacent to the radiator header tank, should be removed and washed in **methylated spirits.** After it has dried off, re-lubricate the wire mesh with **brake fluid.** On 8 inch type servos the air filter is mounted on the control valve assembly. Clean off light dust with low pressure air or fit a new element. **Do not use any type of cleaning fluid.**

Service the air filter on **420 models** every 12,000 miles. Refer to **FIG 11 : 5,** prise off cover 39 and remove washer 37. Wash the filter element 36 in clean, denatured alcohol, dry in air and reassemble. **Do not wet the element with oil or brake fluid.**

Preventive maintenance:

Regularly examine the friction pads. They should be renewed when worn down to a thickness of $\frac{1}{4}$ inch on **S type cars** and $\frac{1}{8}$ inch of **420 models.** Check the tightness of all pipes and unions and the condition of flexible hoses. Change the brake fluid every 2 years or 25,000 miles. Use

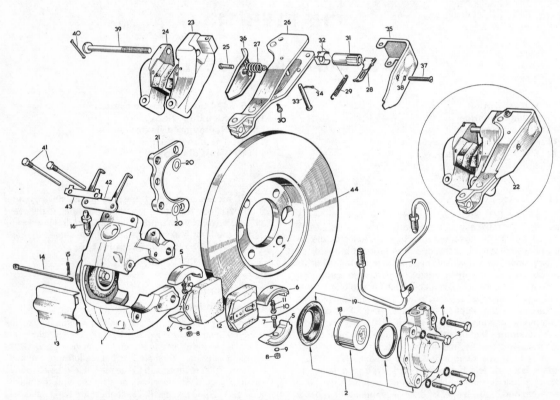

FIG 11:2 Components of the handbrake unit and S type brake caliper (rear illustrated)

Key to Fig 11 : 2   1 Caliper and piston assembly   2 Piston and cylinder assembly   3 Bolt   4 Shakeproof washer
5 Lefthand pad support   6 Righthand pad support   7 Bolt   8 Nut   9 Shakeproof washer   10 Screw
11 Shakeproof washer   12 Friction pad kit   13 Stop plate assembly   14 Pin   15 Clip   16 Bleed screw
17 Bridge pipe assembly   18 Piston   19 Seal kit   20 Shim   21 Adaptor plate   22 Righthand handbrake mechanism assembly
23 Righthand inner pad carrier   24 Righthand outer pad carrier   25 Anchor pin   26 Operating lever   27 Return spring
28 Pawl   29 Tension spring   30 Anchor pin   31 Adjusting nut   32 Friction spring   33 Hinge pin   34 Splitpin
35 Protection cover   36 Protection cover   37 Bolt   38 Washer   39 Bolt   40 Splitpin   41 Bolt
42 Retraction plate   43 Tabwasher   44 Disc

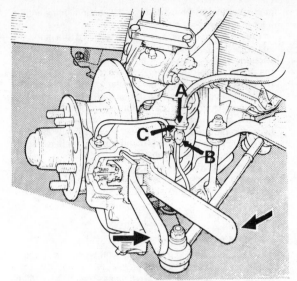

FIG 11:3 Resetting the pistons with special tool No. 10416. Arrows A, B and C are referred to in the text of Section 11:8

only recommended **fluid** and **observe absolute cleanliness** when working on all parts of the hydraulic system.

Handbrake cable adjustment:

This is described in **Section 11:9**.

11:3 S type brakes

Friction pad renewal:

Deal with only **one caliper at a time** so that fluid pressure does not interfere with reassembly.

Access to front pads requires the removal of the road wheel. Access to rear pads is through the forward aperture in the rear suspension crossmember (see **FIG 8:12**) and and requires the car to be on a lift or over a pit.

1 Refer to **FIG 11:1,** withdraw the spring clip and extract the retaining pin, stop plate and, using a hooked tool through the hole in the metal lug, extract the worn pads. These are items 15, 14, 13 and 12 in **FIG 11:2**.

2 Half empty the brake fluid from the reservoir and use special tool No. 10416 to lever back the pistons into their cylinders as shown in **FIG 11:3**. Watch the level in the reservoir and remove more fluid if necessary.

3 Insert the new pads, reassemble, check and top up the fluid level as described in **Section 11:2**.

Automatic adjustment mechanism:

The operation of the automatic adjustment retractor pin mechanism is shown diagramatically in **FIG 11:4**. In position **1** the brakes are off; in **2** the brakes are on and the retractor spring is under compression. In position **3** the brakes are on and the retractor bush has been drawn along the pin by the piston to take up pad wear and in **4** the brakes are off and normal clearance between the discs and the pad has been restored.

Removing and refitting front and rear calipers:

The procedure is as described in **Section 11:5** for 420 models.

Caliper overhaul:

Refer to **FIG 11:2** which shows the components of a rear caliper and note that except for the shape of caliper 1 and bridge pipe 17, items up to 20 are applicable to the front caliper unit.

1 Remove and thoroughly clean the caliper. Remove bridge pipe 17, four bolts 3 and washers 4 which secure each cylinder assembly 2 and dismount them from the caliper.

2 Disengage dust cover 19 from the groove round the cylinder block face, temporarily connect a block to the hydraulic pipe and, by very gentle application of the brake pedal, eject each piston in turn.

3 Extract seal 19 from the retaining groove in the cylinder bore ensuring, in doing so, that the bore is not damaged. Clean the pistons and cylinders with trichoethylene and inspect them. Obtain replacements if there are scores deep enough to result in loss of fluid.

4 Soak the new seal for some minutes in brake fluid and insert it wet into the retaining groove. Smear the bores and piston barrels with Dunlop Preservative Fluid, locate the piston onto the retractor pin, ensure correct alignment and press the piston into the bore. Fit the new dust cover after applying a small amount of Preservative Fluid to prevent corrosion. Check that the cover is correctly located in the piston groove and on the face spigot.

Reassembly and refitment is now the reverse of the earlier operations. On completion, bleed the brake unit as described in **Section 11:7** and check for leakage.

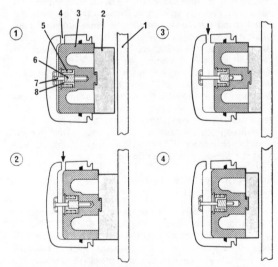

FIG 11:4 Automatic adjustment mechanism (S type cars)

Key to Fig 11:4   1 Brake disc   2 Friction pad   3 Piston
4 Fluid connection   5 Retractor spring   6 Retractor bush
7 Retractor pin   8 Spring retainer

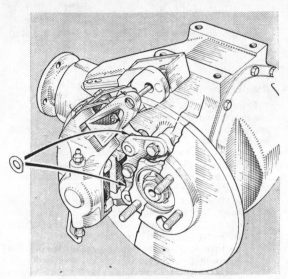

FIG 11:5   Caliper adjustment shims

Removing and refitting a front brake disc:

This procedure applies to S type cars and to 420 models.
Remove the wheel hub as described in **Section 9:3**.
Remove the five self-locking nuts and bolts and separate
the disc from the hub.

Refitting is the reverse of this operation. Disc 'run-out'
should not exceed .006 inch dial gauge reading.

Removing and refitting a rear brake disc:

This procedure applies to S type cars and to 420 models.
Remove the rear suspension unit as described in
Section 8:9. Refer to **Section 8:10** and remove the
road spring and damper units. Remove the four all-metal
self-locking nuts which secure the inner universal halfshaft joint to the final drive output flange and brake disc
and withdraw the halfshaft from the bolts. Note the
number of camber shims (41 in **FIG 8:13**) fitted.
Dismount the handbrake unit as described in **Section
11:9** and dismount the main caliper as described in
Section 11:5. Tap back the four bolts as far as possible,
lift the lower wishbone, hub carrier and halfshaft assembly
until the disc can be withdrawn from the bolts.

Refitting is the reverse of this procedure. Disc 'runout'
should not exceed .006 inch dial gauge reading. Ensure
that the camber shims are refitted.

11:4 S type hydraulic system

Vacuum servo unit:

The vacuum servo unit provides a degree of braking
assistance by boosting the hydraulic pressure which is
generated in the master cylinder when the brake pedal is
applied. It is installed in the hydraulic system between
the master cylinder and the four brake assemblies. The
layout of the system is illustrated diagramatically in
FIG 11:6. A cross-section of the $6\frac{7}{8}$ inch type is shown
in **FIG 11:7**. The unit consists mainly of a servo piston,
a hydraulic slave cylinder and an air control valve. Power
for its operation is derived from the difference between

atmospheric pressure and the partial vacuum in the engine
inlet manifold.

When the servo unit is in the released position, the
servo piston is held 'OFF' by a spring and the partial
vacuum in the reservoir is also present on each side of
the booster piston. When the brake pedal is applied,
hydraulic pressure from the master cylinder causes the
air control valve to admit atmospheric pressure which
acts upon the outer face of the servo piston driving it
inwards and a rod attached to its centre boosts the
hydraulic pressure within the slave cylinder thus assisting
the application of the brakes without any increase in the
load applied to the brake pedal.

An 8 inch type servo unit was introduced at the
following chassis numbers. 3.4 litre, 1B.2102RH and
1B.25286LH; 3.8 litre, 1B.52037RH and 1B.76292LH.
On this type the air filter is mounted directly onto the
control valve assembly.

Removal of servo unit:

This procedure is applicable to both types of servo unit.
Remove the front righthand road wheel and drain the
hydraulic system at that brake caliper. Refer to **FIG 11:6**.

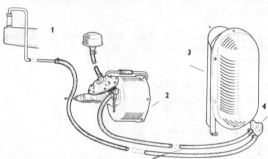

FIG 11:6   Layout of vacuum servo system (S type cars)

Key to Fig 11:6   1 Inlet manifold   2 Vacuum servo
3 Vacuum reservoir   4 Check valve

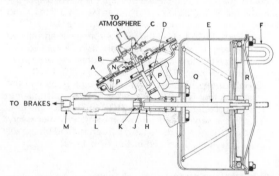

FIG 11:7   Section through $6\frac{7}{8}$ inch type servo unit

Key to Fig 11:7   **A** Diaphragm assembly   **B** Vacuum valve
C Air valve   **D** Air valve piston   **E** Servo piston pushrod
F Cylinder pipe   **H** Slave cylinder piston   **J** Rubber cup
K Spring guide   **L** Slave cylinder   **M** Adaptor
N Chamber above diaphragm assembly   **P** Chamber below
diaphragm assembly   **Q** Chamber inner
(vacuum) side of servo piston   **R** Chamber outer side of
vacuum piston: vacuum when brakes are off, atmospheric
pressure when brakes are being applied

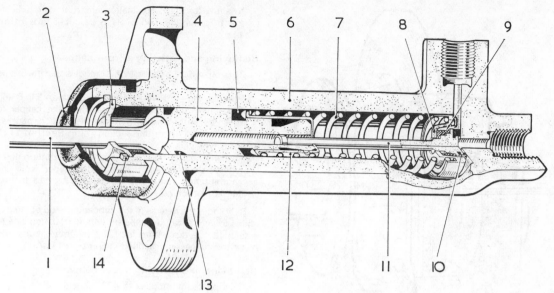

FIG 11:8 Cutaway view of a master cylinder (S type cars)

Key to Fig 11:8   1 Pushrod   2 Dust excluder   3 Dished washer   4 Piston   5 Cup seal   6 Body
7 Return spring   8 Spring support   9 Valve spring   10 Seal   11 Valve   12 Spring support   13 Sealing ring
14 Circlip

Disconnect the air cleaner hose from the air valve cover, the vacuum reserve tank hose at its banjo connection and the two rigid hydraulic pipes. Detach the clamp and support block from the valance inside the engine compartment by removing two nuts and bolts. Remove eight bolts and withdraw the unit. Detach the supporting cowl by removing three nuts.

It is not recommended that a vacuum servo unit be dismantled by an owner and, if internal trouble arises, rectification should be entrusted to a Main Agent or an exchange replacement should be obtained.

Refitting servo unit:

This is the reverse of the removal sequence for both types of servo unit.

The master cylinder:

FIG 11:8 shows a cutaway view of a master cylinder. Two of these units are fitted to S type cars. One operates in the braking system and the other in the clutch system. The removal, dismantling, reassembly and refitting procedures which are described in this section are also, as stated in **Section 5:6**, applicable to the clutch master cylinder.

The brake pedal is connected to the pushrod and **FIG 11:8** shows the master cylinder piston at about mid-stroke. Fluid forced from the cylinder passes to the vacuum servo unit through the pipe connection which is at right-angles to the cylinder bore. The fluid reservoir is connected to the other pipe connection which, in **FIG 11:8,** is shown closed by the seal on the end of the valve. The cup seal prevents reserve fluid flow. When the pedal is released, the return spring pushes the piston to the 'OFF' position. The length of the valve stem is such that the valve seal is held off its seat by the spring

support while the piston is in the 'OFF' position and fluid is free to flow from the reservoir into the cylinder. Immediately the piston starts to move, this port is sealed and fluid passes through the angled pipe connection. To ensure that the piston returns fully to the 'OFF' position, clearance is provided between the pushrod and the piston.

Removing and refitting the master cylinder:

Drain the reservoir and disconnect the two pipes from the master cylinder. Remove the clevis pin from the pushrod, remove the two flange nuts and dismount the unit. Refitting is the reverse of this procedure. Refill the reservoir and bleed the system as described in **Section 11:7.**

Dismantling the master cylinder to fit new seals:

1 Ease the lip of the dust excluder 2 in **FIG 11:8** from its groove. Remove the circlip 14 and withdraw the pushrod 1.

2 Withdraw the piston 4 and remove the two seals 5 and 13. Withdraw the valve assembly complete with springs and spring supports. Remove the seal 10 from the end of the valve.

Reassembly of the master cylinder:

1 Lubricate the new seals and the cylinder bore with brake fluid. Fit the seal to the end of the valve and ensure that the lip registers in the groove. Fit the seals to the piston.

2 Insert the piston into the spring support and ensure that the valve stem 11 enters the bore of the piston. Lubricate the piston with Girling Red Rubber Grease

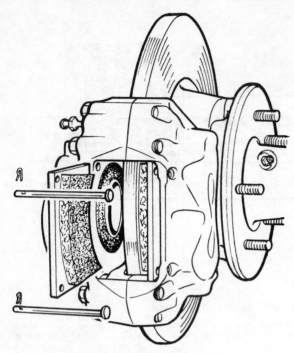

FIG 11:9 Friction pad removal

and slide the complete assembly into the cylinder bore taking care not to trap or distort the seals. Use a fitting sleeve if possible.

3 Position the pushrod and depress the piston so that the dished washer 3 may be fitted. Fit the circlip and check that it is fully engaged into its groove. Fill the dust excluder with Girling Red Rubber Grease and reseat it onto the cylinder

4 Refit the master cylinder as described earlier.

Flushing the hydraulic system:

If the brake fluid becomes thick after long service or if the vehicle has been laid up for some time, the system should be drained, flushed and refilled with fresh fluid. The procedure is described in **Section 11:6**.

11:5 420 type brakes

Friction pad renewal:

Deal with one caliper at a time so that fluid pressure does not interfere with reassembly.

Access to front pads requires the removal of the road wheel. Access to rear pads is through the forward aperture in the rear suspension crossmember (see **FIG 8:12**) and requires the car to be on a lift or over a pit.

1 Refer to **FIG 11:9**, withdraw the spring clips, extract the two retaining pins and withdraw the worn pads.

2 Half empty the brake fluid from the reservoirs and, using a suitable lever, force the pistons back into their cylinders. Watch the levels in the reservoirs and remove more fluid if necessary.

3 Insert new pads and reassemble. Note that the retaining pins must not be forced into their locating holes and check that the pads are free to move slightly

to allow for brake application and automatic adjustment. Top up the fluid levels as described in **Section 11:2**.

Removing and refitting a front caliper:

This procedure applies to 420 models and to S type cars.

1 Remove the road wheel. Refer to **Section 11:8** and disconnect the fluid feed pipe. Plug the caliper to preclude entry of dirt. Remove the friction pads as described earlier in this section (or in **Section 11:3** for S type cars).

2 Discard the locking wire from the two mounting bolts, remove the bolts and dismount the caliper. Note any centralization shims (20 in **FIG 11:2** or 13 in **FIG 11:10**) which may be fitted.

Refitting is the reverse of this procedure. Add or remove shims to centralize the caliper to within .010 inch side to side with the disc. Wire lock the mounting bolts and bleed the caliper as described in **Section 11:7**.

Removing and refitting a rear caliper:

This procedure applies to 420 models and to S type cars.

1 Remove the rear suspension as described in **Section 8:9**. Dismount the handbrake unit as described in **Section 11:9**. Refer to **Section 11:8**, remove the hydraulic feed pipe and blank off the orifice to preclude entry of dirt.

2 Remove the friction pads from the caliper as described earlier in this Section (or in **Section 11:3** for S type cars). Remove the forward road spring and damper unit as described in **Section 8:10**, remove the four all-metal self-locking nuts from the halfshaft inner universal joint, withdraw the joint, allow the hub carrier to move outwards and support it in this position.

3 Ensure that the camber shims (41 in **FIG 8:13**) do not become displaced. Discard the locking wire, remove the two mounting bolts, dismount the caliper and note any centralization shims (20 in **FIG 11:2** or 12 in **FIG 11:11**) which may be fitted at the points shown in **FIG 11:5**.

Refitting is the reverse of this sequence. Before wire locking the mounting bolts, temporarily fit the handbrake pivot bolts (41 in **FIG 11:2** or 16 in **FIG 11:11**) and check that the measurement between each pivot bolt shank and the disc is equal. If not, add or remove shims to centralize the caliper. On completion of reassembly, bleed the caliper as described in **Section 11:7**.

Caliper overhaul:

Each caliper unit comprises two paired halves bolted together by **four bolts which must not be disturbed.**

The components of the front caliper are shown in **FIG 11:10** and those of the rear unit in **FIG 11:11**. It will be noted that the outboard half of the front caliper contains two pistons. Except for this difference, the procedure for the overhaul of front and rear calipers is the same. **No petrol, paraffin or mineral fluid of any kind may be be used for component cleaning.**

1 Remove and thoroughly clean the caliper. Release the dust covers (5 and 7 in **FIG 11:10** and 4 in **FIG 11:11**) from their grooves, pack rag between the pistons, apply

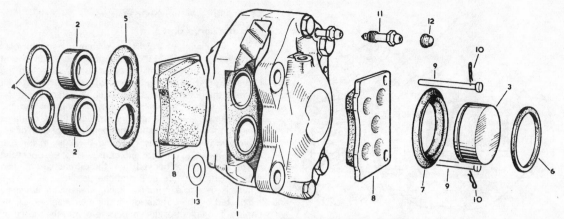

FIG 11:10   Components of 420 type front brake caliper

Key to Fig 11:10   1 Righthand front caliper assembly   2 Outer piston   3 Inner piston   4 Seal   5 Dust seal (outer piston)
6 Seal   7 Dust seal (inner piston)   8 Friction pad kit   9 Pin   10 Clip   11 Bleed screw   12 Dust cap   13 Shim

air pressure to the fluid feed orifice and blow the pistons from their bores. Extract the pistons.

2 Extract seals 4 and 6 or 3 from the retaining groove in the cylinder bore ensuring that, in doing so, the bore is not damaged. Clean the pistons and cylinders with Girling Cleaning Fluid and inspect for serviceability. It may be possible to clean up abrasion or corrosion with fine steel wool (be sure to remove all traces and particles before proceeding) otherwise obtain new parts.

3 Soak the new seals for some minutes in brake fluid and insert them wet. Locate the outer lips of the dust covers into the cylinder bore grooves, lubricate the bores and pistons with brake fluid, smear the bore of the dust

covers with Girling Red Rubber Grease and, as shown in **FIG 11:12**, insert the piston (closed end first) through the dust cover. Engage the dust cover lip into the groove in the piston.

4 Apply even pressure and force the pistons into their cylinders. Further reassembly and refitment is now the reverse of the dismantling and removal procedure.

On completion, bleed the calipers as described in **Section 11:7**, apply full brake pressure and check for leakage.

Removing and refitting a front or rear brake disc:

The procedure is as described in **Section 11:3** for S type models.

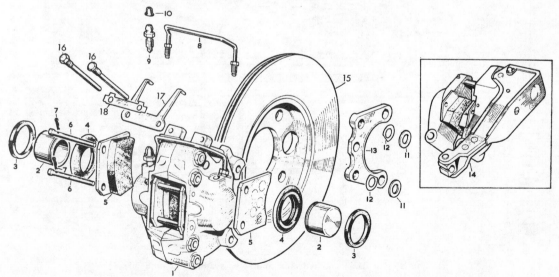

FIG 11:11   Components of the 420 type rear brake caliper. Inset shows the handbrake unit

Key to Fig 11:11   1 Rear caliper assembly   2 Piston   3 Seal   4 Dust seal   5 Friction pad   6 Pin   7 Clip
8 Bridge pipe   9 Bleed screw   10 Dust cap   11 Distance piece   12 Shim   13 Adaptor plate
14 Handbrake mechanism assembly   15 Disc assembly   16 Bolt   17 Retraction plate   18 Tabwasher

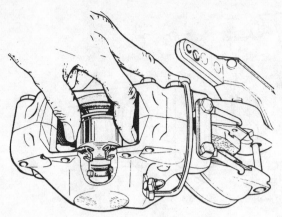

FIG 11:12 Fitting a caliper piston

11:6 420 type hydraulic system

Vacuum servo unit:

The layout of the braking system is shown diagramatically in FIG 11:13. The dual-line vacuum unit provides a degree of braking assistance by boosting the hydraulic pressure which is generated in the master cylinder **N** when the brake pedal is depressed. It is installed in the hydraulic system between the master cylinder and the four brake calipers. The tandem slave cylinder **L** contains two pistons which, operating independently of each other, serve two hydraulic lines. One line, **J** relates to the rear and the other, **K** to the front brakes. Power for the operation of the servo unit is derived from the difference between atmospheric pressure at **F** and the partial vacuum at **E** which is available from the vacuum reservoir which is evacuated by the depression in the inlet manifold of the engine. The layout of the vacuum reservoir, the pipe runs to the inlet manifold, check valve, servo unit and reaction valve are shown in FIG 11:14. The components of the duel-line servo unit are shown in FIG 11:15.

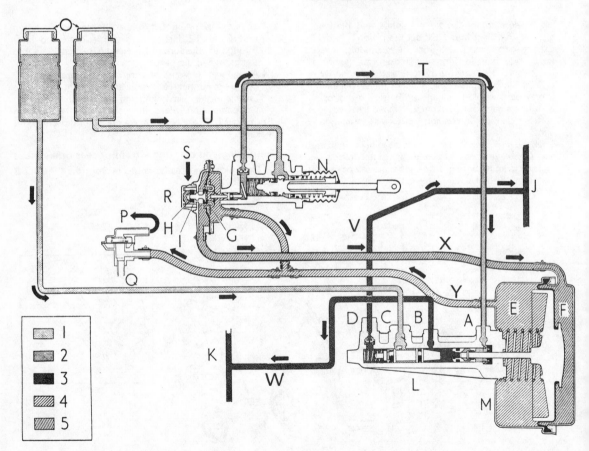

FIG 11:13 Dual-line hydraulic and servo system (420 models)

Key to Fig 11:13   1 Fluid at feed pressure   2 Fluid at master cylinder delivery pressure   3 Fluid at system delivery pressure
4 Vacuum   5 Air at atmospheric pressure   A Primary chamber (slave cylinder)   B Outlet port (front brakes)
C Inlet port (secondary piston)   D Outlet port (rear brakes)   E Vacuum   F Air pressure   G Diaphragm   H Filter
I Air control   J To rear brakes   K To front brakes   L Tandem slave cylinder   M Vacuum cylinder   N Master cylinder
O Fluid reservoir   P To manifold   Q To reserve   R Reaction valve   S Air inlet   T to Y see text

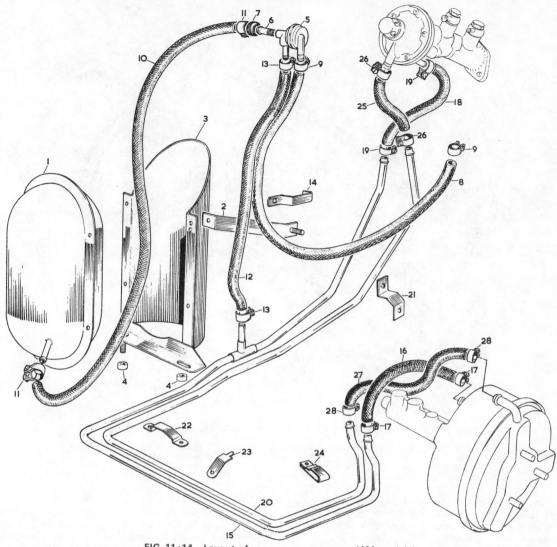

FIG 11:14   Layout of vacuum servo system (420 models)

Key to Fig 11:14   1 Reservac tank assembly   2 Steady bracket   3 Stoneguard   4 Distance piece   5 Check valve
6 Adaptor   7 Grommet   8 Vacuum hose   9 Clip   10 Vacuum hose   11 Clip   12 Vacuum hose   13 Clip   14 Clip
15 Vacuum pipe   16 Vacuum hose   17 Clip   18 Vacuum hose   19 Clip   20 Pipe   21 Clip   22 Clip   23 Clip
24 Clip   25 Hose   26 Clip   27 Hose   28 Clip

In the event of failure of pipe **T** or **U** in **FIG 11:13**, the reaction valve **R** will be actuated mechanically by the master cylinder piston, atmospheric air will pass to **F** and fluid at boosted pressure will actuate both front and rear brakes. Failure of pipe **V** which feeds the rear brakes will result in the slave cylinder secondary piston travelling the full extent of the bore, blanking off the outlet to pipline **V** and allowing the primary piston to feed fluid to the front brakes in the normal way. Failure of pipe **W** which feeds the front brakes results in the primary piston moving down the bore until it contacts the secondary piston. The two pistons will then travel together along the bore to apply the rear brakes. In the event of failure or leakage in pipes

X or **Y**, both front and rear brakes will be applied by fluid at (unboosted) master cylinder pressure.

Removal of servo unit :

Drain the reservoir feeding the servo unit slave cylinder. Remove the lefthand front road wheel. Remove two nuts and two setscrews securing the fibreglass cover and mounting bracket and withdraw the cover. Disconnect three flexible hoses and three pipe unions from the servo unit and slave cylinder and blank off all open orifices to preclude entry of dirt. Remove four screws securing the servo unit mounting bracket, withdraw the unit and bracket as an assembly and separate by unscrewing four nuts.

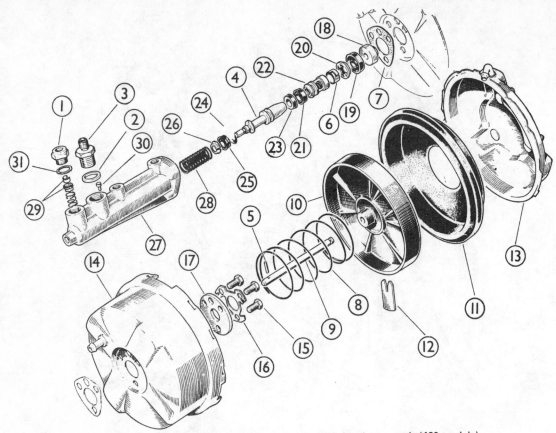

FIG 11:15 Components of the tandem slave cylinder and servo unit (420 models)

Key to Fig **11:15**   1 Outlet connection   2 Gasket   3 Inlet connection   4 Piston   5 Pin   6 Retaining clip   7 Gasket   8 Spring   9 Pushrod   10 Diaphragm support   11 Diaphragm   12 Key   13 Cover   14 Vacuum cylinder shell   15 Screw   16 Locking plate   17 Abutment plate   18 Bearing   19 Seal   20 Spacer   21 Cup   22 Piston   23 Cup   24 Piston washer   25 Seal   26 Retainer   27 Slave cylinder body   28 Spring   29 Trap wire   30 Stop pin   31 Gasket

It is not recommended that a vacuum servo unit be dismantled by an owner and, if internal trouble arises, rectification should be entrusted to a Main Agent or an exchange replacement should be obtained.

Refitting servo unit:

This is the reverse of the removal sequence. Refill the reservoir and bleed the system as described in **Section 11:7**.

The master cylinder and reaction valve:

The components of the master cylinder and reaction valve are illustrated in **FIG 11:16**. Basically the master cylinder functions in the same manner as the S type master cylinder which is described in **Section 11:4** and, when the brake pedal is applied, it generates hydraulic pressure which is then boosted by the servo unit but mounted on the master cylinder is the reaction valve. The function of this valve has been referred to earlier in this Section.

Removing and refitting the master cylinder:

Drain the fluid reservoir feeding the master cylinder. Disconnect hoses 18 and 25 in **FIG 11:14** from the

reaction valve and the two hydraulic pipes from the master cylinder. Remove the splitpin, withdraw the clevis pin and disconnect the pushrod 19 in **FIG 11:16** which is accessible from inside the car. Remove two nuts and washers and detach the master cylinder from the brake pedal housing.

It is not recommended that this type of master cylinder or the reaction valve should be dismantled by an owner and, if internal trouble arises, rectification should be entrusted to a Main Agent or an exchange replacement should be obtained.

Refitting is the reverse of this procedure. Fill the reservoir with recommended brake fluid, bleed the system as described in **Section 11:7** and check for leaks.

Flushing the hydraulic system:

If the brake fluid becomes thick after long service or if the vehicle has been laid up for some time, the system should be drained, flushed and refilled with fresh fluid. The procedure is as follows and is applicable to 420 models and to S type cars.

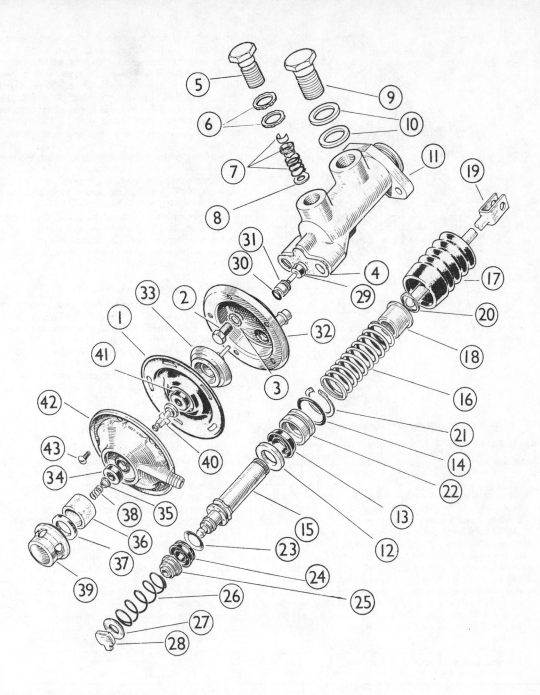

FIG 11:16   Components of the master cylinder and reaction valve (420 models)

Key to Fig 11:16   1 Diaphragm   2 Screw   3 Shakeproof washer   4 Gasket   5 Banjo bolt   6 Washers   7 Trap valve body
8 Washer   9 Banjo bolt   10 Copper gasket   11 Body   12 Bearing   13 Secondary cup   14 Seal   15 Piston
16 Return spring   17 Rubber boot   18 Spring retainer   19 Pushrod   20 Spirolox circlip   21 Circlip   22 Bearing
23 Piston washer   24 Main cup   25 Retainer   26 Spring   27 Retainer   28 Lever   29 Seal   30 Seal   31 Piston
32 Valve housing   33 Diaphragm support   34 Valve rubber   35 Valve cap   36 Filter   37 Sorbo washer   38 Spring
39 Filter cover   40 Valve stem   41 Valve rubber   42 Valve cover   43 Screw

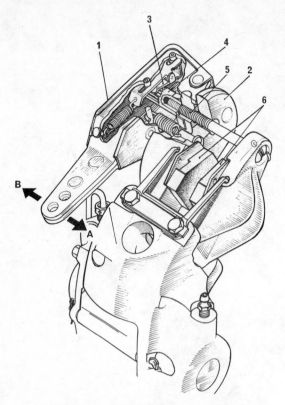

FIG 11:17 The handbrake caliper unit

Key to Fig 11:17   **A** Brakes released   **B** Brakes applied
1 Operating lever   2 Pad carrier assembly   3 Pawl assembly
4 Adjuster nut   5 Adjuster bolt   6 Friction pad

1 Connect one end of a rubber tube to a caliper bleed screw and slacken the screw by a full turn. Lead the other end of the tube into a container.

2 Depress the brake pedal quickly and allow it to return unassisted. Pause, then repeat the cycle until no more fluid is expelled from the caliper. Repeat the operation on the remaining three calipers and discard the fluid.

3 Fill the reservoir(s) with industrial methylated spirit and flush this through the system, one caliper at a time, by pumping the brake pedal as before. Top up the reservoir level(s) repeatedly and continue until at least two pints of spirit has been flushed through each caliper.

4 Ensure that all methylated spirit has finally been expelled before filling the system with fresh recommended brake fluid.

5 Bleed the system as described in **Section 11:7**.

11:7 Bleeding the system

This procedure is only necessary if air has entered the hydraulic system because the level in the brake fluid reservoir(s) has dropped so low that air has been drawn into the system or because part of the system has been dismantled. It is important to keep the reservoir(s) topped up during the bleeding operation to avoid air being drawn into the system. Do not use fluid which has been bleed

through the system to replenish the reservoir(s) as it will be aerated. Use fresh fluid straight from the tin.

Check that all connections are tight and all bleed screws closed. The bleed screws are: **S type** front, arrowed in **FIG 11:1**, rear, item 16 in **FIG 11:2. 420 models** front, item 11 in **FIG 11:10**; rear, item 9 in **FIG 11:11**. Commence the following procedure which requires two operators, with the lefthand rear caliper. Repeat the operation on the righthand rear and then on the front calipers.

1 Attach a rubber tube to the bleed screw and immerse its free end in a small quantity of brake fluid in a clean glass jar. Slacken the bleed screw.

2 Actuate the brake pedal slowly backwards and forwards through its full stroke. When air ceases to bubble through the fluid in the jar, keep the pedal depressed, close the bleed screw firmly and release the pedal.

3 On completion, top up the fluid reservoir(s). Apply normal pressure to the pedal for some minutes and check for fluid leaks.

11:8 Removing a flexible hose

Never attempt to remove a hose by turning either end unless it is disconnected from its metal pipe and from its bracket. Refer to **FIG 11:3** and unscrew the metal pipeline union nut 'B'. Next, hold the flexible hose hexagon 'A' with a spanner, remove locknut 'C' which secures the hose to the bracket. The other end of the flexible hose may now be unscrewed without twisting the hose itself. Fitting a hose is the reverse of this procedure.

11:9 The handbrake
Handbrake calipers:

FIG 11:17 shows a cutaway view of a mechanically operated handbrake caliper unit which is attached to each of the rear main calipers. These units operate on the rear brake discs but form an independent system with their own automatically adjusted friction pads. **FIG 11:2** shows their components which are items 23 to 43 and the assembled unit is shown in the inset in **FIGS 11:2** and **11:11**.

When the handbrake is applied, lever 1 in **FIG 11:17** is pulled away from the pad carrier 2 in the direction of the arrow **B** and the friction pads 6 are drawn together onto the brake disc. Under normal conditions, when the lever is released, pawl 3 returns to its original position and normal running clearance between the disc and the pads is maintained. When the clearance increases due to wear, the pawl rotates ratchet adjuster nut 4 and draws the adjuster bolt 5 inwards. This brings the pads closer together and normal running clearance is restored.

Friction pad renewal:

With the car on a ramp or over a pit, remove and discard the splitpin, withdraw the clevis pin and disconnect the cable fork end from one lever and withdraw the outer cable from the trunnion on the other. Refer to **FIG 11:2**. Untab and remove pivot bolts 41, tabwashers 43 and retractor plates 42. Move the units rearwards around the discs and dismount them. Withdraw the worn pads by slackening the nuts on the outer face of each carrier and, using a hooked tool to engage the hole in the pad securing plate, pull out the pads.

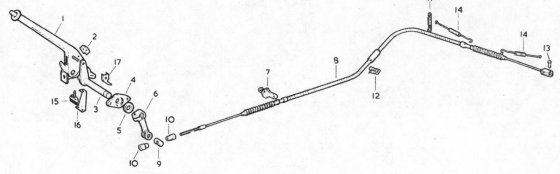

FIG 11:18 Components of the handbrake operating cable

Key to Fig 11:18 1 Handbrake assembly 2 Coverplate 3 Shaft assembly 4 Shaft housing 5 Rubber seal 6 Lever 7 Cable abutment bracket 8 Cable 9 Trunnion 10 Adjusting nut 11 Spring 12 Clip 13 Clevis pin 14 Return spring 15 Handbrake warning light switch 16 Bracket 17 Bracket

Fit new pads, short face upwards, ensure that each locates the head of the retaining bolt and tighten the nuts.

Reposition the units to the main calipers, fit new retraction plates but leave the pivot bolts slack at this stage. Pull and release each lever repeatedly until the ratchet ceases to operate (this indicates that the correct clearance between the new pads and the disc has been obtained), reconnect the outer and inner cables and apply the handbrake reasonably hard. Tighten and retab the pivot bolts.

Should the automatic adjustment mechanism require to be reset, remove splitpin 40 in **FIG 11:2** from the head of the adjuster bolt 39 and slacken this bolts until there is about $\frac{1}{4}$ inch free movement between the bolt head and the carrier. Pull the pad carriers away from the disc, bending the retraction plate fingers until there is $\frac{1}{16}$ inch clearance between each pad and the disc. Take up the free movement of the adjuster bolt, tightening until the head is in light contact with the pad carrier and lock with a new splitpin.

Handbrake cable mechanism:

FIG 11:18 shows the components of the handbrake lever and cable mechanism. The forward end of the cable outer casing is secured to the body bracket 7 and the rear end, by reaction, operates the trunioned lever (26 in **FIG 11:2**) of the righthand brake unit when the inner cable, which is attached to the plain lever of the lefthand unit, is operated.

Handbrake cable adjustment:

Release the handbrake, refer to **FIG 11:18** and back off adjusting nut 10 at the rear of trunnion 9. Check that the handbrake unit levers are in the fully release position (**A** in **FIG 11:17**) and, by means of the forward nut 10, adjust the cable to a point just short of where the caliper levers begin to move. Tighten the rear adjusting nut to lock against the trunnion.

11:10 Fault diagnosis

(a) 'Spongy' pedal

1 Leak in hydraulic system
2 Worn master cylinder
3 Defective master cylinder seals
4 Defective caliper cylinder seals
5 Air in hydraulic system

(b) Excessive pedal movement

1 Check 1 and 5 in (a)
2 Excessive friction pad wear
3 Very low fluid level in reservoir(s)

(c) Brakes grab or pull to one side

1 Distorted discs
2 Wet or oily friction pads
3 Loose caliper unit
4 Disc loose on front hub
5 Worn suspension or steering connections
6 Uneven tyre pressures
7 Seized piston in caliper cylinder
8 Blocked flexible or rigid pipe
9 Seized handbrake caliper unit
10 Seized handbrake cable
11 Broken handbrake pull-off spring

(d) Absence of servo assistance

1 Air filter blocked
2 Vacuum or air pipe blocked or broken
3 Check valve leaking
4 Reaction valve defective (420 models)
5 Vacuum tank punctured
6 Servo unit inoperative due to internal fault

(e) Only front or rear brakes operative (420 models)

1 Only front brakes operative, pipe to rear calipers broken
2 Only rear brakes operative, pipe to front calipers broken

NOTES

CHAPTER 12

THE ELECTRICAL EQUIPMENT

12 : 1 Description

Models covered by this manual have 12-volt electrical systems. Wiring diagrams are given in Technical Data in the Appendix section. **FIG 14 : 1** relates to S type cars and **FIG 14 : 2** to 420 models.

The battery is mounted on the righthand side at the rear of the engine compartment and the charging circuit control on the lefthand side. The fuses are located behind the instrument panel.

Instructions for the servicing of the electrical equipment are given in this chapter. It will be accepted that it is not sensible to try to repair units which are seriously defective, electrically or mechanically. Such equipment should be replaced by new units obtained on an exchange basis. It must be stressed that accurate meters are essential when checking or altering control settings.

S type cars:

The positive battery terminal is earthed. The generator is a DC machine and the charging circuit control box embodies a cut-out, current regulation and voltage regulation. The starter motor engages through a Bendix pinion.

420 models:

The negative battery terminal is earthed. The generator is an AC machine and this three-phase alternator incorporates an air-cooled transistorized (six silicon diodes) rectifier which, since it precludes reverse current flow, eliminates the need for a cut-out. The inherent self-regulating characteristics of the alternator make a current regulator unnecessary. The starter motor incorporates positive engagement of the pinion.

12 : 2 The battery

S type cars have the positive and 420 models have the negative battery terminal earthed. **Serious damage will occur if the terminal connections are reversed.**

To maintain the performance of the 12-volt lead/acid type battery it is essential to carry out the following operations. This is particularly so in winter when heavy current demands have to be met.

Keep the top and surrounding parts of the battery dry and clean as dampness can cause current leakage.

Keep metal parts free of corrosion. Clean, if necessary, with diluted ammonia. Paint the battery mounting with

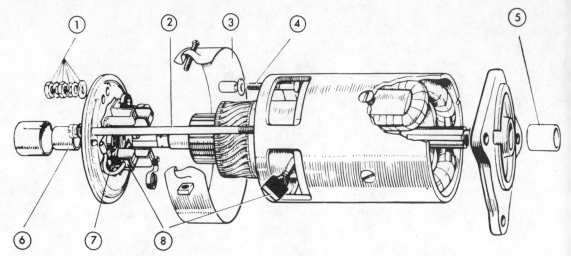

FIG 12:1   Components of the starter motor fitted to S type cars

Key to Fig 12:1   1 Terminal nuts and washers   2 Through-bolt   3 Cover band   4 Terminal post   5 Bearing bush
6 Bearing bush   7 Brush spring   8 Brushes

anti-sulphuric paint and smear the terminal posts, after removing the cables and cleaning, with petroleum jelly. Remake the connections firmly.

Test the condition of the cells with a hydrometer after topping up the electrolyte level with distilled water to just above the separators. **Never add neat acid. If it is necessary to prepare new electrolyte due to loss or spillage, add sulphuric acid to distilled water. It is highly dangerous to add water to acid.**

The indications from the readings of the specific gravity are as follows:

For climates below 80°F or 27°C:

Cell fully charged   Specific gravity 1.270 to 1.290
Cell half-discharged   Specific gravity 1.190 to 1.210
Cell discharged   Specific gravity 1.110 to 1.130

For climates above 80°F or 27°C:

Cell fully charged   Specific gravity 1.210 to 1.230
Cell half-discharged   Specific gravity 1.120 to 1.150
Cell discharged   Specific gravity 1.050 to 1.070

These figures assume an electrolyte temperature of 60°F or 16°C. If the electrolyte temperature exceeds this, add .002 to the reading for each 5°F or 3°C rise. Subtract .002 for any corresponding drop below 60°F or 16°C.

If the charge state of the battery is low, take the car for a long daylight run or put it on a charger at 5 amps with the vent plugs removed until it gasses freely. Refrain from using a naked light when it is gassing. If the battery is to stand unused for long periods, give a freshening-up charge every month. It will be ruined if left uncharged.

12:3 The starter

The components of the M.45G type starter fitted to S type cars are shown in **FIG 12:1**. The solenoid switch is separately mounted. **FIG 12:2** shows the components and integral solenoid of the positive pre-engaged pinion type of starter which is fitted to 420 models.

Examining the commutator and brush gear:

Refer to **FIG 12:1** or **FIG 12:2** and remove the cover band. Hold back each brush spring in turn and pull gently on its flexible connector. Relieve any sluggishness by polishing the side of the brush on a smooth file and replace each brush in its original position. Renew brushes which have worn to less than $\frac{5}{16}$ inch in length by the procedure which is described later. Check that the spring tension on an S type is within the range 30 to 40 oz. and, on a 420 model, 52 oz. Clean the commutator by turning it against a petrol-moistened cloth.

Tests for a starter which does not operate:

Check the condition of the battery and its connections. If it is charged, switch on the lights and operate the starter switch. Current is reaching the starter if the lights go dim. If the lights do not dim, check the switch, solenoid and all cable connections through to the battery. Check the pinion drive as described later. If these are in order, remove the starter.

Removing the starter, S type cars:

Disconnect the battery earth cable and the cable from the starter motor. On automatic transmission models, disconnect the filler tube extension and blank off at the rubber joint to prevent escape of oil. Release the gland at the gearbox and swing the tube away. From below, remove two nuts, support the starter and withdraw the securing strap. From above, remove the top bolt and withdraw the starter from beneath the car.

Removing the starter, 420 models:

Remove the bonnet and oil filter as described in **Sections 1:2** and **1:13**. Remove the battery and disconnect the cables from the starter/solenoid unit. Remove two setscrews and washers, the bottom one from beneath. This will require a socket spanner and approximately 30

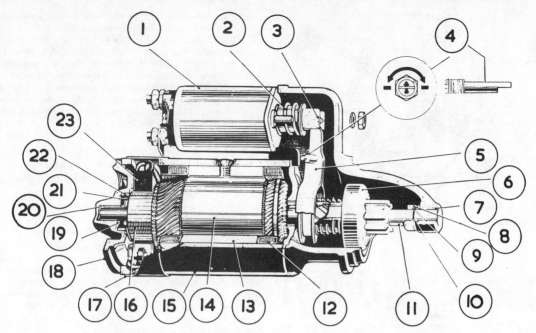

FIG 12:2 Components of the starter motor fitted to 420 models

Key to Fig 12:2   1 Actuating solenoid   2 Return spring   3 Clevis pin   4 Eccentric pivot pin   5 Engaging lever
6 Roller clutch   7 Porous bronze bush   8 Thrust collar   9 Jump ring   10 Thrust ring   11 Armature shaft extension
12 Field ring   13 Pole shoes   14 Armature   15 Yoke   16 Commutator   17 Band cover   18 CE bracket
19 Thrust washer   20 Porous bronze bush   21 Brake shoes and cross-peg   22 Brake ring   23 Brushes

inches of extension. Enter the spanner from behind the gearbox. A second operator must guide the spanner from the engine bay. Dismount the starter unit through the chassis frame.

Dismantling the starter, S type cars:

Refer to **FIG 12:1**. Remove the cover band, hold back the springs 7 and lift out the brushes 8. Remove the terminal nuts and washers 1 and unscrew and withdraw the through-bolts 2. Lift off the commutator end bracket and withdraw the mounting end bracket complete with armature and pinion drive.

Dismantling the starter, 420 models:

1 Disconnect the copper link from between the solenoid terminal and starter yoke. Remove the two securing nuts, detach the extension cable and withdraw the solenoid carefully disengaging the plunger from lever 5 in **FIG 12:2**.

2 Remove the cover band 17, hold back the springs and lift out the brushes. Unscrew and withdraw the two through-bolts, separate the commutator end bracket 18 and yoke 15 from the intermediate and drive end brackets and withdraw the rubber seal.

3 Slacken the pivot securing nut (see inset), unscrew and withdraw the eccentric pin 4. Separate the drive end bracket from the intermediate bracket and armature assembly. Remove thrust collar 8, prise jump ring 9 from its groove and slide the drive assembly and intermediate bracket from the shaft.

Renewing the brushes, both types:

Two brushes (see **FIG 12:3**) are connected to terminal eyelets and two to the field coils. The flexible connectors must be unsoldered and the connectors of the new brushes securely soldered in their place. New brushes are preformed and do not require to be bedded to the commutator.

Servicing the commutator, both types:

Follow the procedure described in **Section 12:4** for the C.42 generator commutator but **do not undercut the insulation between the segments.**

Testing the field coils, both types:

Test the continuity, with the armature removed, using a 12-volt supply and test lamp between the terminal post and each field brush in turn. Follow apparently satisfactory continuity by testing for insulation breakdown with a 110-volt AC supply and test lamp connected between the terminal post and a clean part of the starter body. If the lamp lights, defective coil or terminal post insulation is indicated. Renewal of field coils should be entrusted to a Service Station.

Bearing renewal, both types of end brackets:

Withdraw the worn bearing bushes. New bushes must not be reamed or their porosity will be impaired. Allow the new bushes to stand fully immersed in SAE.30/40 engine oil for 24 hours before pressing them into the brackets. Use

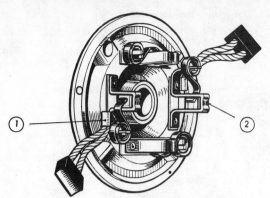

FIG 12:3   Commutator end bracket

Key to Fig 12:3   1 Terminal eyelet   2 Brush box

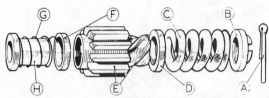

FIG 12:4   Components of the pinion drive (S type cars)

Key to Fig 12:4   A Splitpin   **B** Shaft nut   **C** Main spring
D Washer   **E** Screwed sleeve and pinion   **F** Collar
G Restraining spring   **H** Restraining spring sleeve

a shouldered mandrel with a highly polished pilot of the same diameter as the armature shaft and slightly longer than the bushes.

Bearing renewal, intermediate bracket, 420 models:

Press out the worn indented bronze bearing bush. After pressing in the new bush, lubricate the bearing surface with Rocol 'Molypad' or similar molybdenized non-creep oil.

The pinion drive, S type cars:

Refer to **FIG 12:4**. To dismantle, remove splitpin A, hold the squared shaft extension in a spanner and unscrew shaft nut B. Parts C to H may then be lifted off. Renew broken springs or worn screwed sleeve or pinion. Clean and reassemble but use no lubricant on the screwed sleeve or pinion as this, by causing dirt to adhere, will cause the drive to stick. A jammed starter pinion can usually be released by using a spanner on the square end of the shaft after removing the push-fit cover cap.

The pinion drive and solenoid switch, 420 models:

The components of the drive are shown in **FIG 12:5**. The roller clutch (**B**, **D** and **E**) must provide immediate take-up of drive in one direction and free rotation in the other. The operating bush **H** must slide smoothly on the driving sleeve **I** when compressing spring **G** and the driving sleeve must slide along the shaft splines without any tendency to bind. The trunnion block, pivot pin and engagement lever (see **FIG 12:2**) must pivot freely. All

moving parts of the drive should be smeared liberally with Shell Retinax 'A' or an equivalent grease.

FIG 12:6 shows a cutaway view of the solenoid switch and plunger unit. Initially, both windings **B** and **C** are energized in parallel but, having effected engagement of the pinion, the pull-in winding is shorted out when the starter switch contacts close. The 'lost motion' at **F** allows pinion engagement before energization of the motor rotates the pinion and also allows the solenoid contacts to open before pinion retraction begins.

Reassembling and refitting, S type cars:

These operations are the reverse of the dismantling and removal procedures.

Reassembling and refitting, 420 models:

This is the reverse of the removal and dismantling sequence but the following points must be noted. Torque tighten the nuts on the solenoid copper terminals to 20 lb in, the solenoid fixing bolts to 4.5 lb ft and the motor through-bolts to 8 lb ft. When fitting the commutator end bracket, ensure that the brake shoes (21 in **FIG 12:2**) seat squarely and that the shaft cross-peg engages correctly with the shoe slots.

The eccentric pivot pin 4 in **FIG 12:2** must be adjusted to give .005 to .015 inch clearance between the thrust collar 8 and the face of the pinion in the engaged position. The engaged position is achieved by energizing the solenoid pull-in coil. Connect a 6-volt battery across the starter yoke and, through a switch, the solenoid terminal in **FIG 12:6**. Close the switch, measure the clearance and open the switch. When adjusted, tighten the nut to lock the pivot pin.

When refitting the starter unit, **take great care not to cross the fine threads on the two securing bolts.**

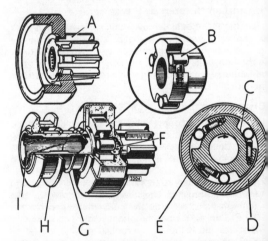

FIG 12:5   Components of the pinion drive (420 models)

Key to Fig 12:5   **A** Alternative construction (pinion pressed and clear-ringed into the drive member)   **B** Spring loaded rollers   **C** Cam tracks   **D** Driven member (with pinion)   **E** Driving member   **F** Bush
G Engagement spring   **H** Operating bush   **I** Driving sleeve

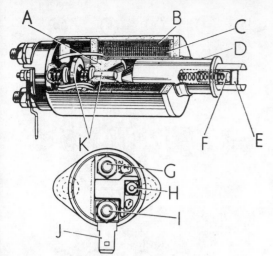

FIG 12:6 Solenoid/starter switch (420 models)

Key to Fig 12:6   **A** Core   **B** Shunt winding
C Series winding   **D** Plunger   **E** Clevis pin
F 'Lost motion' device   **G** Starter terminal   **H** Solenoid
terminal   **I** Battery terminal   **J** Accessories terminal
K Spindle and moving contact terminal

12:4 The generator (S type cars)

FIG 12:7 shows the generator/cooling fan belt drive. On models fitted with power steering, the steering pump is driven from the rear of the generator. **FIG 12:8** illustrates the components of the C.42 which is standard fitment. A C.48 generator of larger capacity may be fitted to special order.

Every 6000 miles, inject a few drops of SAE.30 oil into the end bracket hole marked OIL.

Testing when generator is not charging:

1 Ensure that belt slip is not the cause of the trouble.
2 Check that the larger generator terminal is connected to control box terminal D and the smaller terminal to control box terminal F. Check the brushgear as described later in this section.
3 Switch off all lights and accessories, disconnect the cables from the generator and connect the two terminals with a short length of wire. Disconnect the radio suppression capacitor (if fitted) from between the output terminal and earth. Run the engine at idling speed and clip the negative lead of a 0 to 20-volt moving coil meter to a generator terminal and the positive lead to a good earth on the generator yoke. Gradually increase the engine speed. The meter reading should rise rapidly and without fluctuation. Do not race the engine or allow the reading to reach 20 volts.
4 Reconnect the radio suppression capacitor. If there is now no reading on run-up, the capacitor is defective. Excessive sparking at the commutator indicates a defective armature. A reading of $\frac{1}{2}$ to 1 volt may indicate a faulty field coil.
5 If the generator is in order, check the continuity of the cables to the control box. Remove the temporary link, reconnect the cables and test the control box as described in **Section 12:5**.

Removing the generator:

If power assisted steering is fitted, refer to **Section 10:7** and dismount the pump. Remove the leads from the generator, refer to **FIG 12:7**, loosen the two lower arrowed bolts and remove the top arrowed bolt. Swing the generator towards the engine and disengage the drive belt. Remove the lower bolts and dismount the generator.

Dismantling the generator:

Remove the retaining nut and pull off the driving pulley. Unscrew and remove the two through-bolts. Withdraw the commutator end bracket. Lift off the driving end bracket complete with armature and press the shaft out of the bearing.

Servicing the brushgear:

Lift the brushes up into their boxes and secure them by positioning each spring at the side of its brush. Fit the commutator end bracket over the commutator and release the brushes. Hold back each spring in turn and move the brush by pulling gently on its flexible connector. If a brush moves sluggishly, remove it and ease the sides against a smooth file. Refit in its original position. Renew, and bed to the commutator, any brushes which are less than the permissible minimum of $\frac{1}{4}$ inch. Renew any brush spring which gives a spring balance reading of less than 33 oz with a new brush or 16 oz with a fully worn one.

Servicing the commutator:

A commutator in good condition will be smooth and free from pitting and burned segments. Clean with a cloth and petrol and, if necessary, polish with fine glasspaper while turning the armature. **Do not use emerycloth.** Skim a badly worn commutator in a lathe. Use a high-speed and take a light cut with a sharp tool. Remove the minimum amount to clean up and polish with fine glasspaper. Undercut the insulation between the segments to a depth of $\frac{1}{32}$ inch using a hacksaw blade ground down to the thickness of the insulation.

The armature:

In the absence of armature testing facilities, the only check for a suspected fault which an owner can make is to substitute one which is known to be serviceable.

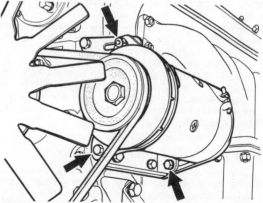

FIG 12:7 Generator mounting and belt drive (S type cars)

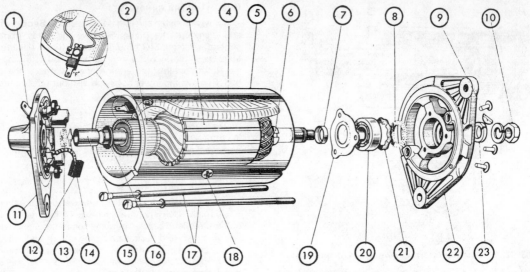

FIG 12:8 Components of the DC generator fitted to S type cars

Key to Fig 12:8 1 Output terminal 'D' 2 Commutator 3 Armature 4 Field coils 5 Yoke 6 Shaft collar 7 Shaft collar retaining cup 8 Felt ring 9 Shaft key 10 Shaft nut 11 Commutator end bracket 12 Brushes 13 Felt ring 14 Felt ring retainer 15 Porous bronze bush 16 Fibre thrust washer 17 Through-bolts 18 Pole shoe securing screws 19 Bearing retaining plate 20 Ballbearing 21 Corrugated washer 22 Drive end bracket 23 Pulley spacer

Testing field coils

When testing with an ohmmeter, the reading should be 4.5 ohms. Alternatively, connect a 12-volt supply in series with the coil and an ammeter. A reading of about 2.7 amps should be obtained. A zero reading indicates that the coil has a break in it. If the reading is much more than 2.7 amps or if the ohmmeter reads much less than 4.5 ohms, the coil insulation has broken down. Renewal of the field coils should be entrusted to a Service Station.

Renewing bearings:

Pull out the old bush with a $\frac{5}{8}$ inch tap which has been screwed in a few turns. The new bush must not be reamed or its porosity will be impaired. Allow the new bush to stand fully immersed in SAE.30 engine oil for 24 hours before pressing it onto the bracket. Use a shouldered mandrel with a highly polished pilot of the same diameter as the armature shaft and slightly longer than the bush.

The drive end ballbearing is pressed out of the bracket after drilling out the rivets and removing the retaining plate. Collect the corrugated and felt washers. Pack the new bearing with high melting point grease before fitting it. Use new rivets inserted from the outer side of the end bracket and open them by means of a punch to secure the retaining plate rigidly.

Reassembling and refitting the generator:

This is the reverse of the dismantling procedure. Ensure that the springs bear correctly on the tops of the brushes before pushing the end bracket finally home. On completion of assembly, inject a few drops of SAE.30 oil into the end bracket hole marked OIL.

12:5 The control box (S type cars)

The RB.340 control box has a voltage regulator, a current regulator and a cut-out all of which are adjustable and are shown in **FIG 12:9** which illustrates the control box with its cover removed.

Checking the charging circuit:

Do not disturb the control box until the 5 checks listed in **Section 12:4** under 'Testing when generator is not charging' have been carried out. It must again be stressed that first grade, accurate, moving coil electrical meters are required to check and make any necessary adjustments to the control box. All checks and adjustments must be completed as rapidly as possible to avoid errors from heating up of the operating coils. Should the control box fail to respond correctly to any adjustment it should be examined at a Service Station.

Adjusting voltage regulator:

Refer to **FIG 12:9** and withdraw cables from terminal blades B and WL. Connect a 0 to 20 voltmeter between terminal WL and a good earth. So that the engine may be started, join together the ignition and battery feeds with a suitable lead. The generator test rev/min is 3000 (1800 engine rev/min) for type C.48 and 4500 (2700 engine rev/min) for type C.42. Adjustment is made by turning the voltage regulator cam by means of the special tool 6 in **FIG 12:9**. To raise the voltage the **tool** is turned clockwise. If necessary, the engine is stopped, adjustment made and the engine run up to the test rev/min to recheck the voltage reading. The correct voltage for the prevailing ambient temperature is given in Technical Data in the Appendix section.

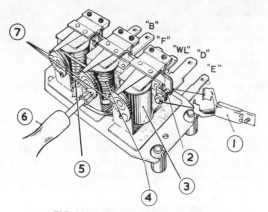

FIG 12:9   The RB.340 control box

Key to Fig 12:9   1 Clip (see text)   2 Voltage regulator contacts   3 Voltage regulator   4 Current regulator   5 Cut-out   6 Special tool   7 Adjustment cams

Adjusting the current regulator:

Render the voltage regulator inoperative by short-circuiting its contacts. Refer to **FIG 12:9** where the method of shortcircuiting the contacts by clip 1 is indicated. Withdraw the cable from terminal B. Connect a first grade 0 to 40 ammeter between this cable and the terminal B which must carry this connection only. The ignition feed must be made to the battery side of the ammeter.

Switch on all lights to provide a load. Run the C.48 generator at 3000 rev/min (1800 engine rev/min). The ammeter should read 35 amps. Run the C.42 generator at 4500 rev/min (2700 engine rev/min). The ammeter should read 30 amps. If adjustment is required, turn the current regulator cam by means of the special tool 6 in **FIG 12:9**. Clockwise rotation of the **tool** raises the setting.

Adjusting the cut-out:

Withdraw the cable from the WL terminal and connect the voltmeter between the WL terminal and a good earth. Switch on the lights to provide a load, start the engine and slowly increase the speed. The voltage should rise steadily to the cut-in voltage of 12.6 to 13.4 and drop slightly as the contacts close. If adjustment is necessary, reduce engine speed, refer to **FIG 12:9** and turn the cut-out cam by means of the special tool 6. Clockwise rotation of the **tool** will raise the cut-in voltage. The drop-off voltage should be 9.3 to 11.2 and is checked by removing the cable from terminal B, connecting the voltmeter between terminal B and earth, slowly decelerating from about 3000 engine rev/min and noting the reading from which the voltage suddenly drops to zero. If adjustment is required, stop the engine and carefully bend the fixed contact bracket. Reducing the gap will raise the drop-off setting. When the contacts 'make' there should be a blade deflection of .010 to .035 inch.

Adjustment of the voltage and current regulator air gap settings:

If an original setting has been disturbed, reset as follows:

1 Disconnect the battery. Refer to **FIG 12:9** and bring the appropriate cam to minimum lift by turning it by means of the special tool 6 which should be turned fully anticlowise.

2 Insert a .045 inch feeler gauge between the armature and core as far back as the two rivet heads on the underside of the armature. Keep the gauge in position, press down squarely on the armature and screw the adjustable contact inwards until it just touches the armature contact.

On completion of these mechanical adjustments, check the electrical settings as described earlier.

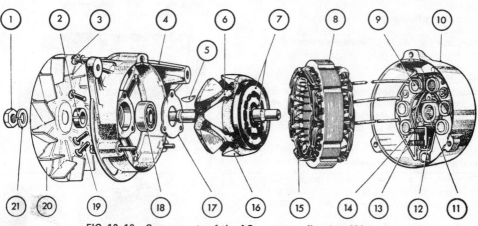

FIG 12:10   Components of the AC generator fitted to 420 models

Key to Fig 12:10   1 Shaft nut   2 Bearing collar   3 Through fixing bolts (3)   4 Drive end bracket   5 Key   6 Rotor (field) winding   7 Slip rings   8 Stator laminations   9 Silicon diodes (6)   10 Slip ring end bracket   11 Needle roller bearing   12 Brush box moulding   13 Brushes   14 Diode heat sink   15 Stator windings   16 Rotor   17 Bearing retaining plate   18 Ballbearing   19 Bearing retaining plate   20 Fan   21 Spring washer

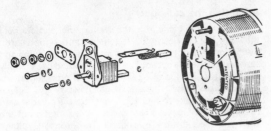

FIG 12:11   Brush removal

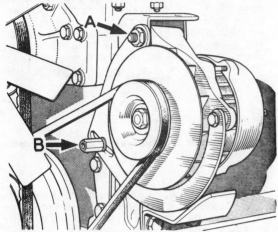

FIG 12:12   Alternator mounting and belt drive (420 models)

Adjustment of cut-out contact 'follow-through' and core gap:

1 Refer to **FIG 12:9**. Press down the cut-out armature against the copper separation on the core. Bend the fixed contact bracket until the 'follow-through' or blade deflection is between .010 and .035 inch. Release the armature.
2 Adjust the armature backstop to give a core gap of .035 to .045 inch.
3 Check the cut-in and drop-off voltages as described earlier.

Cleaning contact points:

Fine carborundum stone or silicon carbide paper may be used on the regulator contacts but **not on the soft cut-out contacts which should be cleaned with fine glasspaper.** Clean off all dust with methylated spirits.

12:6   The alternator (420 models)

The components of the 11AC alternator are shown in **FIG 12:10**. The stationary 3-phase output windings 15 are connected to the built-in rectifier (six silicon diodes 9 in a 3-phase bridge circuit). The rotor 16 which runs in a ballbearing 18 at the drive end and a needle roller bearing 11 at the slip ring end, carries the field windings 6 which are connected to the two slip rings 7. The brushes 13 which run on the slip rings, are shown also in **FIG 12:11**. The alternator is belt driven as shown in **FIG 12:12**.

Precautions:

Never use a 'megger' type of ohmmeter unless the alternator diodes and control unit transistors have been isolated. Never reverse battery connections; **the negative must be earthed.** Never earth the brown/green alternator cable, the main cable or terminal. Never run the alternator on open-circuit with the field windings energized.

Testing when alternator is not charging:

1 Ensure that belt slip is not the cause of the trouble.
2 Disconnect the battery earth cable. Refer to **FIG 13:9**, hinge down the instrument panel, disconnect the brown/white cables from the ammeter and connect the two cables to a moving coil ammeter registering up to 75 amps.
3 Refer to **FIG 12:14**, detach the connector block and (with a length of cable and two 'Lucar' terminals) link the black and the brown/green cables. Reconnect the battery earth.
4 Run the alternator up to 4000 rev/min (2000 engine rev/min). The ammeter should read some 40 amp. A low reading indicates a faulty alternator or poor circuit connections. Correct the latter and recheck.
5 If a low reading persists, test the rotor winding with the external wiring disconnected. Connect a 12-volt

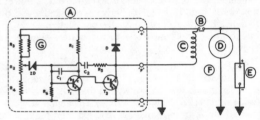

FIG 12:13   Alternator control circuit diagram

Key to Fig 12:13
B Field isolating device
D Alternator (rectified) output   **E** 12-volt battery
G Thermistor
A Control unit
C Rotor field winding
F Stator winding

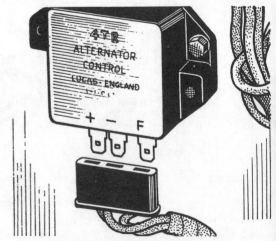

FIG 12:14   The 4TR alternator control

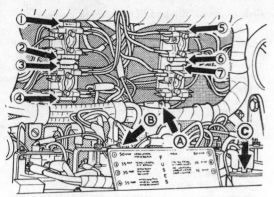

FIG 12:15 1 to 7 are the standard fuses. A and B are extra fuses and C is the instrument voltage stabilizer/regulator

battery, with an ammeter in series, across the winding. 3.2 amp should be recorded. A higher reading indicates failed insulation, a zero reading, an open-circuit in the coil, slip rings or brushgear which should be serviced as described later.

6 If a zero reading is obtained in 4, stop the engine, switch on the ignition use a 0 to 20 voltmeter to check that battery voltage is applied at the rotor windings. Refer to **FIG 14:2** and trace the break in circuit.

It is recommended that a failed alternator should be entrusted to a Specialist for repair or that an exchange replacement be obtained.

Servicing the brushgear:

Refer to **FIG 12:11**. Withdraw the brush box after removing the terminal nuts, washers, insulating pieces and two setscrews and washers. Measure the brush length and renew if worn to $\frac{5}{32}$ inch. Ensure terminal retention by levering up the tongue on the terminal blade. Check that the brushes move freely. If not, ease them against a smooth file.

Removing and refitting an alternator:

If air conditioning is fitted, refer to **Section 13:13** and dismount the compressor. Do not disturb the hose unions. Disconnect the alternator cables, refer to **FIG 12:12**, remove bolts arrowed **A** and **B**, disengage the drive belt and dismount the alternator. Refitting is the reverse of this procedure. When correctly tensioned, there should be $\frac{1}{2}$ inch belt deflection under pressure between the pulleys.

12:7 Alternator control (420 models)

The circuit diagram of the 4TR electronic voltage control unit is illustrated in **FIG 12:13**. No cut-out is required as the alternator diodes preclude reverse current flow. No current regulator is required as the characteristics of the alternator limit current output. The circuit also includes a 3AW warning light control unit.

Precautions:

Incorrect connections will damage the control units and alternator and the precautions given in **Section 12:6** should be noted.

Voltage check and adjustment:

Provided that the alternator and associated wiring circuits have been tested and found satisfactory, that the battery is well charged and the alternator has been run at charging speed for eight minutes to stabilize temperatues, adjusting the voltage may be proceeded with.

1 **Leave normal connections to the alternator and control unit undisturbed.** Connect a high quality suppressed zero 12 to 15 range voltmeter between the + and − control unit terminals. Switch on load of approximately 2 amp (side and tail lights), start the engine and run the alternator at 3000 rev/min (1500 engine rev/min) for eight minutes.

2 The voltmeter should show a stabilized reading of 13.9 to 14.3 at an ambient temperature of 68° to 78°F. If the voltage is outside this range, adjustment may be made provided that the voltage has risen to some degree above battery voltage before stabilizing. If the reading remains unchanged at battery voltage or increases in an uncontrolled manner, the control unit is faulty and an exchange replacement must be obtained.

3 Stop the engine, dismount and invert the control unit. Carefully remove the sealing compound which conceals the potentiometer (R2 in **FIG 12:13**) adjuster. Check that the voltmeter is still connected as before, start the engine, run the alternator at 3000 rev/min and turn the adjuster (clockwise will increase the voltage) until the correct setting is obtained.

4 Recheck by stopping the engine and again running up to speed. If regulated satisfactorily, refit the unit but do not attempt to reseal the adjuster as undue heat may damage the unit.

The warning light unit:

Should this fail, preclude possible recurrence before fitting a replacement by checking the voltage between the brown/yellow cable and earth. At 1500 engine rev/min it should be 7.0 to 7.5 volts. If a higher voltage is registered, the alternator diodes must be suspect.

12:8 Fuses

Access to the fuses is by hinging down the instrument panel as described in **Section 13:9**. The circuits served

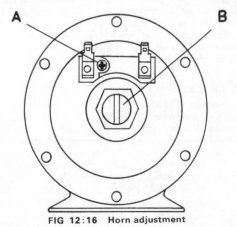

FIG 12:16 Horn adjustment

Key to Fig 12:16   A Adjustment screw
B Central screw (do not disturb)

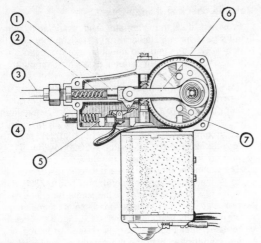

FIG 12:17 Windscreen wiper motor and gearbox components

Key to Fig 12:17
1 Crosshead 2 Cable rack 3 Cable tube 4 Adjusting nut 5 Self-parking switch 6 Connecting rod 7 Final gear

by each fuse is given on the identification panel on which the numbering is as shown in **FIG 12:15**. Fuses **A** and **B** serve certain optional extras (if fitted) as follows: **A** Heated backlight (15 amp), Radio (5 amp) and Traffic hazard warning (USA only, 35 amp). **B** Air conditioning on 420 models (30 amp). Each fuse unit carries two spares. Replace a blown fuse by one of the correct value and ensure that the spare is replaced.

12:9 The horns

The horn circuit operates through a Lucas 6RA relay as shown in **FIGS 14:1** and **14:2**. This type of horn cannot be conveniently adjusted in position. Remove and securely mount on a test fixture. **Do not disturb the central screw.** A small serrated adjusting screw (**A** in **FIG 12:16**) is located adjacent to the horn terminals. Connect a 0 to 25 ammeter in series with the horn and a 12-volt supply. Protect the ammeter from overload by connecting an ON-OFF switch across it and switch OFF only while taking a reading (when the horn is sounding). Adjust the serrated screw until the horn operates within the range of 6.5 to 7.0 amps.

12:10 Windscreen wipers

Apart from the renewal of wiper blades, the windscreen wipers require no routine maintenance. The motor is a two-speed, thermostatically protected, self-parking, cable rack unit. The cable rack passes through protective tubing to a pair of scuttle mounted wheelboxes which drive the wiper arm spindles. If overloading causes the motor windings to overheat, the thermostat cuts the supply to the motor and, should this occur, the cause of the overload must be located as reconnection is made automatically when the motor windings have cooled.

The self-parking switch 5 in **FIG 12:17** is adjusted by turning knurled nut 4 by small amount and checking the effect.

Checking voltage and light running current:

Poor performance may be electrical or mechanical in origin. Connect a first grade 0 to 20 voltmeter to the motor supply terminal (to which the green cable is connected) and to earth. With the motor working normally, the reading should be 11.5 volts. If the reading is low, check the battery, switch, cables and their connections.

To check the light running current, refer to **FIG 12:17** and proceed as follows:

1 Remove the setscrews and lift off the gearbox coverplate. Uncouple the connecting rod by removing the circlip, washer, spring and plate from the crankpin.

2 Disconnect the green cable from the motor and insert a first grade ammeter between this cable and the terminal from which is was disconnected.

3 If, with the motor running normally at 45 to 50 cycles/min, the light running current exceeds 3.4 amps, the motor is faulty.

Removing and refitting the motor:

Remove the wiper arms, unscrew the large nut connecting the cable rack tubing to the motor, remove the setscrew securing the earth wire to the motor and, noting their colours, disconnect the cables at the snap connectors. Remove the three screws, accessible from beneath the righthand front wing, which retain the motor to the valance. Dismount the motor and withdraw the cable rack from its tubing. Uncouple the cable rack as described earlier and lift out the cable ferrule. Refitting is the reverse of this procedure. Turn each wheelbox spindle in turn to engage the cable rack as it is fed through the tubing.

Checking the cable rack and its tubing:

With the wiper arms removed and the connecting link uncoupled, the force to move the cable rack in its tubing should not exceed 6 lb measured by pulling on the crosshead with a spring balance. Excessive load may be due to the cable rack or a wheelbox being seized, the tubing may be damaged or a wheelbox may be loose and misaligned.

Removal of wheelboxes:

1 On **S type cars**, refer to **Section 13:8** and remove the screen rail, hinge down the instrument panel and release the two main harness clips. Detach the fabric cover (held by upholstry solution) between the demister ducts and the panels. On **420 models**, withdraw the facia panel as described in **Section 13:9**. Support it and ensure that the covering is protected.

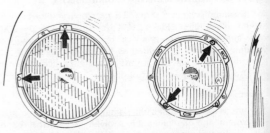

FIG 12:18 Headlamp beam setting screws

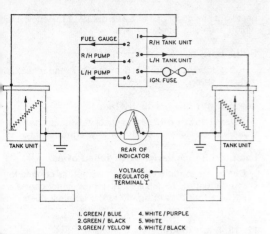

I. GREEN / BLUE   4. WHITE / PURPLE
2. GREEN / BLACK   5. WHITE
3. GREEN / YELLOW   6. WHITE / BLACK

IG 12 : 19   Wiring diagram of fuel gauge and tank units

2 Remove the wiper arms, unscrew the large nuts which secure the wheelboxes to the scuttle and remove the chrome distance pieces and rubber seals. Remove the motor and cable as described earlier.

3 Remove the two screws which retain each wheelbox backplate, pull the cable rack away from the worm wheels, slide off the spacer tube and withdraw the wheelboxes and spacers.

Refitting is the reverse of this procedure. Ensure that he flared ends of the tubes register with the narrow slots n the backplates. The cable rack and wheelboxes should be lubricated with Duckhams HBB grease.

Servicing the motor :

Withdraw the two through-bolts and remove the cover. Inspect the brushes and springs. Ensure that the brushes are free and that the springs function adequately. If the brush assembly is to be removed, mark it so that it may be refitted in its original position. Clean the commutator with a petrol-moistened cloth.

2 : 11   Headlamps

With the car normally loaded the undipped headlamp beams should be parallel to each other and to the road. For correct beam adjustment, aiming pads are mounted into the lenses for use on a mechanical aimer such as a Lev-L-Lite. If this facility is not available, set the car on level ground facing square to and 25 ft from a wall. Adjust the lamps so that the centre of the 'hot spot' is 2 inches below the horizontal height of the lamps. On **420 models**, cover the inner lamps while adjusting the outer and vice versa.

FIG 12 : 18 shows the **420 model** setting screws. The screws on **S type** headlamps are as illustrated on the left with the adjusters at right angles to each other. Access to the setting screws requires the removal of the rims which are each retained by a single screw at the bottom.

2 : 12   Flasher and traffic hazard warning units

Flasher unit :

The flasher unit, in which a switch is operated automatically by alternate heating and cooling of an actuating wire, is housed in a small cylindrical container located

behind the instrument panel. A small relay to flash the pilot light is incorporated and operation is audible inside the car.

In case of trouble, check the bulbs for serviceability. Check fuse No. 3 (see **Section 12 : 8**). With a voltmeter, check that battery voltage exists between terminal **B** and earth when the ignition is switched on. Connect terminals **L** and **B**, switch on the ignition and operate the direction indicator switch. If the direction indicator lamps now light, the flasher unit is defective and must be renewed. Mark the leads and ensure that the new unit is correctly connected. If the unit is not defective, refer to wiring diagram **FIG 14 : 1** or **FIG 14 : 2** and check all flasher circuit cables and connections.

Traffic hazard warning unit :

This system, which is fitted to cars for the USA market only, operates in conjunction with the flashing direction indicator lights. Operation of the toggle switch on the sub-panel causes all four lights to flash simultaneously. A red pilot light is incorporated to indicate that the system is in operation. A 35 amp fuse is included in the circuit. The flasher unit differs in internal circuit from the direction indicator flasher unit although it is of similar appearance. In the event of failure, a new unit of the correct type must be fitted. The wiring diagram is included in **FIGS 14 : 1** and **14 : 2**.

12 : 13   Panel and warning lights

Access to the panel instrument illumination bulbs requires the panel to be hinged down as described in **Section 13 : 9**. Access to the speedometer and revolution counter illumination bulbs, ignition, fuel and headlamp beam warning lights is from below these instruments. Flasher indicator and overdrive or automatic transmission selector bulbs are accessible after removing the upper switch cover (43 in **FIG 10 : 13**) which is secured from below by two screws. The heated backlight indicator bulb and the handbrake warning bulb (note that this bulb holder is spring-loaded) is accessible after removing the bezel.

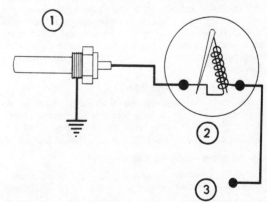

FIG 12 : 20   Temperature transmitter and gauge wiring diagram

Key to Fig 12 : 20   1 Temperature transmitter   2 Gauge
3 Voltage regulator terminal 'I'

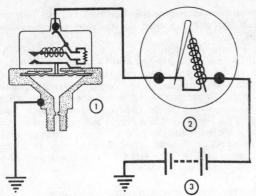

FIG 12:21 Oil pressure transmitter and gauge wiring diagram

Key to Fig 12:21   1 Pressure transmitter   2 Gauge
3 Battery

12:14 Gauges and clock

To avoid accidental shortcircuits, it is advisable to **disconnect the battery earth cable** before inspecting or removing an instrument or gauge.

To gain access to the fuel, pressure or temperature gauges or to the ammeter, refer to **Section 13:9** and hinge down the instrument panel. If a gauge is to be removed, disconnect the leads, withdraw the illumination bulb, unscrew the two knurled nuts and remove the U-bracket. Withdraw the gauge from the front. A voltage stabilizer (arrowed **C** in **FIG 12:15**) provides a stable 10-volt supply to the fuel and temperature gauges and the wiring of these is shown in **FIGS 12:19** and **12:20**. The voltage stabilizer is located at the top righthand side of the centre instrument panel. The wiring diagram for the oil pressure gauge is shown in **FIG 12:21**. This, it will be seen is not in circuit with the voltage stabilizer as it is not so critical to supply voltage.

The speedometer and revolution counter are retained by U-brackets and knurled nuts. To provide clearance, the speedometer must be withdrawn before the revolution counter can be removed. The clock may be detached from the revolution counter on **S type** cars by removing the two retaining nuts. The separate transistorized clock fitted to **420 models** is powered by a mercury cell which must be renewed every 18 months. Access to the cell is by hinging down the instrument panel as described in **Section 13:9**.

12:15 Impulse tachometer

The revolution counter fitted to 420 models is an indicator head actuated by a pulse lead (coloured white) which is wired in circuit with the 'SW' terminal of the ignition coil. The wiring circuit is included in **FIG 14:2**.

12:16 Electrically heated backlight

FIG 12:22 shows the wiring diagram of the electrically heated backlight which may be fitted as an optional extra.

12:17 Lighting circuits

Lamps give poor light :

Refer to **Section 12:2** and check the condition of the battery. Recharge if necessary. Check the setting of the headlights as described in **Section 12:11**. Renew bulbs which have darkened with age.

Bulbs burn out frequently :

Refer to **Sections 12:5** and **12:7** and check the voltage setting.

Lamps light but gradually fade :

Refer to **Section 12:2** and check the battery as it is not capable of supplying current for any legnth of time.

Lamp brilliance varies with speed of car :

Check the condition of the battery and its connections. Clean the battery terminal posts, renew faulty cables and make sure that they fit tightly to the terminal posts.

12:18 Fault diagnosis

(a) Battery discharged

1 Terminal connections loose or dirty
2 Shorts in lighting circuit
3 Generator or alternator not charging
4 Control box or control unit faulty
5 Battery internally defective

(b) Insufficient charging rate

1 Check 1 and 4 in (a)
2 Driving belt slipping

(c) Battery will not hold charge

1 Low electrolyte level
2 Battery plates sulphated
3 Electrolyte leakage from cracked case
4 Battery plate separators defective

(d) Battery overcharged

1 Control box needs adjusting, S type cars

(e) Generator or alternator output low or nil

1 Drive belt broken or slipping
2 Control box or control unit out of adjustment
3 Worn bearings, loose polepieces
4 Commutator or slip rings worn, burned or shorted
5 Armature or rotor shaft bent or worn
6 Insulation proud between commutator segments, S type cars
7 Brushes sticking, springs weak or broken
8 Field coil or rotor windings broken, shorted or burned

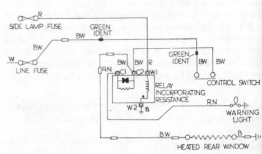

FIG 12:22   Electrically heated backlight wiring diagram

f) Starter motor lacks power or will not operate

  Battery discharged, loose cable connections
2 Starter pinion jammed in flywheel gear, S type cars
3 Starter switch or solenoid faulty
4 Brushes worn or sticking, leads detached or shorting
5 Commutator or slip rings worn, burned or shorted
6 Motor shaft bent
7 Engine abnormally stiff, perhaps due to rebore

g) Starter motor runs but does not turn engine

1 Pinion sticking on screwed sleeve, S type cars
2 Broken teeth on pinion or flywheel gear
3 Defective roller clutch, 420 models

h) Noisy starter pinion when engine is running

1 Restraining spring weak or broken, S type cars

(j) Starter motor inoperative

1 Check 1 and 4 in (f)
2 Armature, rotor or field coils faulty

(k) Starter motor rough or noisy

1 Mounting bolts loose
2 Damaged pinion or flywheel gear teeth
3 Main pinion spring broken, S type cars

(l) Lamps inoperative or erratic

1 Battery low, bulbs burned out
2 Faulty earthing of lamps or battery
3 Lighting switch faulty, loose or broken connections

(m) Wiper motor sluggish, taking high current

1 Faulty armature
2 Commutator dirty or shortcircuiting
3 Brushes worn or sticking, spring broken
4 Wheelbox binding, cable rack tight in its tubing
5 Lack of lubrication
6 Motor gearbox binding, no end float to armature shaft

(n) Wiper motor runs but does not drive

1 Wheelbox gear and spindle worn
2 Cable rack faulty
3 Motor gearbox components worn

(o) Fuel, temperature or pressure gauges do not work

1 Check wiring for continuity
2 Voltage stabilizer faulty
3 Check instruments and transmitters for continuity

CHAPTER 13

THE BODYWORK

13:1 Bodywork finish

Large-scale repairs to body panels are best left to expert panel beaters. Even small dents can be tricky, as too much hammering will stretch the metal and make things worse instead of better. Filling minor dents and scratches is probably the best method of restoring the surface. The touching-up of paintwork is well within the powers of most owners, particularly as self-spraying cans of paint in the correct colours are now readily available. paint may change colour with age and it is better to spray a whole wing rather than to touch-up a small area.

Before spraying, remove all traces of wax polish with white spirit. More drastic treatment is required if silicone polishes have been applied. Use a primer surfacer or paste stopper according to the amount of filling required, and when it is dry, rub it down with 400 grade 'Wet or dry' paper until the surface is smooth and flush with the surrounding area. Spend time on getting the best finish as this will control the final effect. Apply the retouching paint keeping it wet in the centre and light and dry round the edges. After a few hours of drying, use a cutting compound to remove the dry spray and finish with liquid polish.

13:2 Removing door trims

Insert a screwdriver between the door handle and the spring cap, press inwards and tap out the retaining pin. Remove the handle, cap and escutcheon. Close the window fully and repeat this procedure on the winder handle. On front doors, remove two screws and washers and detach the armrest. Remove the centre screw and detach the locking turn-button.

Refer to **FIG 13:1** and detach the wood capping which is retained by the four screws arrowed in the top part of the illustration. Detach the waist rail by removing the three screws arrowed in the centre of the illustration and, on 420 models, withdraw four screws and remove two wooden fillets. Pull away the fabric (attached with upholstery adhesive) from the bottom of the window. Remove the six screws (five on rear doors) shown in the lower part of **FIG 13:1** which secure the top of the casing to the door. Prise off the casing which is retained by spring clips. On front doors unhook the map pocket tensioning.

Refitting is this sequence in reverse.

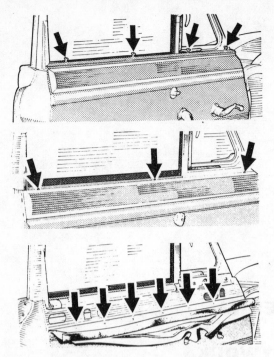

FIG 13:1 Removing door trims

13:3 Window winding mechanism

Remove the door casing as described in **Section 13:2** and lift off the piece of felt from the winding spindle. Remove the eight screws and serrated washers which are arrowed in **FIG 13:2**. Four of these, on both front and rear doors, secure the window regulator to the door frame and four, on front doors only, secure the regulator spring. The window winding mechanism can now be withdrawn as shown in **FIG 13:3**.

Refitting is the reverse of this procedure.

13:4 Door hinges and lock mechanism

Door hinge removal and refitment:

Mark the position of the hinges on the door and remove the splitpin and clevis pin from the check strap bracket. On front doors remove six bolts, on rear doors remove seven cross-headed screws securing the hinges to the door and remove the door. Remove each hinge by unscrewing two cross-headed screws plus, on front hinges only, one bolt. Refitting is the reverse of this procedure.

Lock mechanism removal and refitment:

The components of the lock mechanism are shown in **FIG 13:4**. Remove the door trim as described in **Section 13:2** and expose the mechanism as seen in **FIG 13:5**.

On a front door, release the spring clip and disconnect link **A** in **FIG 13:4** from the dowel on lever **B**. Disconnect the remote control link by removing the wire clip, plain and wavy washers and removing the link from the latch lever **E**. Remove three screws **F** and dismount the control

unit. Detach the locking rod by removing the clip which secures it to the lever **G**. Two screws **H** retain the turn-button control. Remove the lower glass run channel bolt together with its washers and packing pieces then, when removing the lock it may be pressed inwards so that the latch passes inside the shut face. On a rear door, remove the starlock washer and disconnect link **C** from cross-shaft **D**. Collect the plain washer from behind the link. Remove three screws **I**, collect plate **J** and remove the lock. The press button unit may be withdrawn after removing two bolts **K**. Unless a replacement is required, do not remove the outside handle. Do not disturb screws **L** unless adjusting or replacing the striker unit.

Refitment is the reverse of the removal sequence but note the following. The clearance between plunger bolt **Q** and contactor **S** should be $\frac{1}{32}$ inch and may be adjusted by releasing locknut **R**, turning bolt **Q** as required and re-tightening the locknut. Use the nearest hole in link **A** (three at the top) or **C** (three at the bottom) to compensate for any assembly variation. On rear locks provision is made for temporarily pegging lever **B** in the locked position prior to connecting the link **C** by inserting a short piece of $\frac{1}{8}$ inch diameter rod through the rectangular

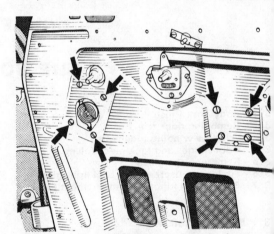

FIG 13:2 Window winding mechanism securing screw

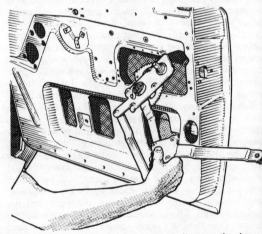

FIG 13:3 Removing window winding mechanism

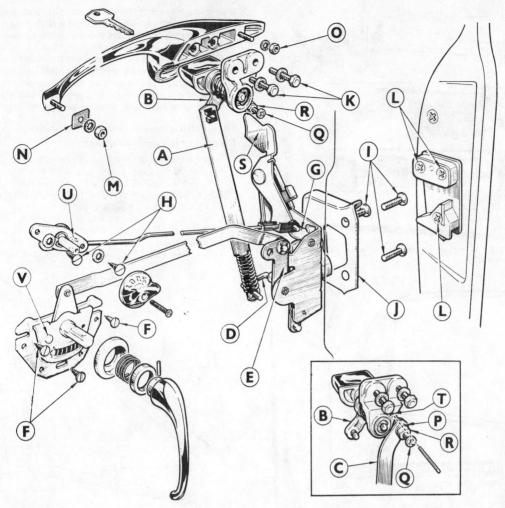

FIG 13:4   Components of the door lock mechanism

Key to Fig 13:4   **A** Connecting link (front door)   **B** Operating lever   **C** Connecting link (rear door)   **D** Cross-shaft
E Latch operating lever   **F** Screw   **G** Locking lever   **H** Screw   **I** Screw   **J** Dovetail plate   **K** Bolt   **L** Screw
M Nut   **N** Packing washer   **O** Nut   **P** Washer   **Q** Plunger bolt   **R** Locknut   **S** Lock contactor
T Rectangular hole   **U** Stop   **V** Stop

hole **T**. After connecting the link, remove the rod and, by depressing the push button, check that the plunger bolt **Q** clears contactor **S**.

13:5 Removing and refitting door glass

The following procedure applies to both front and rear door windows.

1 Remove the door trim as described in **Section 13:2**. Remove the screws, serrated and plain washers from below the top of the door panel, collect the packing pieces and identify them to position. Remove the two bolts, serrated and plain washers which secure the two legs of the window frame to the door and collect the wooden packing pieces. These screws and bolts are shown arrowed in **FIG 13:5** which illustrates a front door.

2 Unclip the weatherstrip, which is secured by four clips, from the door frame and withdraw the window frame from the door frame, as shown in **FIG 13:6**.

3 Slide the glass out of the retaining channel.

Refitting is the reverse of this procedure. Place a layer of sealing compound on the door frame below the NDV. On rear doors, wind up the glass about one third of the way before inserting the window frame. Ensure that all packing pieces are refitted. Position the frame to clear the screen pillar (or, on a rear window, the door pillar) by $\frac{1}{16}$ inch. When this has been done, tighten the screws and bolts which are arrowed in **FIG 13:5**.

Adjusting no draught ventilators:

On front doors, refer to **Section 13:2** and carry out the door trim removal procedure up to the point at which

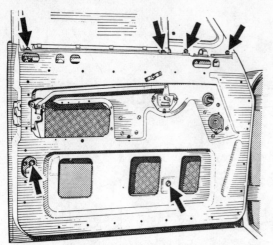

FIG 13:5 Window frame securing screws and bolts are arrowed

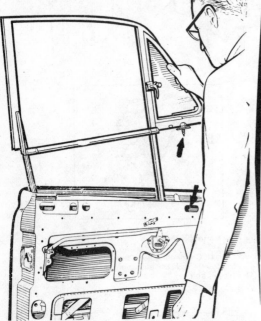

FIG 13:6 Removing a front window frame. The NDV adjustment nut is arrowed

the small aperture arrowed in **FIG 13:6** is uncovered. Through this aperture the adjustment nut (also arrowed in **FIG 13:6**) can be tightened until there is a positive feel between the segment and the quadrant when the NDV is moved to any of its three positions. The rear NDV is provided with a catch arm and adjustment is not applicable.

Removing and refitting NDV's:

On a front door proceed as for NDV adjustment described earlier and, through the aperture, remove the locknut, nut and washer securing the spring against

the quadrant post. Remove the pin and segment. Remove two screws which retain the NDV hinge to the window frame and withdraw the NDV as shown in **FIG 13:7**.

On a rear window disconnect the catch arm by removing the nut screw and fibre washer and open the NDV. Remove the five screws which secure the NDV hinge to the window frame and withdraw the NDV.

Refitting, in each case, is the reverse of this procedure.

13:6 Fitting windscreen and backlight glass

Removing the original glass:

1 Prise off the two chrome finisher pieces and the chrome finisher itself. Extract one end of the rubber insert (shown black in **FIG 13:8**) and withdraw it completely. Run a thin bladed tool round the aperture to break the seal between the rubber and the flange.

2 In the case of a heated backlight, disconnect the two cables in the luggage compartment and take care not to break them where they pass through the sealing rubber (see **FIG 13:8**) when removing the backlight.

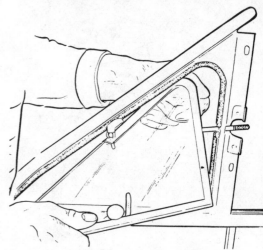

FIG 13:7 Removing a front NDV glass

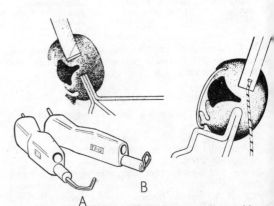

FIG 13:8 Windscreen and backlight sealing rubbers. A and B are special tools used for fitting sealing rubbers and sealing strips (Churchill tool set No. JD23)

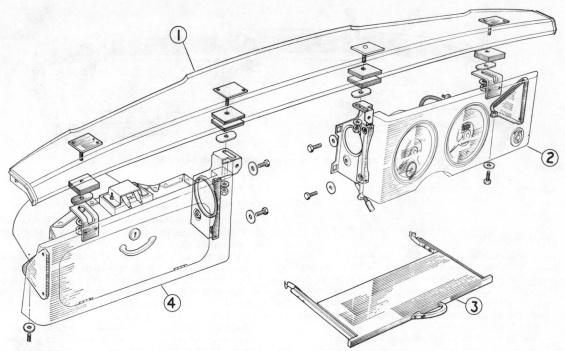

FIG 13:9   Side facia panel, glove box and screenrail. S type cars

Key to Fig 13:9   1 Screenrail   2 Side facia panel   3 Tray   4 Glove box

3 Strike the glass with the flat of the hand from inside the car. Start at one corner, work towards the bottom and continue round until the glass can be withdrawn outwards.

Fitting new glass:

1 Remove old sealer, ensure that all particles of glass are removed from the sealing rubber and that it is thoroughly clean. If there is any doubt, use new sealing rubber as small particles of glass may break the glass again. Check that the aperture flange is undamaged. File away any bump or the glass may break again.

2 Attach the rubber to the aperture flange with its flat side towards the inside of the car and the joint at the bottom. In the case of a heated backlight, pierce the rubber in two appropriate places and feed the electrical wires through the holes. Offer up the glass to the aperture from outside. **Fit it equally. Do not fit one end and then try to fit the other.** Use the special hook tool **A** in **FIG 13:8** and insert the glass into the groove in the rubber starting along the bottom edge. Use the special threading tool **B** in **FIG 13:8** to fit the rubber insert (shown black in **FIG 13:8**) into the the rubber seal with its rounded wide edge outwards.

3 Use a pressure gun fitted with a copper nozzle (which will not scratch the glass) and inject sealing compound between the glass and the rubber and between the rubber and the flange. Remove excess compound with a rag and white spirit. Do not use thinners as this will damage the paintwork.

4 Offer up the chrome finisher to the sealing rubber and bend to suit the contour if necessary. Note that on the windscreen the finisher is fitted under both lips of the wide groove in the rubber but, on the backlight, under the inner lip only and round the outer periphery of the sealing rubber. When the contour is correct, coat the inside of the chrome strip with Bostik 1251 and, when tacky, fit it to the rubber seal. With hook tool **A** feed both rubber lips over it in the case of a windscreen and the inner lip in the case of a backlight. To facilitate fitting the finisher round the outer periphery of the backlight, insert small lengths of $\frac{1}{8}$ inch diameter stiff piping cord at points where the rubber bends hard onto the depression. Finally fit the two chrome finishing pieces.

13:7 Bonnet and luggage compartment locks

Adjusting bonnet lock:

Slacken the locknut and rotate the striker peg with a screwdriver until there is approximately $\frac{1}{16}$ inch movement between the catch plate and the peg. Retighten the locknut.

Adjusting luggage compartment lock:

Slacken the four setscrews securing the striker to the lid. Move the striker in the elongated holes until the lock operates correctly and does not rattle. Retighten the setscrews.

13:8 Removing the facia, S type cars

The instrument panel:

Pull out the picnic tray fully, press both clips which are at the back edge of the tray towards each other and

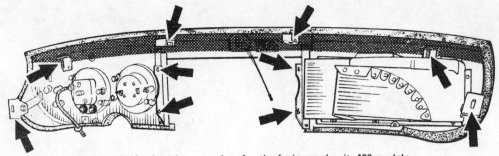

FIG 13:10 Attachment points for the facia panel unit. 420 models

withdraw the tray. Refer to **Section 13:9**. The procedure from this point is identical with that described for 420 models.

The screen rail:

To remove, refer to **FIG 13:9** and remove four nuts, one at each end and one at each side of the instrument panel. The nut located above the glove box is accessible through a hole in the top of the glove box. The central nuts are accessible after hinging down the instrument panel. Disconnect the two leads to the maplight and lift off the rail.

Refitting is the reverse of the removal procedure.

The side facia panel:

This unit is 2 in **FIG 13:9**. Before removing, detach the battery earth lead, remove the screen rail and hinge down the instrument panel. Remove the upper switch cover (43 in **FIG 10:13**) from the steering column. It is retained from below by two screws. Disconnect the snap connectors and withdraw the flasher light harness. Remove two screws and detach the fabric covered steering column casing. Lower the column to the parcel tray by releasing two nuts which secure it to the body. Detach the fabric (held with upholstery adhesive) between the demister ducts and the facia panel. Remove the setscrew securing the panel to the bracket below the screen pillar and withdraw the two screws located in the instrument panel aperture. Disconnect the speedometer drive cable, all leads from revolution counter, illumination and warning lights and withdraw the side facia panel.

Refitting is this procedure in reverse. Check that leads are correctly reconnected and use **FIG 14:1** for colour coding if necessary.

The glove box:

This unit is 4 in **FIG 13:9**. Before removing, detach the battery earth lead, withdraw the picnic tray, hinge down the instrument panel and remove the screen rail as described earlier in this section. Detach the fabric (held with upholstery adhesive) between the demister ducts and the glove box. Remove the setbolt securing the glove box to the bracket below the screen pillar and the two screws located in the instrument panel aperture. Disconnect the two leads to the illumination light and withdraw the glove box.

Refitting is the reverse of this sequence.

13:9 Removing the facia, 420 models

The instrument panel:

The following procedure also applies to the instrument panel on S type cars (after picnic tray removal as described in **Section 13:8**).

Detach the earth lead from the battery. Remove the ignition key and cigar lighter, remove the screw from each top corner and hinge down the panel. If air conditioning equipment is fitted it will be necessary to dismount the controls sub-panel before the instrument panel can be lowered.

The panel may now be removed as follows. Identify and remove the leads from the instruments, cigar lighter and all switches. Remove the electrical harness and its clips from the panel and withdraw the bolts from the extensions of the hinges which are accessible from beneath.

Refitting is the reverse of this procedure. Check that leads are correctly reconnected. Use **FIG 14:2** (**FIG 14:1** on S type cars) for colour coding reference if necessary.

The facia panel:

The facia panel, glove box and screenrail are removed as a complete unit.

Detach the earth lead from the battery. Remove the console and parcel tray as described in **Section 13:10** and hinge down the instrument panel. Disconnect the flasher light harness at the snap connectors above the steering column and withdraw the harness. Remove the two nuts which secure the column to its mounting bracket, lower the column and collect any packing washers which may be fitted at the bracket.

Disconnect the speedometer drive cable. Disconnect the earth lead from the clock fixing strap and the snap connector from the maplight lead.

Refer to **FIG 13:10** which shows the facia panel attachment points. The four points immediately below the screen rail are retaining nuts (the nut above the glove box is accessible through a hole in the top of the glove box) and the other six points are setscrews. Remove the four nuts and six setscrews and pull the panel forward.

Disconnect the remaining cables noting their colours and locations for reference when refitting and withdraw the facia panel unit. If necessary, the side facia panel and glove box can be separated from the screen rail by removing the appropriate screws.

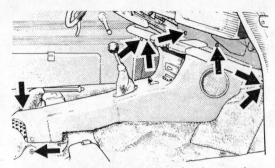

FIG 13:11 Attachment points for the console

Refitting is the reverse of this procedure. Check that the leads are correctly reconnected and use **FIG 14:2** for colour coding if necessary.

13:10 Removing the console and parcel tray

The console and parcel tray is a unit the attachment points of which are shown in **FIG 13:11**.

1 On **S type cars,** remove the two crash rolls which are each retained by two domed nuts. On **420 models,** withdraw the screws and remove both side kick-panels and the air conditioning control sub-panel (if fitted) from its mounting studs.

2 On all models, remove four nylon retaining pins and withdraw the perforated heater control guard. Refer to **FIG 13:12** and, on **S type cars,** pull off the heater flap control lever knob 5, disconnect the lever from the inner cable, remove the pivot pin and washer and withdraw the lever. On **420 models,** disconnect the lever from the inner cable and release the clip securing the outer cable.

3 On all models, disconnect the control cables from the air direction boxes 4 by releasing the locking screws which secure the inner cables to the spindles, remove the locknuts securing the outer cables to the boxes, disconnect the cables and collect the adaptors. On **S type cars,** unscrew the outer cables from the tray centre finisher, withdraw the complete assemblies and remove the finisher by removing the domed and plain nuts and washers from the two outer studs and the nuts and washers from the two inner studs.

4 On all models, remove the button control escutcheon 6 which is retained by two pegs to the control and remove the two screws now exposed. Lift the tray trimming and remove two round-headed screws from

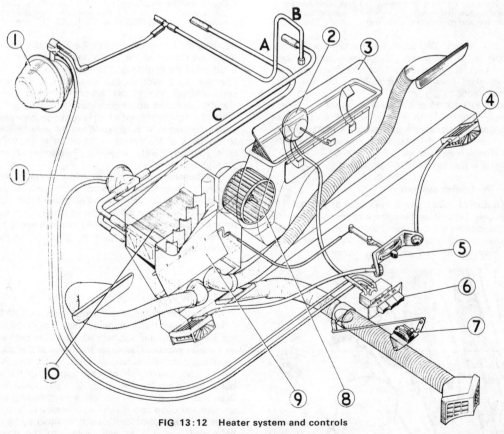

FIG 13:12 Heater system and controls

Key to Fig 13:12   1 Reservac tank   2 Vacuum actuator   3 Scuttle vent   4 Air direction box   5 Heater flap control
6 Three-button control   7 Rear air supply control   8 Fan   9 Flap   10 Heater box   11 Vacuum water valve
A Heater box to pump   **B** To induction manifold   **C** Water manifold to heater box

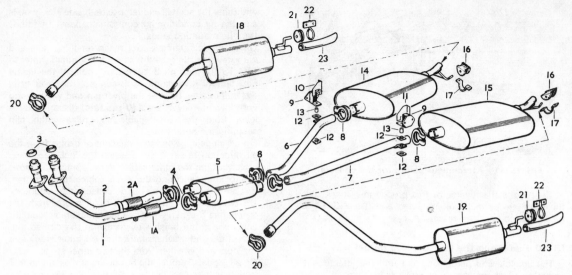

FIG 13:13   Components of the exhaust system

the tray recess. Withdraw the button panel facia, identify and disconnect the three rubber pipes. Disconnect the heater duct at the front junction. On standard transmission models remove the gearchange knob.

5 Refer to **FIG 13:11** and remove the eight attachment screws. Slide the unit rearwards to clear the front fixings and lift out over the gearlever. If, on **420 models,** the crash rail is to be detached, remove twelve nuts, two of which are domed.

Refitting is the reverse of this sequence.

13:11 The heater system

The layout of the system is illustrated in **FIG 13:12.** Engine coolant circulates through the heater box matrix 10 when the vacuum servo operated water valve 11 is open. Air, blown through the matrix by the electrically driven fan 8, may be directed in varying degrees by flap 9

FIG 13:14 Compressor drive belt adjustment. 420 models

between the air direction boxes 4 and the demister ducts which are located at the base of the windscreen. The flap is adjusted by control 5. The external scuttle vent 3 is operated by a vacuum servo actuator 2. The vacuum servo units 2 and 11 are button-controlled at 6. The vacuum tank and non-return valve 1 (which is located under the righthand front wing) is continuously evacuated while the engine is running. Warm air may be directed to the back of the car and its amount is controlled by lever 7 which operates a valve in the ducting which runs through the console.

If it becomes necessary to adjust controls 4 or 5, slacken the inner cable connector, set the unit and control at a corresponding position and retighten the locking.

When draining and refilling the cooling system, valve 11 must be open, that is in the HEAT position and it may be necessary to run the engine to generate vacuum to operate the valve.

13:12 The exhaust system

The layout of the exhaust system is shown in **FIG 13:13.**

To disconnect the downpipes 1 and 2 from the engine, remove four nuts and washers which secure each pipe to its exhaust manifold, separate the pipes at the clamping strap adjacent to the flexible sections 1A and 2A and remove the bolt which attaches pipe 2 to the clutch housing. Collect sealing rings 3. The pipes may be detached from the front silencer 5 by removing clips 4. On lefthand drive cars it will be necessary to remove the steering column joint heat shield (retained by two nuts, bolts and washers) to gain access to the downpipe flange nuts. Renew sealing rings 3 when refitting and retighten the flange nuts after running the engine.

To remove the silencers, tail pipes and intermediate pipes, proceed as follows. Slacken clips 20 and remove rear silencers 18 and 19 and their tail pipes. Remove two nuts, bolts and washers which secure each main silencer rubber mounting 16 and bracket 17. Slacken two clips 8 at the front of the main silencers 14 and 15 and remove the silencers. Slacken clips 8 at the rear of the front silencer, remove the bolts in the rubber mounting bracket 9 and remove the intermediate pipes. Slacken two clips 4 (unless the downpipes have already been removed) and dismount the front silencer 5.

13:13 Air conditioning equipment

Every 6000 miles, check the tension of the compressor drive belt. Release the nut arrowed in **FIG 13:14**

sufficiently to allow the pivot to be moved upwards when a spanner is applied to the pivot hexagon. When adjusted retighten the securing nut. Belt tension is correct when it can be depressed $\frac{1}{2}$ inch between the pulleys.

Do not loosen or attempt to remove any of the unions or hoses in the air conditioning system. Such dismantling must be carried out only by Authorised Jaguar Agents or qualified Refrigeration Engineers.

It is necessary to dismount parts of the air conditioning system to give access for the removal of certain other equipment and this can and must be done without loosening unions or removing hoses.

NOTES

APPENDIX

TECHNICAL DATA

Dimensions are in inches unless otherwise stated

ENGINE

Bore and stroke:

3.4 litre	...	...	...	...	...	83 x 106 mm
3.8 litre	...	...	...	...	...	87 x 106 mm
4.2 litre	...	...	...	...	...	92 x 106 mm

Compression ratio:

3.4 and 3.8 litre	...	...	...	...	7:1, 8:1 or 9:1
4.2 litre	...	...	...	...	8:1 or 9:1

Crankshaft:

Number of main journals	...	...	...	Seven
Main journal diameter ...	...	...	...	2.7500 to 2.7505
Main bearings ...	...	...	...	Thinwall, steel-backed

Material:

3.4 and 3.8 litre	...	...	...	Whitemetal
4.2 litre	...	...	...	Lead/bronze

Diametral clearance:

3.4 and 3.8 litre	...	...	...	.0015 to .003
4.2 litre	...	...	...	.0025 to .0042
Undersizes	...	...	...	—.010, —.020, —.030, —.040

Thrust washers:

Location	...	...	...	Centre journal
Thickness	...	...	...	.091 to .093 or .095 to .097
End float	...	...	...	.004 to .006
Crankpin journal diameter	...	...	...	2.0866 to 2.0860
Minimum regrind diameter	...	...	...	2.0460

Connecting rods:

Length between centres	...	...	...	7.750
Big-end bearings	...	...	...	Thinwall, steel-backed

Material:

3.4 and 3.8 litre	...	...	Lead/bronze, lead/indium coated
4.2 litre	...	...	Lead/bronze
Diametrical clearance ...	...	...	.0015 to .0033
End float	...	...	.0058 to .0087
Bore diameter for big-end bearing	...	...	2.2330 to 2.2335
Small-end bush material	...	...	Phosphor/bronze, steel-backed
Small-end bore diameter	...	...	.8750 to .8752

Pistons:

Type:

3.4 and 3.8 litre	...	...	...	Aluminium, semi-split skirt
4.2 litre, 8:1 CR	...	...	...	Aluminium, solid skirt
4.2 litre, 9:1 CR	...	...	...	Aluminium, semi-split skirt
Gudgeon pin bore diameter	...	...	...	.8750 to .8752

Suitable bore size (standard):

3.4 litre	...	...	...	82.9936 to 83.0127 mm
3.8 litre	...	...	...	86.9936 to 87.0127 mm
4.2 litre	...	...	...	92.0686 to 92.0877 mm

Bore size for piston grade letter:

3.4 litre	F	...	...	...	...	3.2673 to 3.2676
	G	...	...	...	...	3.2677 to 3.2680
	H	...	...	...	...	3.2681 to 3.2684
	J	...	...	...	...	3.2685 to 3.2688
	K	...	...	...	...	3.2689 to 3.2692

3.8 litre	F ...	...	...	...	...	3.4248 to 3.4251
	G ...	...	...	...	...	3.4252 to 3.4255
	H ...	...	...	...	...	3.4256 to 3.4259
	J ...	...	...	...	...	3.4260 to 3.4263
	K ...	...	...	...	...	3.4264 to 3.4267
4.2 litre	F ...	...	...	...	...	3.6250 to 3.6253
	G ...	...	...	...	...	3.6254 to 3.6257
	H ...	...	...	...	...	3.6258 to 3.6261
	J ...	...	...	...	...	3.6262 to 3.6265
	K ...	...	...	...	...	3.6266 to 3.6269

Oversizes available	...	...	...	...	+.010, +.020, +.030
Piston rings	...	...	...	...	Two compression, one oil control
Top ring	...	...	...	...	Tapered and chrome faced
Second ring	...	...	...	...	Tapered
Oil control	...	...	...	...	Maxiflex

Compression ring width:

3.4 and 3.8 litre	...	...	...	...	.0772 to .0777
4.2 litre	...	...	...	...	.0770 to .0780

Oil control ring width:

3.4 and 3.8 litre	...	...	...	...	.150 to .154
4.2 litre	...	...	...	...	.151 to .158
Fitted gap, compression	...	...	...	...	.015 to .020
Fitted gap, Maxiflex	...	...	...	...	.015 to .033
Ring to groove clearance	...	...	...	...	.001 to .003
Gudgeon pin type	...	...	...	...	Fully floating
Gudgeon pin diameter	...	...	...	...	.8750 to .8752

Compression height:

3.4 litre—7:1	...	...	...	...	...	1.690 to 1.695
	8:1	...	...	...	...	2.163 to 2.168
	9:1	...	...	...	...	2.258 to 2.263
3.8 litre—7:1	...	...	...	...	...	1.841 to 1.846
and	8:1	...	...	...	...	2.064 to 2.069
4.2 litre	9:1	...	...	...	...	2.242 to 2.247

Compression pressures:

7:1 ...	...	...	...	...	...	125 lb/sq in
8:1 ...	...	...	...	...	...	155 lb/sq in
9:1 ...	...	...	...	...	...	180 lb/sq in

Cylinder block:

Maximum rebore size	...	...	...	...	+.030
Liner interference fit	...	...	...	...	.001 to .005
Main bearings bore	...	...	...	...	2.9165 to 2.9170

Material:

3.4 litre	...	...	...	...	Chromium iron
3.8 litre	...	...	...	...	'Brivadium' dry liners
4.2 litre	...	...	...	...	4KG dry liners

Camshafts:

Journals	...	...	...	...	Four thinwall, steel-backed
Bearing material	...	...	...	...	Whitemetal
Journal diameter	...	...	...	...	.9990 to .9995
End float	...	...	...	...	.004 to .006
Bearing diametrical clearance	...	...	...	...	.0005 to .0020

Drive:

Type	...	...	...	...	Duplex chain, $\frac{3}{8}$ pitch
Top chain	...	...	...	...	100 pitches
Bottom chain	...	...	...	...	82 pitches

Tappets, guides and pads:

Tappet diameter	1.3738 to 1.3742
Guide diameter	1.375 to 1.382
Guide to head shrink fit	.003
Adjusting pads:	
Thickness of pad 'A'	.085
Available in thickness steps of .001 to pad 'Z' which has a thickness of .110	

Valves:

Seat angle, inlet and exhaust	45 deg.
Head diameter:	
Inlet...	1.748 to 1.752
Exhaust	1.6248 to 1.6252
Stem diameter	.309 to .310
Valve lift	.375

Valve guides:

Bore diameter:	
Inlet...	.311 to .312
Exhaust	.312 to .313
Length:	
Inlet with stem seal	1.860
Inlet without stem seal	1.8125
Exhaust	1.9375
Guide to head interference fit	.0005 to .0022
Fitted height above head	.3125
Bore diameter of valve seat insert:	
Inlet...	1.499 to 1.503
Exhaust	1.379 to 1.383
Insert shrink fit to head	.003

Valve springs:

Free length	1.9375 outer, 1.6565 inner
Fitted length	1.3125 outer, 1.2187 inner
Load at fitted length	48 lb outer, 30 lb inner

Valve timing and clearances:

Valve clearance:	
Inlet...	.004
Exhaust	.006

Valve timing:

Inlet opens	15 deg. BTDC
Inlet closes	57 deg. ABDC
Exhaust opens	57 deg. BBDC
Exhaust closes...	15 deg. ATDC

Oil pump:

Type	Eccentric rotor
Outer rotor/body clearance	.010 maximum
Lobe tip clearance	.010 maximum
End clearance	.004 maximum

Oil filter...	Fullflow with renewable element

FUEL SYSTEM

Carburetters:

3.4 and 3.8 litre	SU HD6, 1¾ inch size
Jet needle type	TL
Jet size	.10
4.2 litre	SU HD8, 2 inch size
Jet needle type	UM
Jet size	.125

Starting carburetter needle:

Type	425/8
Fuel pumps	Two AUF.301

COOLING SYSTEM

Thermostat:
3.4 and 3.8 litre, standard type:
    Initial opening ... ... 70°C to 75°C
    Fully open ... ... 85°C
3.4 and 3.8 litre, type for extreme winter conditions:
    Initial opening ... ... 80°C to 84°C
    Fully open ... ... 93°C
4.2 litre, standard type:
    Initial opening ... ... 70.5°C
    Fully open ... ... 75.5°C
4.2 litre, type for extreme winter conditions:
    Initial opening ... ... 78.8°C
    Fully open ... ... 83.7°C

IGNITION SYSTEM

Sparking plugs:
3.4 and 3.8 litre ... ... Champion UN.12Y
4.2 litre ... ... Champion N.11Y
Distributor ... ... Lucas 22.D6
Contact points gap ... ... .014 to .016 inch
Firing order ... ... 1,5,3,6,2,4. No.1 is the rear cylinder

CLUTCH

Early 3.4 and 3.8 litre ... ... Borg and Beck 10 A6–G
Diameter of plate... ... ... 9.85 inch Borglite
Number of coil springs 12
Colour of springs:
    3.4 litre ... ... Yellow/light green
    3.8 litre ... ... Black
Later 3.4 and 3.8 litre ... ... Borg and Beck diaphragm spring clutch
4.2 litre ... ... Borg and Beck diaphragm spring clutch

TRANSMISSION

Gearbox:
    Number of forward speeds ... ... Four
    Synchromesh, early 3.4 and 3.8 litre ... ... Second, third and top gears
    Synchromesh, later 3.4 and 3.8 litre ... ... All forward gears
Gearbox ratios:
    Prefix GB or GBN, suffix JS:
        Top 1:1
        Third 1.283:1
        Second 1.860:1
        First 3.377:1
        Reverse 3.377:1
    Prefix JC or JCN:
        Top 1:1
        Third 1.328:1
        Second 1.973:1
        First 3.040:1
        Reverse 3.490:1

	S type cars	420 models
Automatic:		
Top	1:1	1:1
Intermediate...	1.435:1	1.46:1
Low...	2.308:1	2.40:1
Reverse	2.009:1	2.00:1

Torque converter:

Type ... ... Three-element
Ratio:
    S type cars ... ... 2.15 maximum
    420 models ... ... 2.0 maximum

Overdrive:

Make ... ... Laycocke de Normanville
Fitted to prefix GBN gearboxes ... ... Type A
Fitted to prefix JCN ... ... Compact type A
Ratio ... ... .778

Differential ratios:

Standard transmission:
    S type cars 3.54:1
    420 models 3.31:1
Overdrive models:
    S type cars 3.77:1
    420 models 3.77:1
Automatic transmission:
    S type cars 3.54:1
    420 models 3.31:1

SUSPENSION

Front suspension:

Type ... ... Independent, one coil spring per wheel
Camber ... ... zero to 1 deg. positive
Castor ... ... $\frac{1}{2}$ deg. negative to $\frac{1}{2}$ deg. positive
Swivel inclination ... ... $3\frac{1}{2}$ deg.

Rear suspension:

Type ... ... Independent, two coil springs per wheel
Camber—$\frac{1}{2}$ deg. to 1 deg. negative with the suspension locked in the mid-laden position.
    See text, page 99.

Road springs:

Front (one per wheel):
    Number of coils ... ... $6\frac{1}{2}$
    Diameter of wire ... ... .610
Rear (two per wheel):
    Number of coils ... ... $8\frac{3}{4}$
    Diameter of wire ... ... .475
    Free length 11.395
    Identification colour... ... ... Red/Yellow

Dampers ... ... Hydraulic, telescopic, one per road spring

STEERING

Manual ... ... Burman F3, recirculating ball
Ratio ... ... 20.3 at centre of travel
Number of wheel turns ... ... $4\frac{1}{4}$ lock to lock
Turning circle ... ... 33 ft 6 in
Toe-in ... ... Parallel to $\frac{1}{8}$ total toe-in
Power-assisted, S type cars ... ... Burman, recirculating ball
Pump ... ... Hobourn-Eaton mounted on rear of generator
Power-assisted, 420 models ... ... Adwest, Marles Varamatic
Ratio ... ... 21.6 at centre of travel
Number of wheel turns ... ... $2\frac{7}{8}$ lock to lock
Pump ... ... Saginaw

BRAKES

S type cars—Dunlop hydraulic, disc front and rear with quick change pads

Disc diameter, front	11
Disc diameter, rear	$10\frac{3}{8}$
Pad material	Mintex M.59
Servo unit (early cars)	Lockheed $6\frac{7}{8}$ inch type
Servo unit (later cars)	Lockheed 8 inch type

420 models—Girling hydraulic, disc front and rear with quick change pads

Disc diameter, front	11.1875
Disc diameter, rear	10.395
Pad material	Mintex M.33
Servo unit	Lockheed type 8, dual line
Hydraulic fluid	Castrol/Girling Crimson
Handbrake pad material	Mintex M.34

ELECTRICAL EQUIPMENT

Battery:

Voltage	12 volt

Earthing system:

S type cars	Positive
420 models	Negative

Type:

S type cars	BV.11A
Capacity (20 hour rate)	67 amp/hr
420 models	S11/9/8
Capacity (20 hour rate)	67 amp/hr

Starter motor:

3.4 and 3.8 litre	M.45G with Bendix pinion drive
4.2 litre	M.45G with positive pre-engagement of pinion drive

Generator ... ... Lucas

3.4 and 3.8 litre	C.42 or, to special order, C.48
4.2 litre	11AC alternator with integral rectifier

Generator maximum DC output:

C.42	30 amps
C.48	35 amps
11AC	45 amps

Control unit type ... ... Lucas

With C.42 and C.48	RB.340
With 11AC	4TR

Voltage regulator settings:

Type RB.340

With C.42 generator:

50°F	14.9 to 15.5
68°F	14.7 to 15.3
86°F	14.5 to 15.1

With C.48 generator:

50°F	15.0 to 15.6
68°F	14.8 to 15.4
86°F	14.6 to 15.2

Cut-out:

Cut-in voltage	12.6 to 13.4
Drop-off voltage	9.3 to 11.2

Voltage setting on 4TR unit:

At 68°F to 78°F	13.9 to 14.3

CAPACITIES

	Imperial	USA	Litres
Engine	12 pints	14½ pints	6.75
Gearbox:			
Standard	2½ pints	3 pints	1.5
With overdrive	4 pints	4¾ pints	2.25
Automatic transmission:			
S type cars	15 pints	18 pints	8.5
420 models	16 pints	19 pints	9.0
Final drive unit	2¾ pints	3¼ pints	1.5
Cooling system with heater:			
S type cars	22 pints	26½ pints	12.5
420 models	25½ pints	30½ pints	14.5
Petrol total (two tanks)	14 galls.	16½ galls.	63.5

DIMENSIONS

Overall length	15 ft 7⅞ in
Overall width	5 ft 6¾ in
Overall height	4 ft 6½ in
Ground clearance	7 in
Wheelbase	8 ft 11⅜ in
Track:	
Front, disc wheels	4 ft 7¼ in
Front, wire wheels	4 ft 7¼ in
Rear, disc wheels	4 ft 6¼ in
Rear, wire wheels	4 ft 4⅞ in

TORQUE WRENCH SETTINGS

Engine:

Cylinder head stud nuts:	
3.4 and 3.8 litre	54 lb ft
4.2 litre	58 lb ft
Big-end bolts	37 lb ft
Main bearing bolts	83 lb ft
Camshaft bearing nuts	15 lb ft
Flywheel bolts	67 lb ft

Final drive unit:

Drive gear bolts	70 to 80 lb ft
Differential bearing cap bolts	60 to 65 lb ft
Pinion nut	120 to 130 lb ft
Thornton 'Power-Lok' differential bolts	40 to 45 lb ft

Starter motor (420 models):

Copper terminal nut on solenoid	20 lb in
Solenoid fixing bolts	4.5 lb ft
Through bolts	8 lb ft

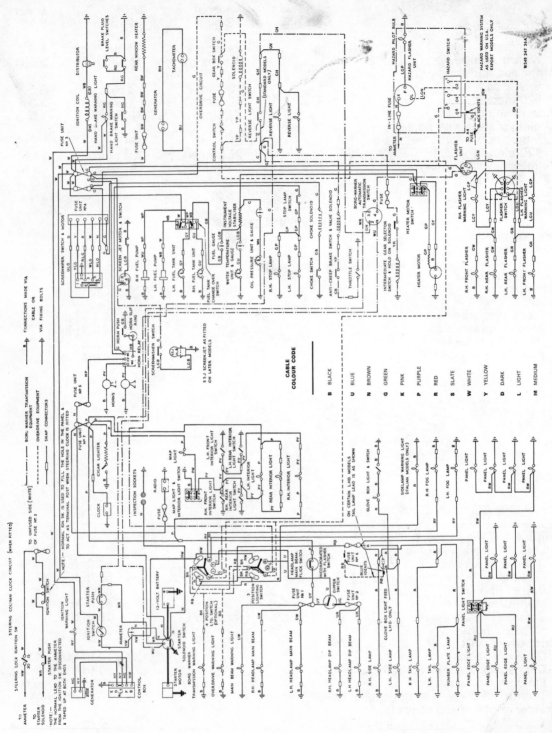

FIG 14:1 Wiring diagram for S type cars

166

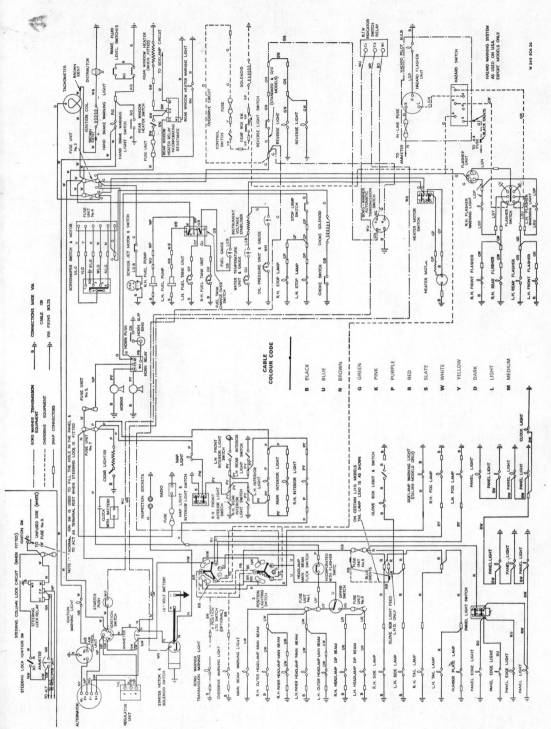

FIG 14:2 Wiring diagram for 420 models

Inches	Decimals	Milli-metres	Inches to Millimetres (Inches)	(mm)	Millimetres to Inches (mm)	(Inches)
1/64	.015625	.3969	.001	.0254	.01	.00039
1/32	.03125	.7937	.002	.0508	.02	.00079
3/64	.046875	1.1906	.003	.0762	.03	.00118
1/16	.0625	1.5875	.004	.1016	.04	.00157
5/64	.078125	1.9844	.005	.1270	.05	.00197
3/32	.09375	2.3812	.006	.1524	.06	.00236
7/64	.109375	2.7781	.007	.1778	.07	.00276
1/8	.125	3.1750	.008	.2032	.08	.00315
9/64	.140625	3.5719	.009	.2286	.09	.00354
5/32	.15625	3.9687	.01	.254	.1	.00394
11/64	.171875	4.3656	.02	.508	.2	.00787
3/16	.1875	4.7625	.03	.762	.3	.01181
13/64	.203125	5.1594	.04	1.016	.4	.01575
7/32	.21875	5.5562	.05	1.270	.5	.01969
15/64	.234375	5.9531	.06	1.524	.6	.02362
1/4	.25	6.3500	.07	1.778	.7	.02756
17/64	.265625	6.7469	.08	2.032	.8	.03150
9/32	.28125	7.1437	.09	2.286	.9	.03543
19/64	.296875	7.5406	.1	2.54	1	.03937
5/16	.3125	7.9375	.2	5.08	2	.07874
21/64	.328125	8.3344	.3	7.62	3	.11811
11/32	.34375	8.7312	.4	10.16	4	.15748
23/64	.359375	9.1281	.5	12.70	5	.19685
3/8	.375	9.5250	.6	15.24	6	.23622
25/64	.390625	9.9219	.7	17.78	7	.27559
13/32	.40625	10.3187	.8	20.32	8	.31496
27/64	.421875	10.7156	.9	22.86	9	.35433
7/16	.4375	11.1125	1	25.4	10	.39370
29/64	.453125	11.5094	2	50.8	11	.43307
15/32	.46875	11.9062	3	76.2	12	.47244
31/64	.484375	12.3031	4	101.6	13	.51181
1/2	.5	12.7000	5	127.0	14	.55118
33/64	.515625	13.0969	6	152.4	15	.59055
17/32	.53125	13.4937	7	177.8	16	.62992
35/64	.546875	13.8906	8	203.2	17	.66929
9/16	.5625	14.2875	9	228.6	18	.70866
37/64	.578125	14.6844	10	254.0	19	.74803
19/32	.59375	15.0812	11	279.4	20	.78740
39/64	.609375	15.4781	12	304.8	21	.82677
5/8	.625	15.8750	13	330.2	22	.86614
41/64	.640625	16.2719	14	355.6	23	.90551
21/32	.65625	16.6687	15	381.0	24	.94488
43/64	.671875	17.0656	16	406.4	25	.98425
11/16	.6875	17.4625	17	431.8	26	1.02362
45/64	.703125	17.8594	18	457.2	27	1.06299
23/32	.71875	18.2562	19	482.6	28	1.10236
47/64	.734375	18.6531	20	508.0	29	1.14173
3/4	.75	19.0500	21	533.4	30	1.18110
49/64	.765625	19.4469	22	558.8	31	1.22047
25/32	.78125	19.8437	23	584.2	32	1.25984
51/64	.796875	20.2406	24	609.6	33	1.29921
13/16	.8125	20.6375	25	635.0	34	1.33858
53/64	.828125	21.0344	26	660.4	35	1.37795
27/32	.84375	21.4312	27	685.8	36	1.41732
55/64	.859375	21.8281	28	711.2	37	1.4567
7/8	.875	22.2250	29	736.6	38	1.4961
57/64	.890625	22.6219	30	762.0	39	1.5354
29/32	.90625	23.0187	31	787.4	40	1.5748
59/64	.921875	23.4156	32	812.8	41	1.6142
15/16	.9375	23.8125	33	838.2	42	1.6535
61/64	.953125	24.2094	34	863.6	43	1.6929
31/32	.96875	24.6062	35	889.0	44	1.7323
63/64	.984375	25.0031	36	914.4	45	1.7717

UNITS	Pints to Litres	Gallons to Litres	Litres to Pints	Litres to Gallons	Miles to Kilometres	Kilometres to Miles	Lbs. per sq. In. to Kg. per sq. Cm.	Kg. per sq. Cm. to Lbs. per sq. In.
1	.57	4.55	1.76	.22	1.61	.62	.07	14.22
2	1.14	9.09	3.52	.44	3.22	1.24	.14	28.50
3	1.70	13.64	5.28	.66	4.83	1.86	.21	42.67
4	2.27	18.18	7.04	.88	6.44	2.49	.28	56.89
5	2.84	22.73	8.80	1.10	8.05	3.11	.35	71.12
6	3.41	27.28	10.56	1.32	9.66	3.73	.42	85.34
7	3.98	31.82	12.32	1.54	11.27	4.35	.49	99.56
8	4.55	36.37	14.08	1.76	12.88	4.97	.56	113.79
9		40.91	15.84	1.98	14.48	5.59	.63	128.00
10		45.46	17.60	2.20	16.09	6.21	.70	142.23
20				4.40	32.19	12.43	1.41	284.47
30				6.60	48.28	18.64	2.11	426.70
40				8.80	64.37	24.85		
50					80.47	31.07		
60					96.56	37.28		
70					112.65	43.50		
80					128.75	49.71		
90					144.84	55.92		
100					160.93	62.14		

UNITS	Lb ft to kgm	Kgm to lb ft	UNITS	Lb ft to kgm	Kgm to lb ft
1	.138	7.233	7	.967	50.631
2	.276	14.466	8	1.106	57.864
3	.414	21.699	9	1.244	65.097
4	.553	28.932	10	1.382	72.330
5	.691	36.165	20	2.765	144.660
6	.829	43.398	30	4.147	216.990

HINTS ON MAINTENANCE AND OVERHAUL

There are few things more rewarding than the restoration of a vehicle's original peak of efficiency and smooth performance.

The following notes are intended to help the owner to reach that state of perfection. Providing that he possesses the basic manual skills he should have no difficulty in performing most of the operations detailed in this manual. It must be stressed, however, that where recommended in the manual, highly-skilled operations ought to be entrusted to experts, who have the necessary equipment, to carry out the work satisfactorily.

Quality of workmanship:

The hazardous driving conditions on the roads to-day demand that vehicles should be as nearly perfect, mechanically, as possible. It is therefore most important that amateur work be carried out with care, bearing in mind the often inadequate working conditions, and also the inferior tools which may have to be used. It is easy to counsel perfection in all things, and we recognize that it may be setting an impossibly high standard. We do, however, suggest that every care should be taken to ensure that a vehicle is as safe to take on the road as it is humanly possible to make it.

Safe working conditions:

Even though a vehicle may be stationary, it is still potentially dangerous if certain sensible precautions are not taken when working on it while it is supported on jacks or blocks. It is indeed preferable not to use jacks alone, but to supplement them with carefully placed blocks, so that there will be plenty of support if the car rolls off the jacks during a strenuous manoeuvre. Axle stands are an excellent way of providing a rigid base which is not readily distrubed. Piles of bricks are a dangerous substitute. Be careful not to get under heavy loads on lifting tackle, the load could fall. It is preferable not to work alone when lifting an engine, or when working underneath a vehicle which is supported well off the ground. To be trapped, particularly under the vehicle, may have unpleasant results if help is not quickly forthcoming. Make some provision, however humble, to deal with fires. Always disconnect a battery if there is a likelihood of electrical shorts. These may start a fire if there is leaking fuel about. This applies particularly to leads which can carry a heavy current, like those in the starter circuit. While on the subject of electricity, we must also stress the danger of using equipment which is run off the mains and which has no earth or has faulty wiring or connections. So many workshops have damp floors, and electrical shocks are of such a nature that it is sometimes impossible to let go of a live lead or piece of equipment due to the muscular spasms which take place.

Work demanding special care:

This involves the servicing of braking, steering and suspension systems. On the road, failure of the braking system may be disastrous. Make quite sure that there can be no possiblity of failure through the bursting of rusty brake pipes or rotten hoses, nor to a sudden loss of pressure due to defective seals or valves.

Problems:

The chief problems which may face an operator are:
1 External dirt.
2 Difficulty in undoing tight fixings.
3 Dismantling unfamiliar mechanisms.
4 Deciding in what respect parts are defective.
5 Confusion about the correct order for reassembly.
6 Adjusting running clearance.
7 Road testing.
8 Final tuning.

Practical suggestions to solve the problems:

1 Preliminary cleaning of large parts—engines, transmissions, steering, suspensions, etc.,—should be carried out before removal from the car. Where road dirt and mud alone are present, wash clean with a high-pressure water jet, brushing to remove stubborn adhesions, and allow to drain and dry. Where oil or grease is also present, wash down with a proprietary compound (Gunk, Tepol etc.,) applying with a stiff brush—an old paint brush is suitable—into all crevices. Cover the distributor and ignition coil with a poly-thene bag and then apply a strong water jet to clear the loosened deposits. Allow to drain and dry. The assemblies will then be sufficiently clean to remove and transfer to the bench for the next stage.

On the bench, further cleaning can be carried out, first wiping the parts as free as possible from grease with old newspaper. Avoid using rag or cotton waste which can leave clogging fibres behind. Any remaining grease can be removed with a brush dipped in paraffin. If necessary, traces of paraffin can be removed by carbon tetrachloride. Avoid using paraffin or petrol in large quantities for cleaning in enclosed areas, such as garages, on account of the high fire risk.

When all exteriors have been cleaned, and not before, dismantling can be commenced. This ensures that dirt will not enter into interiors and orifices revealed by dismantling. In the next phases, where components have to be cleaned, use carbon tetrachloride in preference to petrol and keep the containers covered except when in use. After the components have been cleaned, plug small holes with tapered hard wood plugs cut to size and blank off larger orifices with grease-proof paper and masking tape. Do not use soft wood plugs or matchsticks as they may break.

2 It is not advisable to hammer on the end of a screw thread, but if it must be done, first screw on a nut to protect the thread, and use a lead hammer. This applies particularly to the removal of tapered cotters. Nuts and bolts seem to 'grow' together, especially in exhaust systems. If penetrating oil does not work, try the judicious application of heat, but be careful of starting a fire. Asbestos sheet or cloth is useful to isolate heat.

Tight bushes or pieces of tail-pipe rusted into a silencer can be removed by splitting them with an open-ended hacksaw. Tight screws can sometimes be started by a tap from a hammer on the end of a suitable screwdriver. Many tight fittings will yield to the judicious use of a hammer, but it must be a soft-faced hammer if damage is to be avoided, use a heavy block on the opposite side to absorb shock. Any parts of the steering system which have been damaged should be renewed, as attempts to repair them may lead to cracking and subsequent failure, and steering ball joints should be disconnected using a recommended tool to prevent damage.

3 It often happens that an owner is baffled when trying to dismantle an unfamiliar piece of equipment. So many modern devices are pressed together or assembled by spinning-over flanges, that they must be sawn apart. The intention is that the whole assembly must be renewed. However, parts which appear to be in one piece to the naked eye, may reveal close-fitting joint lines when inspected with a magnifying glass, and, this may provide the necessary clue to dismantling. Left-handed screw threads are used where rotational forces would tend to unscrew a right-handed screw thread.

Be very careful when dismantling mechanisms which may come apart suddenly. Work in an enclosed space where the parts will be contained, and drape a piece of cloth over the device if springs are likely to fly in all directions. Mark everything which might be reassembled in the wrong position, scratched symbols may be used on unstressed parts, or a sequence of tiny dots from a centre punch can be useful. Stressed parts should never be scratched or centre-popped as this may lead to cracking under working conditions. Store parts which look alike in the correct order for reassembly. Never rely upon memory to assist in the assembly of complicated mechanisms, especially when they will be dismantled for a long time, but make notes, and drawings to supplement the diagrams in the manual, and put labels on detached wires. Rust stains may indicate unlubricated wear. This can sometimes be seen round the outside edge of a bearing cup in a universal joint. Look for bright rubbing marks on parts which normally should not make heavy contact. These might prove that something is bent or running out of truth. For example, there might be bright marks on one side of a piston, at the top near the ring grooves, and others at the bottom of the skirt on the other side. This could well be the clue to a bent connecting rod. Suspected cracks can be proved by heating the component in a light oil to approximately 100°C, removing, drying off, and dusting with french chalk, if a crack is present the oil retained in the crack will stain the french chalk.

4 In determining wear, and the degree, against the permissible limits set in the manual, accurate measurement can only be achieved by the use of a micrometer. In many cases, the wear is given to the fourth place of decimals; that is in ten-thousandths of an inch. This can be read by the vernier scale on the barrel of a good micrometer. Bore diameters are more difficult to determine. If, however, the matching shaft is accurately measured, the degree of play in the bore can be felt as a guide to its suitability. In other cases, the shank of a twist drill of known diameter is a handy check.

Many methods have been devised for determining the clearance between bearing surfaces. To-day the best and simplest is by the use of Plastigage, obtainable from most garages. A thin plastic thread is laid between the two surfaces and the bearing is tightened, flattening the thread. On removal, the width of the thread is compared with a scale supplied with the thread and the clearance is read off directly. Sometimes joint faces leak persistently, even after gasket renewal. The fault will then be traceable to distortion, dirt or burrs. Studs which are screwed into soft metal frequently raise burrs at the point of entry. A quick cure for this is to chamfer the edge of the hole in the part which fits over the stud.

5 **Always check a replacement part with the original one before it is fitted.**

If parts are not marked, and the order for reassembly is not known, a little detective work will help. Look for marks which are due to wear to see if they can be mated. Joint faces may not be identical due to manufacturing errors, and parts which overlap may be stained, giving a clue to the correct position. Most fixings leave identifying marks especially if they were painted over on assembly. It is then easier to decide whether a nut, for instance, has a plain, a spring, or a shakeproof washer under it. All running surfaces become 'bedded' together after long spells of work and tiny imperfections on one part will be found to have left corresponding marks on the other. This is particularly true of shafts and bearings and even a score on a cylinder wall will show on the piston.

6 Checking end float or rocker clearances by feeler gauge may not always give accurate results because of wear. For instance, the rocker tip which bears on a valve stem may be deeply pitted, in which case the feeler will simply be bridging a depression. Thrust washers may also wear depressions in opposing faces to make accurate measurement difficult. End float is then easier to check by using a dial gauge. It is common practice to adjust end play in bearing assemblies, like front hubs with taper rollers, by doing up the axle nut until the hub becomes stiff to turn and then backing it off a little. Do not use this method with ballbearing hubs as the assembly is often preloaded by tightening the axle nut to its fullest extent. If the splitpin hole will not line up, file the base of the nut a little.

Steering assemblies often wear in the straight-ahead position. If any part is adjusted, make sure that it remains free when moved from lock to lock. Do not be surprised if an assembly like a steering gearbox, which is known to be carefully adjusted outside the car, becomes stiff when it is bolted in place. This will be due to distortion of the case by the pull of the mounting bolts, particularly if the mounting points are not all touching together. This problem may be met in other equipment and is cured by careful attention to the alignment of mounting points.

When a spanner is stamped with a size and A/F it means that the dimension is the width between the jaws and has no connection with ANF, which is the designation for the American National Fine thread. Coarse threads like Whitworth are rarely used on cars to-day except for studs which screw into soft aluminium or cast iron. For this reason it might be found that the top end of a cylinder head stud has a fine thread and the lower end a coarse thread to screw into the cylinder block. If the car has mainly UNF threads then it is likely that any coarse threads will be UNC, which are not the same as Whitworth. Small sizes have the same number of threads in Whitworth and UNC, but in the $\frac{1}{2}$ inch size for example, there are twelve threads to the inch in the former and thirteen in the latter.

7 After a major overhaul, particularly if a great deal of work has been done on the braking, steering and suspension systems, it is advisable to approach the problem of testing with care. If the braking system has been overhauled, apply heavy pressure to the brake pedal and get a second operator to check every possible source of leakage. The brakes may work extremely well, but a leak could cause complete failure after a few miles.

Do not fit the hub caps until every wheel nut has been checked for tightness, and make sure the tyre pressures are correct. Check the levels of coolant, lubricants and hydraulic fluids. Being satisfied that all is well, take the car on the road and test the brakes at once. Check the steering and the action of the handbrake. Do all this at moderate speeds on quiet roads, and make sure there is no other vehicle behind you when you try a rapid stop.

Finally, remember that many parts settle down after a time, so check for tightness of all fixings after the car has been on the road for a hundred miles or so.

8 It is useless to tune an engine which has not reached its normal running temperature. In the same way, the tune of an engine which is stiff after a rebore will be different when the engine is again running free. Remember too, that rocker clearances on pushrod operated valve gear will change when the cylinder head nuts are tightened after an initial period of running with a new head gasket.

Trouble may not always be due to what seems the obvious cause. Ignition, carburation and mechanical condition are interdependent and spitting back through the carburetter, which might be attributed to a weak mixture, can be caused by a sticking inlet valve.

For one final hint on tuning, never adjust more than one thing at a time or it will be impossible to tell which adjustment produced the desired result.

NOTES

GLOSSARY OF TERMS

AF — Across Flats. Width across the flats of nut or bolt heads, or between jaws of associated spanners.

Allen key — Cranked wrench of hexagonal section for use with socket-head screws.

Alternator — Electrical generator producing alternating current. Rectified to direct current for battery charging.

Ambient temperature — Surrounding atmospheric temperature.

ANF — American National Fine screw thread.

Annulus — Used in engineering to indicate the outer ring gear of an epicyclic gear train.

Armature — The shaft carrying the windings, which rotates in the magnetic field of a generator or starter motor. That part of a solenoid which is activated by the magnetic field.

Asymmetrical — Not symmetrical.

Axial — In line with, or pertaining to, an axis.

BA — British Association screw thread.

Backlash — Play in meshing gears.

Balance lever — A bar where force applied at the centre is equally divided between connections at the ends.

Banjo axle — Axle casing with large diameter housing for the crownwheel and differential.

Bendix pinion — A self-engaging and self-disengaging drive on a starter motor shaft.

Bevel pinion — A conical shaped gearwheel, designed to mesh with a similar gear with an axis usually at 90 deg. to its own.

bhp — Brake horse power, measured on a dynamometer.

bmep — Brake mean effective pressure. Average pressure on a piston during the working stroke.

Brake cylinder — Cylinder with hydraulically operated piston(s) acting on brake shoes or pad(s).

Brake regulator — Control valve fitted in hydraulic braking system which limits brake pressure to rear brakes during heavy braking to prevent rear wheel locking.

BSF — British Standard Fine screw thread.

BSW — British Standard Whitworth screw thread.

Bypass filter — Oil filter—one which cleans a small volume of oil from the pump and returns it to the sump.

Camber — Angle at which a wheel is tilted from the vertical.

Capacitor — Modern term for an electrical condenser. Part of distributor assembly, connected across contact breaker points, acts as an interference suppressor.

Castellated — Top face of a nut, slotted across the flats, to take a locking splitpin.

Castor — Angle at which the kingpin or swivel pin is tilted when viewed from the side.

cc — Cubic centimetres. Engine capacity is arrived at by multiplying the area of the bore in sq cm by the stroke in cm by the number of cylinders.

Clevis — U-shaped forked connector used with a clevis pin, usually at handbrake connections.

Clockwise — In the direction of rotation of the hands of a clock, movement in the opposite direction is normally referred to as anti-clockwise.

Collet — A type of collar, usually split and located in a groove in a shaft, and held in place by a retainer. The arrangement used to retain the spring(s) on a valve stem in most cases.

Commutator — Rotating segmented current distributor between armature windings and brushes in generator or motor.

Compression ratio — The ratio, or quantitative relation, of the total volume (piston at bottom of stroke) to the unswept volume (piston at top of stroke) in an engine cylinder.

Condenser — See capacitor.

Core plug — Plug for blanking off a manufacturing hole in a casting.

Crownwheel — Large bevel gear in rear axle, driven by a bevel pinion attached to the propeller shaft. Sometimes called a 'ring wheel'.

'C' Spanner — Like a 'C' with a handle. For use on screwed collars without flats, but with slots or holes.

Damper — Modern term for shock-absorber used in vehicle suspension systems to damp out spring oscillations.

Depression — The lowering of atmospheric pressure as in the inlet manifold and carburetter.

Dowel — Close tolerance pin, peg, tube, or bolt, which accurately locates mating parts.

Drag link — Rod connecting steering box drop arm (pitman arm) to nearest front wheel steering arm in certain types of steering systems.

Dry liner — Thinwall tube pressed into cylinder bore.

Dry sump	Lubrication system where all oil is scavenged from the sump, and returned to a separate tank.	**HT**	High Tension. Applied to electrical current produced by the ignition coil for the sparking plugs.
Dynamo	See Generator.	**Hydrometer**	A device for checking specific gravity of liquids. Used to check specific gravity of electrolyte.
Electrode	Terminal part of an electrical component, such as the points or 'electrodes' of a sparking plug.	**Hypoid bevel gears**	A form of bevel gear used in the rear axle drive gears. The bevel pinion meshes below the centre line of the crownwheel, giving a lower propeller shaft line.
Electrolyte	In lead-acid car batteries a solution of sulphuric acid and distilled water.		
End float	Or end play. The endwise movement between associated parts.	**Idler**	A device for passing on movement. A free running gear between driving and driven gears. A lever transmitting track rod movement to a side rod in steering gear
EP	Extreme pressure. In lubricants, special grades for heavily loaded bearing surfaces, such as gear teeth in a gearbox, or crownwheel and pinion in a rear axle.	**IFS**	Idenpendent Front Suspension.
		Impeller	A centrifugal pumping element. Used in water pumps to stimulate flow.
Fade	Of brakes. Reduced efficiency due to overheating.	**Journals**	Those parts of a shaft that are in contact with the bearings.
Field coils	Windings on the polepieces of motors and generators.	**Kerosene**	Paraffin.
Fillets	Narrow finishing strips usually applied to interior bodywork.	**Kingpin**	The main vertical pin which carries the front wheel spindle, and permits steering movement. May be called 'steering pin' or 'swivel pin'.
First motion shaft	Input shaft from clutch to gearbox.		
Fullflow	Oil filters. Filters all the oil pumped to the engine. If the element becomes clogged, a bypass valve operates to pass unfiltered oil to the engine.	**Layshaft**	The shaft which carries the laygear in the gearbox. The laygear is driven by the first motion shaft and drives the third motion shaft according to the gear selected. Sometimes called the 'Countershaft' or 'Second motion shaft'.
FWD	Front wheel drive.		
Gear pump	Two meshing gears in a close fitting casing. Oil is carried from the inlet round the outside of both gears in the spaces between the gear teeth and the casing to the outlet, the meshing gear teeth prevent oil passing back to the inlet, and the oil is forced through the outlet port.	**lb ft**	A measure of twist or torque. A pull of 10 lb at a radius of 1 ft is a torque of 10 lb ft.
		lb/sq in	Pounds per square inch.
		LC	Low Compression. See 'Compression ratio'.
Generator	Modern term for 'dynamo'. When rotated produces electrical current.	**Little end**	The small, or piston end of a connecting rod. Sometimes called the 'Small end'.
Grommet	A ring of protective or sealing material. Can be used to protect pipes or leads passing through bulkheads.	**ls**	Leading shoe in brake drum. Tends to wedge into drum, when applied, so increasing the braking effect.
Gudgeon pin	Shaft which connects a piston to its connecting rod. Sometimes called 'wrist pin', or 'piston pin'.	**LT**	Low Tension. The current output from battery.
Halfshaft	One of a pair transmitting drive from the differential gearing to the wheel hubs.	**Mandrel**	Accurately manufactured bar or rod used for test or centring purposes.
HC	High-compression. See Compression ratio.	**Manifold**	A pipe, duct, or chamber, with several branches.
Helical	In spiral form. The teeth of helical gears are cut at a spiral angle to the side faces of the gear wheel.	**Needle rollers**	Bearing rollers with a length many times their diameter.
		Oil bath	Reservoir which lubricates parts by immersion. In air filters, a separate oil supply for wetting a wiremesh element and holding the dust.
Hot spot	Hot area that assists vapourisation of fuel on its way to cylinders. Often provided by close contact between inlet and exhaust manifolds.	**Oil wetted**	In air filters, a wiremesh element lightly oiled to trap and hold airborne dust.

Overlap	Period during which inlet and exhaust valves are open together.	**Solenoid**	A coil of wire creating a magnetic field when electric current passes through it. Used with a soft iron core to operate contacts or a mechanical device.
Panhard rod	Bar connected between fixed point on chassis and another on axle to control sideways movement.	**Spur gear**	A gear with teeth cut axially across the periphery.
Pawl	Pivoted catch which engages in the teeth of a ratchet to permit movement in one direction only.	**Stator tube**	A stationary tube inside the steering column, carrying wiring to steering wheel controls.
Peg spanner	Tool with pegs, or pins, to engage in holes in the part to be turned.	**Stub axle**	Short axle fitted at one end only.
Pendant pedals	Pedals with levers that are pivoted at the top end.	**Tachometer**	An instrument for accurate measurement of rotating speed. Usually indicates in revolutions per minute.
Phillips screwdriver	A cross-point screwdriver for use with the cross-slotted heads of Phillips screws.	**TDC**	Top Dead Centre. The highest point reached by a piston in a cylinder, with the crank and connecting rod in line.
Pinion	A small gear, usually in relation to another gear.	**Thermostat**	Automatic device for regulating temperature. Used in vehicle coolant systems to open a valve which restricts circulation at low temperatures.
Piston-type damper	Shock absorber in which damping is controlled by a piston working in a closed oil filled cylinder.	**Third motion shaft**	Output shaft of gearbox.
Preloading	Preset static pressure on ball or roller bearings not due to working loads.	**Three-quarter floating axle**	Outer end of rear axle halfshaft flanged and bolted to wheel hub, which runs on bearing mounted on outside of axle casing. Vehicle weight is not carried by the axle shaft.
Radial	Radiating from a centre, like the spokes of a wheel.		
Radius rod	Pivoted arm confining movement of a part to an arc of fixed radius.	**Thrust bearing or washer**	Used to reduce friction in rotating parts subject to axial loads.
Ratchet	Toothed wheel or rack which can move in one direction only, movement in the other being prevented by a pawl.	**Torque**	Turning or twisting effort. See lb ft.
Ring gear	A gear toothed ring attached to outer periphery of flywheel. Starter pinion engages with it during starting.	**Track rod**	The bar(s) across the vehicle which connect the steering arms and maintain the front wheels in their correct alignment.
Runout	Amount by which a rotating part is out of truth.	**ts**	Trailing shoe, in a drum brake assembly. Tends to be pushed away from drum.
SAE	Society of Automotive Engineers.	**UJ**	Universal joint. A coupling between shafts which permits angular movement.
Semi-floating axle	Outer end of rear axle halfshaft is carried on bearing inside axle casing. Wheel hub is secured to end of shaft.	**UNF**	Unified National Fine screw thread.
Servo	A hydraulic or pneumatic system for assisting, or augmenting a physical effort. See 'Vacuum Servo'.	**Vacuum Servo**	Device used in brake system, using difference between atmospheric pressure and inlet manifold depression to operate a piston which acts to augment pressure as required. See 'Servo'.
Setscrew	One which is threaded for the full length of the shank.		
Shackle	A coupling link, used in the form of two parallel pins connected by side plates to secure the end of the master suspension spring, and absorb the effects of deflection.	**Venturi**	A restriction or 'choke' in a tube, as in a carburetter, used to increase velocity to obtain a reduction in pressure.
		Vernier	A sliding scale for obtaining fractional readings of the graduations of an adjacent scale.
Shell bearing	Thin walled, steel shell lined with anti-friction metal. Usually semi-circular and used in pairs for main and big-end bearings.	**Welch plug**	A domed thin metal disc which is partially flattened to lock in a recess. Used to plug core holes in castings.
Shock absorber	See 'damper'.	**Wet liner**	Removable cylinder barrel, sealed against coolant leakage, where the coolant is in direct contact with the outer surface.
Silentbloc	Rubber bush bonded to inner and outer metal sleeves.		
Socket-head screw	Screw with hexagonal socket for an Allen key.	**Wet sump**	A reservoir attached to the crankcase to hold the lubricating oil.

INDEX

NOTES

Alfa Romeo Giulia 1600,
1750 1962 on
Aston Martin 1921-58
Auto Union Audi 70, 80,
Super 90, 1966 on
Audi 100 1969 on
Austin, Morris etc.
1100 Mk. 1 1962-67
Austin, Morris etc. 1100
Mk. 2, 3, 1300 Mk. 1, 2, 3
America 1968 on
Austin A30, A35, A40
Farina
Austin A55 Mk. 2, A60
1958-69
Austin A99, A110 1959-68
Austin J4 1960 on
Austin Maxi 1969 on
Austin, Morris 1800
1964 on
Austin, Morris 2200 1972 on
Austin, Morris 1300, 1500
Nomad 1969 on

BMC 3 (Austin A50, A55
Mk. 1, Morris Oxford
2, 3 1954-59)
Austin Healey 100/6,
3000 1956-68
Austin Healey, MG
Sprite, Midget 1958 on
Bedford Beagle HA Vans
1964 on
BMW 1600 1966 on
BMW 1800 1964 on
BMW 2000, 2002 1966 on
Chevrolet Corvair 1960-69
Chevrolet Corvette V8
1957-65
Chevrolet Corvette V8
1965 on
Chevrolette Vega 2300
1970 on
Chrysler Valiant V8
1965 on
Chrysler Valiant Straight
Six 1966-70
Citroen DS 19, ID 19
1955-66
Citroen ID 19, DS 19, 20,
21 1966 on
Daf 31, 32, 33, 44, 55
1961 on
Datsun 1200 1970 on
Datsun 1300, 1400, 1600
1968 on
Datsun 240C 1971 on
Datsun 240Z Sport 1970 on
De Dion Bouton
1899-1907
Fiat 124 1966 on
Fiat 124 Sport 1966 on
Fiat 125 1967 on
Fiat 128 1969 on
Fiat 500 1957 on
Fiat 600, 600D 1955-69
Fiat 850 1964 on
Fiat 1100 1957-69
Fiat 1300, 1500 1961-67

Ford Anglia Prefect 100E
1953-62
Ford Anglia 105E, Prefect
107E 1959-67
Ford Capri 1300, 1600 OHV
1968 on
Ford Capri 1300, 1600,
2000 OHC 1972 on
Ford Capri 2000, 3000
1969 on
Ford Classic, Capri
1961-64
Ford Consul, Zephyr,
Zodiac, 1, 2 1950-62
Ford Corsair Straight
Four 1963-65
Ford Corsair V4 1965-68
Ford Corsair V4 2000
1969-70
Ford Cortina 1962-66
Ford Cortina 1967-68
Ford Cortina 1969-70
Ford Cortina Mk. 3
1970 on
Ford Escort 1967 on
Ford Falcon 6 1964-70
Ford Falcon XK, XL
1960-63
Ford Falcon 6 XR/XA
1966 on
Ford Falcon V8 (U.S.A.)
1965-71
Ford Falcon V8 (Aust.)
1966 on
Ford Pinto 1970 on
Ford Maverick 1969 on
Ford Mustang V8 1965-71
Ford Thames 10, 12,
15 cwt 1957-65
Ford Transit 1965 on
Ford Zephyr Zodiac Mk. 3
1962-66
Ford Zephyr Zodiac V4,
V6, Mk. 4 1966-72
Ford Consul, Granada 1972
Hillman Avenger 1970 on
Hillman Hunter 1966 on
Hillman Imp 1963-68
Hillman Imp 1969 on
Hillman Minx 1 to 5
1956-65
Hillman Minx 1965-67
Hillman Minx 1966-70
Hillman Super Minx
1961-65
Holden V8 1968 on
Holden Straight Six
1948-66
Holden Straight Six
1966 on
Holden Torana 4 Series
HB 1967-69
Jaguar XK120, 140, 150,
Mk. 7, 8, 9 1948-61
Jaguar 2.4, 3.4, 3.8 Mk.
1, 2 1955-69
Jaguar 'E' Type 1961 on
Jaguar 'S' Type 420
1963-68

Jaguar XJ6 1968 on
Jowett Javelin Jupiter
1947-53
Landrover 1, 2 1948-61
Landrover 2, 2a, 3 1959 on
Mazda 616 1970 on
Mazda 1200, 1300 1969 on
Mazda 1500, 1800 1967 on
Mercedes-Benz 190b,
190c, 200 1959-68
Mercedes-Benz 220
1959-65
Mercedes-Benz 220/8
1968 on
Mercedes-Benz 230
1963-68
Mercedes-Benz 250
1965-67
Mercedes-Benz 250
1968 on
Mercedes-Benz 280
1968 on
MG TA to TF 1936-55
MGA MGB 1955-68
MGB 1969 on
Mini 1959 on
Mini Cooper 1961 on
Morgan 1936-69
Morris Marina 1971 on
Morris (Aust) Marina
1972 on
Morris Minor 2, 1000
1952-71
Morris Oxford 5, 6 1959-71
NSU 1000 1963 on
NSU Prinz 1 to 4 1957 on
Opel Ascona, Manta
1970 on
Opel GT 1900 1968 on
Opel Kadett, Olympia 993cc
1078cc 1962 on
Opel Kadett, Olympia 1492,
1698, 1897cc 1967 on
Opel Rekord C 1966 on
Peugeot 204 1965 on
Peugeot 304 1970 on
Peugeot 404 1960 on
Peugeot 504 1968-70
Porsche 356A, B, C 1957-65
Porsche 911 1964-69
Porsche 912 1965-69
Porsche 914 S 1969 on
Reliant Regal 1952 on
Renault R4, R4L, 4 1961 on
Renault 6 1968 on
Renault 8, 10, 1100 1962 on
Renault 12, 1969 on
Renault R16 1965 on
Renault Dauphine
Floride 1957-67
Renault Caravelle 1962-68
Rover 60 to 110 1953-64
Rover 2000 1963 on
Rover 3 Litre 1958-67
Rover 3500, 3500S 1968 on

Saab 95, 96, Sport
1960-68
Saab 99 1969 on
Saab V4 1966 on

Simca 1000 1961 on
Simca 1100 1967 on
Simca 1300, 1301, 1500,
1501 1963 on
Skoda One (440, 445, 450)
1955-70
Sunbeam Rapier Alpine
1955-65
Toyota Corolla 1100 1967 on
Toyota Corona 1500 Mk. 1
1965-70
Toyota Corona 1900 Mk. 2
1969 on
Triumph TR2, TR3, TR3A
1952-62
Triumph TR4, TR4A
1961-67
Triumph TR5, TR250,
TR6 1967 on
Triumph 1300, 1500
1965 on
Triumph 2000 Mk. 1, 2.5 PI
Mk. 1 1963-69
Triumph 2000 Mk. 2, 2.5 PI
Mk. 2 1969 on
Triumph Dolomite 1972 on
Triumph Herald 1959-68
Triumph Herald 1969-71
Triumph Spitfire, Vitesse
1962-68
Triumph Spitfire Mk. 3, 4
1969 on
Triumph GT6, Vitesse
2 Litre 1969 on
Triumph Toledo 1970 on
Vauxhall Velox, Cresta
1957-72
Vauxhall Victor 1, 2, FB
1957-64
Vauxhall Victor 101
1964-67
Vauxhall Victor FD 1600,
2000 1967 on
Vauxhall Victor 3300,
Ventora 1968 on
Vauxhall Victor FE
Ventora 1972 on
Vauxhall Viva HA 1963-66
Vauxhall Viva HB 1966-70
Vauxhall Viva, HC Firenza
1971 on
Volkswagen Beetle 1954-67
Volkswagen Beetle 1968 on
Volkswagen 1500 1961-66
Volkswagen 1600 Fastback
1965 on
Volkswagen Transporter
1954-67
Volkswagen Transporter
1968 on
Volkswagen 411 1968 on
Volvo 120 1961-70
Volvo 140 1966 on
Volvo 160 series 1968 on
Volvo 1800 1960 on

NOTES

NOTES

NOTES